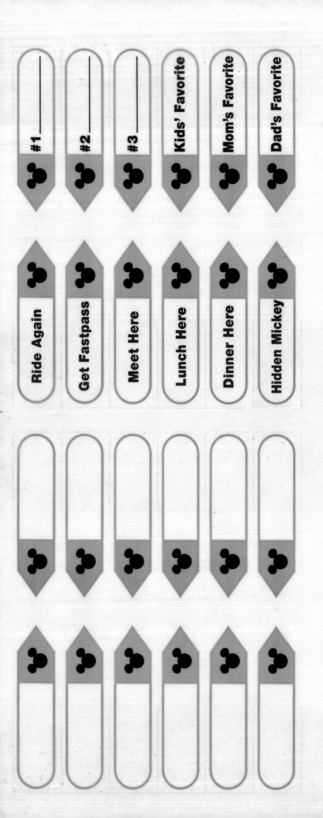

ZAGAT®

Walt Disney World®

Insider's Guide
2008/09

Covering:
- **Attractions**
- **Dining**
- **Character Dining**
- **Nightlife**
- **Shopping**
- **Hotels**
- **Golf**
- **Disney Cruise Line**

CONSULTING EDITOR
David Downing
STAFF EDITOR
Carol Diuguid

Published and distributed by
Zagat Survey, LLC
4 Columbus Circle
New York, NY 10019
T: 212.977.6000
E: disneyworld@zagat.com
www.zagat.com

ACKNOWLEDGMENTS

We thank Pam Brandon, Caren Weiner Campbell, Andrew Collins, Jay Conner, Richard Dworkin, Carolyn Heller, Constance Jones, Bernard Onken, Joe Passov, John Rambow and Kerry Speckman, as well as the following members of our staff: Kelly Stewart (assistant editor), Brian Albert, Sean Beachell, Maryanne Bertollo, Sandy Cheng, Reni Chin, Larry Cohn, Alison Flick, Jeff Freier, Michelle Golden, Tricia Heinz, Alexandra Herbert, Roy Jacob, Brendan Jacobson, Natalie Lebert, Mike Liao, Dave Makulec, Andre Pilette, Josh Rogers, Kimberly Rosado, Becky Ruthenburg, Sharon Yates, Anna Zappia and Kyle Zolner.

The reviews published in this guide are based on public opinion surveys. The numerical ratings reflect the average scores given by all survey participants who voted on each establishment. The text is based on direct quotes from, or fair paraphrasings of, participants' comments. Phone numbers, addresses and other factual information were correct to the best of our knowledge when published in this guide.

Contents

About This Survey

This **2008/09 Walt Disney World Insider's Guide** is an update reflecting significant developments since our last Survey was published. It represents all that the legendary Orlando vacation destination has to offer, including the big four theme parks (**Magic Kingdom, Epcot, Disney's Hollywood Studios** and **Disney's Animal Kingdom**) and water parks (**Blizzard Beach** and **Typhoon Lagoon**). Covering everything from attractions to dining, nightlife, shopping, resorts and more, it offers reliable advice on how to spend your time and money from thousands of savvy people who have been there before you. As a bonus, there are sections covering **WDW Golf Courses** and the **Disney Cruise Line.**

WHO PARTICIPATED: Input from over 4,800 Disney-goers forms the basis for the ratings and reviews in this guide (their comments are shown in quotation marks within the reviews). We sincerely thank each of these participants – this book is really "theirs." We are also grateful to the Walt Disney Company, which provided assistance with photos, maps and other information.

HELPFUL LISTS: Whether you're a first-time visitor to WDW or a seasoned regular, our lists can help you make the right choices for you and your family. Accordingly, we have provided Top Ratings lists at the start of each section of this guide, as well as eight handy indexes. For WDW park maps and photos – including a look at the Top 20 Thrills – see the color section at the back of the book,

ABOUT ZAGAT: This marks our 29th year reporting on the shared experiences of consumers like you. What started in 1979 as a hobby involving 200 of our friends has come a long way. Today we have well over 300,000 surveyors and now cover dining, entertaining, golf, hotels, movies, music, nightlife, resorts, shopping, spas, theater and tourist attractions worldwide.

SHARE YOUR OPINION: We invite you to join any of our upcoming surveys – just register at **ZAGAT.com,** where you can rate and review establishments year-round. Each participant will receive a free copy of the resulting guide when published.

AVAILABILITY: Zagat guides are available in all major bookstores, by subscription at **ZAGAT.com,** and for use on web-enabled mobile devices via **ZAGAT TO GO** or **ZAGAT.mobi.** The latter two products allow you to contact your choice among many thousands of establishments by phone with just one click.

FEEDBACK: There is always room for improvement, thus we invite your comments and suggestions about any aspect of our performance. Is there something more you would like us to include in our guides? We really need your input! Just contact us at **disneyworld@zagat.com.**

New York, NY
May 20, 2008

Nina and Tim

Nina and Tim Zagat

What's New

A year has passed since we published our first-ever guide to WDW, and it has been a busy one.

GOODBYE MGM, HELLO, HOLLYWOOD! In 2007 WDW announced a rare rebranding of one of its parks, recasting Disney-MGM Studios as **Disney's Hollywood Studios,** a move it characterized as widening its focus on the Golden Age of movies to encompass all that today's Hollywood has to offer. At its core, WDW's leonine liaison had consisted manely of a licensing deal that allowed use of the MGM name and logo in marketing the park (as well as film footage in its **Great Movie Ride**), so most park-goers aren't likely to feel much of a loss.

PARKS PROMOTING POPULAR PIXAR PICS: A fair number of WDW's newest – and very popular – attractions are themed around Pixar's animated blockbusters, including this year's most notable Hollywood Studios newcomers: **Toy Story Mania!,** an interactive dark ride hosted by Buzz, Woody and friends, and the riotous **Block Party Bash parade,** a California Adventure import boasting a potpourri of Pixar peeps. Other examples of this trend are recent *Nemo*-themed additions, including Epcot's **The Seas With Nemo & Friends** and Disney's Animal Kingdom's **Finding Nemo: The Musical.**

THE MOUSE THAT ROARED: Industry analysts had been predicting a 2007 theme park slump, but WDW reportedly bucked the trend. Disney, like most if its competitors, closely guards attendance figures, but a 2008 gate-count study by an industry research company/trade association concluded that in 2007 the **Magic Kingdom** retained its title as the world's most popular theme park with more than 17 million visitors. And over the same period, **Disney's Animal Kingdom,** riding on the popularity of **Expedition Everest,** increased its attendance by 6.5%, the highest growth rate of any park in Florida, according to the report.

FUTURE WORLDS: As speculation persists about a possible WDW project in the emirate of Dubai and competition continues to heat up closer to home, Disney is preparing for the much-anticipated makeover of its 1970s-era Magic Kingdom icon **Space Mountain,** which is slated to close in early 2009. Also on the drawing board for this winter is an *American Idol* attraction at Disney's Hollywood Studios, which will have parkgoers competing with one another in a setting that promises "all the glitz and glamour" of the Fox TV juggernaut. On the food and fun fronts, Downtown Disney adds to its offerings with the upcoming debut of **T-Rex,** an interactive dino-themed eatery and retail space; it will join other WDW arrivals **Yak & Yeti,** a Pan-Asian eatery that has brought table-service dining to Animal Kingdom, and the upscale **Rix Lounge,** which has introduced hip nightlife to the Coronado Springs Resort. Also on the horizon is **Kingdom Tower,** a new 15-story timeshare near the Contemporary Resort, and the **Four Seasons Golf Resort,** a luxury hotel and 18-hole golf course, which is being developed with the Toronto-based chain and is slated to open in late 2010.

St. Petersburg, FL
May 20, 2008

David Downing

A Disney Primer

WHO, WALT, WHEN, WHERE, WHY? It may come as a surprise to Disneyophytes that Walt Disney World isn't in Orlando – and that there isn't even a park called "Walt Disney World." Rather, the behemoth that operates under that name is like a small city with four theme parks, two water parks, more than 30 resorts, 300 dining options, myriad stores and five golf courses, as well as a professional sports complex, a campground, recreational activities and Downtown Disney, a shopping and entertainment district. All told, this occupies an area twice the size of Manhattan in Lake Buena Vista, a half hour southwest of Orlando (yet the company itself often calls Orlando home).

ORIGINS: Disney World was the original name of the attraction Walter Elias Disney planned to build on huge tracts of central Florida swampland he covertly bought in the early 1960s. But he died five years before the park opened in 1971, so his brother, Roy, changed the name to *Walt* Disney World as a memorial. However, in 1982 when Disney Company opened its second Florida park, Epcot, the original that visitors had come to know as Walt Disney World reverted to its lesser-known name, The Magic Kingdom: in a kind of theme-park mitosis, one entity became two cells of a larger organism known as Walt Disney World, which continued to grow and divide with the addition of Disney-MGM Studios – now Disney's Hollywood Studios – and Typhoon Lagoon in 1989, Blizzard Beach in 1995 and Disney's Animal Kingdom in 1998.

SIBLING RIVALRY: To better understand the differences between the four major theme parks, think of them as siblings. Magic Kingdom, with nine of WDW's 20 Most Popular attractions, is the oldest – the popular, pretty one that's long been beloved by visitors from around the world. Epcot is the smart second child that many say takes a while to get to know. Hollywood Studios is the third child that shows off to get attention. And Animal Kingdom is the youngest, still finding itself and blazing new paths in the process – such as the addition of Expedition Everest, the Survey's top-rated attraction for Adult Appeal. It's also WDW's only park with live animals. Water parks Typhoon Lagoon and Blizzard Beach might appear to be different from their siblings on the surface, but their imaginative theming and attractions prove their distinctly Disney lineage. (For photos plus surveyor-based reviews of each park, see page A2.)

IT'S A BIG WORLD: For a WDW Resort overview see the map on page A16. Though it's possible to drive between parks, it's often more convenient to use the system of buses, water launches and rail lines connecting them. For example, a monorail connects Magic Kingdom to Epcot four miles to its south, making travel between the two points easy. Hollywood Studios is just southwest of Epcot, about a mile away by car. Occupying about 500 acres, Animal Kingdom is set off in a secluded area to the west of Hollywood Studios. Downtown Disney, the nightlife, dining and shopping district, is the farthest east. Typhoon Lagoon is near Downtown Disney; Blizzard Beach is near Hollywood Studios. Walt Disney World still has about as much undeveloped land as it does developed land, which allows the resort to be ever-expanding.

DISNEYSPEAK: "**Cast members**" are WDW employees, whether maintenance staff or park managers; they're "**on stage**" whenever they can be seen by guests. "**Imagineers**" are the designers responsible for the creation of all Disney attractions, resorts and cruise ships. "**Hidden Mickeys**" are sometimes obscure images of Mickey Mouse that are incorporated into everything from the carpet at Animal Kingdom Lodge to the famous "mouse trap" on the 6th hole of the Magnolia Golf Course. An "**E-ticket**" ride is one that is very popular; it's a holdover from the early days when each attraction required a separate ticket (labeled "A" through "E"), the most expensive being "E-tickets." "**DAK**" is short for Disney's Animal Kingdom.

WHEN TO VISIT: There is no real "slow" season at WDW, though crowds tend to peak whenever school is out of session: Christmas holidays (mid-December through New Year), Presidents' Day weekend (late February), spring break (March–April) and summer (June through Labor Day). The ideal time to visit is September, once kids are back in school. It's not as hot and skies are mostly sunny – though hurricane season extends through November.

WHAT IT COSTS: A single-day one-park ticket is $71 for adults and $60 for ages three–nine (kids under three get in free), but most visitors opt for multiday and multipark tickets such as the Park Hopper and Magic Your Way. (See page 16 for more information.) Admission prices are tightly regulated, so any "discounts" you may find rarely amount to more than a few dollars per day. (Some in-park attractions, such as tours and scuba diving, require additional fees, as do all out-of-park activities; those are noted in the reviews.) In contrast to ticket prices, lodging costs at WDW cover a wide range. Options start at $82 a night for motellike "Value" accommodations at slower times of year and run to 10 times that amount for "Deluxe" resorts with spas, room service and views of fireworks over Cinderella Castle in peak season. Dining choices are similarly diverse, but due to WDW's family-friendly nature, quick, casual budget eateries and snack stands outnumber fancy dining options.

KID CARE: Strollers are for rent at all four parks, and you pay only once per day – if you go to another park, just show your receipt for a new stroller. Changing tables are in many restrooms, and Baby Care Centers in all four parks carry diapers, formula and other needs at a nominal cost (check with Guest Relations for locations). At the resorts, in-room child care is available 24/7 by calling the front desk, and some hotels have supervised activity centers for $11 an hour per child. Given Disney's focus on kids, much of WDW is designed to give youngsters (and grown-ups) a serious case of the "gimmes," with merchandise often stocked at kid-level.

SAFETY FIRST: Though you might not see it (and you're not supposed to), security is tight at WDW, which makes for a safe environment for kids of all ages who may wander away from the family. If you do become separated from a family member, Disney cast members are trained to never refer to a "lost child" – only a "lost parent." Expect bag searches at every park entrance; guests sans bags can use a separate, faster line.

Ratings & Symbols

Ratings and Reviews

All **ratings** throughout this guide are on the Zagat 0 to 30 scale as follows:

0	– 9	poor to fair
10	– 15	fair to good
16	– 19	good to very good
20	– 25	very good to excellent
26	– 30	extraordinary to perfection
∇		low response | less reliable

Ratings apply to the key aspects of each category covered, for example, Food, Decor and Service in the Dining category. See Ratings & Symbols in each section. Places without ratings are **newcomers** or survey **write-ins.**

Cost is covered differently, as noted in the Ratings & Symbols keys at the beginning of each section. Admission to Attractions is included in park tickets; any additional fees are spelled out in the reviews.

Surveyor comments are shown in quotation marks within reviews.

Symbols

Z Zagat Top Spot (highest ratings, popularity and importance)

See also the Ratings & Symbols key in each section.

Top Lists and Indexes

Throughout Top Lists and Indexes, names are followed by their WDW location.

Most Popular lists reflect surveyors' choices when asked to name their five favorite places within each category.

All attractions, restaurants, etc. are listed alphabetically, with their page numbers, in the Alphabetical Index at the back of the book.

Helpful Phone Numbers

We have included addresses and phone numbers with reviews only where it makes sense; in the parks, most places don't have a street address. To get information on virtually everything in WDW, just call 407-824-4321 or visit Disneyworld.com.

The following phone numbers can also be helpful for information and reservations:

Dining and Character Dining:	407-939-3463
Shopping:	407-363-6200
Hotels:	407-934-7639
Golf:	407-939-4653
Disney Cruise Line:	800-910-3659

Top-Rated Attractions

MOST POPULAR

1. Soarin' | *Epcot, Future World*
2. Rock 'n' Roller Coaster | *Hollywood Studios, Sunset Boulevard*
3. Twilight Zone Tower of Terror | *Hollywood Studios, Sunset Boulevard*
4. Pirates of the Caribbean | *Magic Kingdom, Adventureland*
5. Space Mountain | *Magic Kingdom, Tomorrowland*
6. Test Track | *Epcot, Future World*
7. Expedition Everest | *Animal Kingdom, Asia*
8. Splash Mountain | *Magic Kingdom, Frontierland*
9. Haunted Mansion | *Magic Kingdom, Liberty Square*
10. Big Thunder Mountain | *Magic Kingdom, Frontierland*
11. Buzz Lightyear's Spin | *Magic Kingdom, Tomorrowland*
12. Mickey's PhilharMagic | *Magic Kingdom, Fantasyland*
13. IllumiNations | *Epcot, World Showcase*
14. Wishes Spectacular | *Magic Kingdom Parkwide*
15. Fantasmic! | *Hollywood Studios, Sunset Boulevard*
16. Kilimanjaro Safaris | *Animal Kingdom, Africa*
17. it's a small world | *Magic Kingdom, Fantasyland*
18. Festival of the Lion King | *Animal Kingdom, Camp Minnie-Mickey*
19. Spaceship Earth | *Epcot, Future World*
20. Mission: SPACE | *Epcot, Future World*

BY THRILL RATING

29 Summit Plummet | *Blizzard Beach*
Twilight Zone Tower of Terror | *Hollywood Studios, Sunset Boulevard*
Rock 'n' Roller Coaster | *Hollywood Studios, Sunset Boulevard*
Expedition Everest | *Animal Kingdom, Asia*
28 Mission: SPACE | *Epcot, Future World*
27 Space Mountain | *Magic Kingdom, Tomorrowland*
Humunga Kowabunga | *Typhoon Lagoon*
26 Splash Mountain | *Magic Kingdom, Frontierland*
Crush 'n' Gusher | *Typhoon Lagoon*
Test Track | *Epcot, Future World*
25 DINOSAUR | *Animal Kingdom, DinoLand*
Soarin' | *Epcot, Future World*
24 Big Thunder Mountain | *Magic Kingdom, Frontierland*
Slush Gusher | *Blizzard Beach*
Richard Petty Driving | *Magic Kingdom Area*
23 Typhoon Lagoon Surf Pool | *Typhoon Lagoon*
Downhill Double Dipper | *Blizzard Beach*
Kali River Rapids | *Animal Kingdom, Asia*
Lights, Motors, Action! | *Hollywood Studios, Streets of America*
22 Cirque du Soleil | *Downtown Disney, West Side*

BY ADULT APPEAL

29 Expedition Everest | *Animal Kingdom, Asia*
Soarin' | *Epcot, Future World*
Cirque du Soleil | *Downtown Disney, West Side*
Rock 'n' Roller Coaster | *Hollywood Studios, Sunset Boulevard*
Twilight Zone Tower of Terror | *Hollywood Studios, Sunset Boulevard*
Wishes Spectacular | *Magic Kingdom Parkwide*

28 Summit Plummet | *Blizzard Beach*
Space Mountain | *Magic Kingdom, Tomorrowland*
Disney's Keys to the Kingdom | *Magic Kingdom Parkwide*
IllumiNations | *Epcot, World Showcase*
Splash Mountain | *Magic Kingdom, Frontierland*
Test Track | *Epcot, Future World*
Around the World Segway Tour | *Epcot, World Showcase*
Kilimanjaro Safaris | *Animal Kingdom, Africa*

27 Mission: SPACE | *Epcot, Future World*
Crush 'n' Gusher | *Typhoon Lagoon*
Fantasmic! | *Hollywood Studios, Sunset Boulevard*
Mickey's PhilharMagic | *Magic Kingdom, Fantasyland*
Festival of the Lion King | *Animal Kingdom, Camp Minnie-Mickey*
Typhoon Lagoon Surf Pool | *Typhoon Lagoon*

BY CHILD APPEAL

29 Wishes Spectacular | *Magic Kingdom Parkwide*
Turtle Talk with Crush | *Epcot, Future World*
Buzz Lightyear's Spin | *Magic Kingdom, Tomorrowland*
Playhouse Disney | *Hollywood Studios, Animation Courtyard*

28 SpectroMagic Parade | *Magic Kingdom Parkwide*
Festival of the Lion King | *Animal Kingdom, Camp Minnie-Mickey*
Soarin' | *Epcot, Future World*
Camp Minnie-Mickey Trails | *Animal Kingdom, Camp Minnie-Mickey*
Disney Dreams | *Magic Kingdom Parkwide*
Barnstormer Goofy's | *Magic Kingdom, Toontown Fair*
Voyage of The Little Mermaid | *Hollywood Studios, Animation Courtyard*

27 Mickey's PhilharMagic | *Magic Kingdom, Fantasyland*
Kilimanjaro Safaris | *Animal Kingdom, Africa*
Many Adventures of Pooh | *Magic Kingdom, Fantasyland*
Judge's Tent | *Magic Kingdom, Toontown Fair*
Dream with Mickey | *Magic Kingdom, Fantasyland*
DisneyQuest | *Downtown Disney, West Side*
Fantasmic! | *Hollywood Studios, Sunset Boulevard*
Seas with Nemo & Friends | *Epcot, Future World*
Splash Mountain | *Magic Kingdom, Frontierland*
IllumiNations | *Epcot, World Showcase*
Toontown Hall of Fame | *Magic Kingdom, Toontown Fair*
Peter Pan's Flight | *Magic Kingdom, Fantasyland*
Dumbo | *Magic Kingdom, Fantasyland*
Muppet Vision 3-D | *Hollywood Studios, Streets of America*

Top-Rated Restaurants

MOST POPULAR

1. California Grill | *Contemporary Resort, Magic Kingdom Area*
2. Le Cellier Steak | *Epcot, World Showcase*
3. 50's Prime Time | *Hollywood Studios, Echo Lake*
4. Boma | *Animal Kingdom Lodge, Animal Kingdom Area*
5. Jiko/Cooking Place | *Animal Kingdom Lodge, Animal Kingdom Area*
6. Hollywood Brown Derby | *Hollywood Studios, Hollywood Boulevard*
7. Victoria & Albert's | *Grand Floridian, Magic Kingdom Area*
8. Flying Fish Cafe | *BoardWalk, Epcot Area*
9. Chefs de France | *Epcot, World Showcase*
10. 'Ohana | *Polynesian Resort, Magic Kingdom Area*
11. Artist Point | *Wilderness Lodge, Magic Kingdom Area*
12. Liberty Tree | *Magic Kingdom, Liberty Square*
13. Coral Reef | *Epcot, Future World*
14. San Angel Inn | *Epcot, World Showcase*
15. Rose & Crown | *Epcot, World Showcase*
16. Wolfgang Puck Café | *Downtown Disney, West Side*
17. Sci-Fi Dine-In Theater | *Hollywood Studios, Echo Lake*
18. Rainforest Cafe | *multiple locations*
19. Restaurant Marrakesh | *Epcot, World Showcase*
20. Yachtsman Steak | *Yacht Club Resort, Epcot Area**

TOP FOOD RATINGS

27	Victoria & Albert's	*Grand Floridian, Magic Kingdom Area*
26	California Grill	*Contemporary Resort, Magic Kingdom Area*
25	Jiko/Cooking Place	*Animal Kingdom Lodge, Animal Kingdom Area*
24	Boma	*Animal Kingdom Lodge, Animal Kingdom Area*
	Yachtsman Steak	*Yacht Club Resort, Epcot Area*
	Todd English's bluezoo	*Dolphin, Epcot Area*
	Artist Point	*Wilderness Lodge, Magic Kingdom Area*
	Flying Fish Cafe	*BoardWalk, Epcot Area*
23	Ghirardelli	*Downtown Disney, Marketplace*
	Boulangerie Pâtisserie	*Epcot, World Showcase*
	Cítricos	*Grand Floridian, Magic Kingdom Area*
	Shula's Steak	*Dolphin, Epcot Area*
	Le Cellier Steak	*Epcot, World Showcase*
	Kona Cafe	*Polynesian Resort, Magic Kingdom Area*
22	Hollywood Brown Derby	*Hollywood Studios, Hollywood Boulevard*
	Tokyo Dining	*Epcot, World Showcase*
	Earl of Sandwich	*Downtown Disney, Marketplace*
	Narcoossee's	*Grand Floridian, Magic Kingdom Area*
	Teppan Edo	*Epcot, World Showcase*
	Tangierine	*Epcot, World Showcase*

* Indicates a tie with place above

TOP FOOD RATINGS BY CATEGORY

AMERICAN

27 Victoria & Albert's | *Grand Floridian, Magic Kingdom Area*
24 Flying Fish Cafe | *BoardWalk, Epcot Area*
22 Hollywood Brown Derby | *Hollywood Studios, Hollywood Boulevard*

BREAKFAST

24 Boma | *Animal Kingdom Lodge, Animal Kingdom Area*
23 Kona Cafe | *Polynesian Resort, Magic Kingdom Area*
21 Whispering Canyon | *Wilderness Lodge, Magic Kingdom Area*

BUFFET

24 Boma | *Animal Kingdom Lodge, Animal Kingdom Area*
21 Biergarten/Sommerfest | *Epcot, World Showcase*
20 Cape May Cafe | *Beach Club Resort, Epcot Area*

CHILD APPEAL

19 50's Prime Time | *Hollywood Studios, Echo Lake*
17 Pizzafari | *Animal Kingdom, Discovery Island*
16 Cosmic Rays Cafe | *Magic Kingdom, Tomorrowland*

FRENCH

23 Boulangerie Pâtisserie | *Epcot, World Showcase*
22 Bistro de Paris | *Epcot, World Showcase*
Chefs de France | *Epcot, World Showcase*

HOTEL DINING

27 Victoria & Albert's | *Grand Floridian, Magic Kingdom Area*
26 California Grill | *Contemporary Resort, Magic Kingdom Area*
24 Boma | *Animal Kingdom Lodge, Animal Kingdom Area*

ITALIAN

21 Portobello Yacht Club | *Downtown Disney, Pleasure Island*
20 Mama Melrose's | *Hollywood Studios, Streets of America*
17 Tony's Town Square | *Magic Kingdom, Main Street*

JAPANESE

22 Tokyo Dining | *Epcot, World Showcase*
Teppan Edo | *Epcot, World Showcase*
21 Kimonos | *Swan, Epcot Area*

OUTDOOR DINING

22 Hollywood Brown Derby | *Hollywood Studios, Hollywood Blvd.*
21 Portobello Yacht Club | *Downtown Disney, Pleasure Island*
Wolfgang Puck Café | *Downtown Disney, West Side*

ROMANCE

27 Victoria & Albert's | *Grand Floridian, Magic Kingdom Area*
26 California Grill | *Contemporary Resort, Magic Kingdom Area*
24 Todd English's bluezoo | *Dolphin, Epcot Area*

SEAFOOD

24 Todd English's bluezoo | *Dolphin, Epcot Area*
Flying Fish Cafe | *BoardWalk, Epcot Area*
22 Narcoossee's | *Grand Floridian, Magic Kingdom Area*

STEAKHOUSES

24 Yachtsman Steak | *Yacht Club Resort, Epcot Area*
23 Shula's Steak | *Dolphin, Epcot Area*
 Le Cellier Steak | *Epcot, World Showcase*

TEEN APPEAL

23 Ghirardelli | *Downtown Disney, Marketplace*
21 Beaches & Cream | *Beach Club Resort, Epcot Area*
20 Sunshine Season | *Epcot, World Showcase*

VIEWS

26 California Grill | *Contemporary Resort, Magic Kingdom Area*
23 Cítricos | *Grand Floridian, Magic Kingdom Area*
22 Narcoossee's | *Grand Floridian, Magic Kingdom Area*

WINNING WINE LISTS

27 Victoria & Albert's | *Grand Floridian, Magic Kingdom Area*
26 California Grill | *Contemporary Resort, Magic Kingdom Area*
25 Jiko/Cooking Place | *Animal Kingdom Lodge, Animal Kingdom Area*

TOP DECOR RATINGS

27 Victoria & Albert's | *Grand Floridian, Magic Kingdom Area*
26 Todd English's bluezoo | *Dolphin, Epcot Area*
25 Jiko/Cooking Place | *Animal Kingdom Lodge, Animal Kingdom Area*
 Coral Reef | *Epcot, Future World*
 California Grill | *Contemporary Resort, Magic Kingdom Area*
 Sci-Fi Dine-In Theater | *Hollywood Studios, Echo Lake*
 50's Prime Time | *Hollywood Studios, Echo Lake*
24 Rainforest Cafe | *multiple locations*
 Boma | *Animal Kingdom Lodge, Animal Kingdom Area*
 Raglan Road | *Downtown Disney, Pleasure Island*
23 Restaurant Marrakesh | *Epcot, World Showcase*
 Cítricos | *Grand Floridian, Magic Kingdom Area*
 Artist Point | *Wilderness Lodge, Magic Kingdom Area*
 Hollywood Brown Derby | *Hollywood Studios, Hollywood Boulevard*
 Flying Fish Cafe | *BoardWalk, Epcot Area*

TOP SERVICE RATINGS

27 Victoria & Albert's | *Grand Floridian, Magic Kingdom Area*
25 Jiko/Cooking Place | *Animal Kingdom Lodge, Animal Kingdom Area*
24 California Grill | *Contemporary Resort, Magic Kingdom Area*
23 Artist Point | *Wilderness Lodge, Magic Kingdom Area*
 Yachtsman Steak | *Yacht Club Resort, Epcot Area*
 Cítricos | *Grand Floridian, Magic Kingdom Area*
 Todd English's bluezoo | *Dolphin, Epcot Area**
 Le Cellier Steak | *Epcot, World Showcase*
 Whispering Canyon | *Wilderness Lodge, Magic Kingdom Area*
 50's Prime Time | *Hollywood Studios, Echo Lake*
 Biergarten/Sommerfest | *Epcot, World Showcase*
22 Boma | *Animal Kingdom Lodge, Animal Kingdom Area*
 Teppan Edo | *Epcot, World Showcase*
 Flying Fish Cafe | *BoardWalk, Epcot Area*
 Narcoossee's | *Grand Floridian, Magic Kingdom Area*

MOST POPULAR NIGHTLIFE

1. Adventurers Club | *Downtown Disney, Pleasure Island*
2. Comedy Warehouse | *Downtown Disney, Pleasure Island*
3. 8 TRAX | *Downtown Disney, Pleasure Island*
4. Raglan Road | *Downtown Disney, Pleasure Island*
5. Rose & Crown | *Epcot, World Showcase*
6. ESPN Club | *BoardWalk, Epcot Area*
7. Jellyrolls | *BoardWalk, Epcot Area*
8. House of Blues | *Downtown Disney, West Side*
9. California Grill | *Contemporary Resort, Magic Kingdom Area*
10. Mannequins | *Downtown Disney, Pleasure Island*
11. Victoria Falls | *Animal Kingdom Lodge, Animal Kingdom Area**
12. Portobello Yacht Club | *Downtown Disney, Pleasure Island*

MOST POPULAR SHOPPING

1. World of Disney Store | *Downtown Disney, Marketplace*
2. Disney's Days of Christmas | *Downtown Disney, Marketplace*
3. Art of Disney | *multiple locations*
4. Emporium | *Magic Kingdom, Main Street*
5. Mouse Gear | *Epcot, Future World*
6. Animation Gallery | *Hollywood Studios, Animation Courtyard*
7. Once Upon a Toy | *Downtown Disney, Marketplace**
8. Disney Studio Store | *Hollywood Studios, Animation Courtyard*
9. LEGO Imagination | *Downtown Disney, Marketplace*
10. Disney's Pin Traders | *Downtown Disney, Marketplace*

MOST POPULAR HOTELS

1. Disney's Animal Kingdom Lodge | *Animal Kingdom Area*
2. Disney's Wilderness Lodge | *Magic Kingdom Area*
3. Disney's Polynesian Resort | *Magic Kingdom Area*
4. Disney's Grand Floridian Resort & Spa | *Magic Kingdom Area*
5. Disney's Pop Century Resort | *Animal Kingdom Area*
6. Disney's Port Orleans Resort - Riverside | *Downtown Disney Area*
7. Disney's Contemporary Resort | *Magic Kingdom Area*
8. Disney's Beach Club Resort | *Epcot Area*
9. Disney's BoardWalk Villas | *Epcot Area*
10. Disney's Saratoga Springs Resort & Spa | *Downtown Disney Area*

TOP HOTELS OVERALL

25	Disney's Grand Floridian Resort & Spa	*Magic Kingdom Area*
24	Disney's Animal Kingdom Lodge	*Animal Kingdom Area*
	Disney's Yacht Club Resort	*Epcot Area*
	Disney's BoardWalk Inn	*Epcot Area*
23	Disney's Wilderness Lodge	*Magic Kingdom Area*

subscribe to ZAGAT.com

ATTRACTIONS

Attractions

Your theme park ticket includes unlimited admission to attractions and shows during regular park hours. For information on park hours, showtimes, which attractions are closed for refurbishment and more, pick up a park map and "Times Guide & New Information" brochure near the entrance turnstiles, or visit www.disneyworld.com.

TICKET TACTICS: The **Magic Your Way** plan lets you create customized tickets tailored to the length of your stay and your interests. The more days you buy, the cheaper the daily price. Base tickets for each park start at $71 per day ($60 ages three-nine), but with a three-day base ticket the price drops to $67.67 a day ($57 ages three-nine). You can add a **Park Hopper** option for $45 per ticket, which allows unlimited access to all four major parks for up to 10 days. The **Water Parks Fun & More** ticket includes between three and six visits (depending on the number of days you've purchased) to Blizzard Beach, Typhoon Lagoon, DisneyQuest, Pleasure Island and Disney's Wide World of Sports for $50 more and is good for up to 14 days. For an extra fee starting at $15 for a two-day ticket and going up to $180 for a 10-day ticket, a "no expiration" feature can be added to any multiday ticket; otherwise all tickets expire 14 days after first use.

PICK A PARK: For the most rides, especially for kids under 12, head to the Magic Kingdom. Teens might prefer Hollywood Studios with its two thrillers: **Rock 'n' Roller Coaster** and **Twilight Zone Tower of Terror.** Epcot's top attractions include **Mission: SPACE** and **Test Track,** and a casual stroll around the globe in **World Showcase.** As for animal lovers, they tout Disney's Animal Kingdom, with everything from gorillas and lions to dinosaur fossils, as well as **Expedition Everest,** WDW's newest (and most extreme) roller coaster. For surveyor-based reviews of each park plus photos, see page A2.

PARK HOURS: The Disney theme parks and resorts are open 365 days a year, rain or shine. Hours vary seasonally, but generally the Magic Kingdom, Epcot Future World, Hollywood Studios and Animal Kingdom open at 9 AM and Epcot World Showcase at 11 AM. In peak season – spring break, summertime and winter holidays – the parks remain open until about 11 PM (except DAK, which puts the animals to bed earlier). In less-busy times (late January or September, for instance) the parks can close as early as 7 PM. Typhoon Lagoon and Blizzard Beach are usually open 10 AM–5 PM, but unlike the theme parks, these are limited in capacity, so go early or you may find the gates already closed (they reopen as early arrivals depart). They're usually packed most weekends, especially in summer; hours can be curtailed during winter cold snaps.

CROWD CONTROL: Generally, the Magic Kingdom is most crowded on Mondays as visitors are just arriving for the week. Epcot World Showcase has the lightest crowds when it opens (11 AM), and tends to be more crowded on weekends when more locals add to the mix. The throngs hit Animal Kingdom early in the morning, since that's the best time to view the wildlife on the savannah. Crowds are generally lighter in late afternoon at Hollywood Studios. Nighttime shows in the theme parks are always crowded, but there's no hurry to find a

subscribe to ZAGAT.com

choice spot at Epcot for IllumiNations – there's good viewing from almost anywhere around World Showcase Lagoon. In the Magic Kingdom, the crowds for Wishes fireworks are heaviest on Main Street, U.S.A., but you can catch the show from almost anywhere (Adventureland is often least crowded). At Hollywood Studios, the Fantasmic! amphitheater starts filling up an hour before showtime. But to make it easy, reserve for the Fantasmic! Dining Experience, which assures seats for the post-dinner show.

RIDE DETAILS: Height and age restrictions are noted in reviews where applicable, and posted at the entrance to major attractions in all four parks. The duration (in minutes) of each attraction is listed with reviews too, as are surveyors' estimates of wait time: Short, Moderate, Long, Very Long. Tip boards in each park also give wait times (usually very accurate) for popular attractions. In the Magic Kingdom the tip board is on Main Street, U.S.A., near Cinderella Castle; at Epcot on a digital board in Innoventions Plaza; at Disney's Hollywood Studios on Hollywood Boulevard and Streets of America; and on Discovery Island at DAK. Tip: often the best time to ride is during a parade or fireworks, when others are watching the show.

TIME SAVERS: To avoid long lines at popular attractions get a **Fastpass** ticket – it's free and easy to use. Just insert your park ticket into the Fastpass dispenser in front of the attraction and you'll receive a pass indicating a one-hour window of time in which you can return to the dedicated Fastpass line. There's a limited supply for each attraction, so don't wait to get yours. Some attractions have **single rider** lines that can shave as much as 40% off wait times. Also, guests with children too young to ride can take advantage of the **switch off** option: just tell a cast member at the attraction that you want to "switch off," which means one adult rides and one stays with the kids, then the second grown-up rides when the first returns.

REFUELING: See our "In the Parks" Dining section, starting on page 56, for a rundown on in-park eating options, which range from burger-and-fries quick serves to an around-the globe sampling of cuisines at Epcot's World Showcase. If you're looking to have a midday meal in any of the parks, plan to dine promptly at 11:30 AM or wait until after 1:30 PM to avoid the crush. Keep in mind that you can enjoy food and beverages while waiting in line for rides, but they are not permitted on the rides themselves (you can bring them into shows, however).

Adult Appeal

MAGIC KINGDOM

29| Wishes Spectacular | *Parkwide*
28| Space Mountain | *Tomorrowland*
Disney's Keys to the Kingdom | *Parkwide*
Splash Mountain | *Frontierland*
27| Mickey's PhilharMagic | *Fantasyland*
Big Thunder Mountain | *Frontierland*

EPCOT

29| Soarin' | *Future World*
28| IllumiNations | *World Showcase*
Test Track | *Future World*
Around the World Segway Tour | *World Showcase*
27| Mission: SPACE | *Future World*
26| Off Kilter | *World Showcase*

DISNEY'S HOLLYWOOD STUDIOS

29| Rock 'n' Roller Coaster | *Sunset Boulevard*
Twilight Zone Tower of Terror | *Sunset Boulevard*
27| Fantasmic! | *Sunset Boulevard*
Lights, Motors, Action! | *Streets of America*
26| Backstage Magic | *Parkwide*
25| Walt Disney: One Man's Dream | *Pixar Place*

DISNEY'S ANIMAL KINGDOM

29| Expedition Everest | *Asia*
28| Kilimanjaro Safaris | *Africa*
27| Festival of the Lion King | *Camp Minnie-Mickey*
26| Backstage Safari | *Parkwide*
DINOSAUR | *DinoLand*
Kali River Rapids | *Asia*

BLIZZARD BEACH

28| Summit Plummet
26| Teamboat Springs
25| Slush Gusher
Downhill Double Dipper
Runoff Rapids
Toboggan Racers

TYPHOON LAGOON

27| Crush 'n' Gusher
Typhoon Lagoon Surf Pool
Humunga Kowabunga
26| Shark Reef
Castaway Creek
23| Storm Slides

Child Appeal

MAGIC KINGDOM
29 Wishes Spectacular | *Parkwide*
Buzz Lightyear's Spin | *Tomorrowland*
28 SpectroMagic Parade | *Parkwide*
Disney Dreams | *Parkwide*
Barnstormer Goofy's | *Toontown Fair*
27 Mickey's PhilharMagic | *Fantasyland*

EPCOT
29 Turtle Talk with Crush | *Future World*
28 Soarin' | *Future World*
27 Seas with Nemo & Friends | *Future World*
IllumiNations | *World Showcase*
26 Test Track | *Future World*
Kidcot Fun Stops | *World Showcase*

DISNEY'S HOLLYWOOD STUDIOS
29 Playhouse Disney | *Animation Courtyard*
28 Voyage of The Little Mermaid | *Animation Courtyard*
27 Fantasmic! | *Sunset Boulevard*
Muppet Vision 3-D | *Streets of America*
Beauty & the Beast | *Sunset Boulevard*
Honey, I Shrunk the Kids | *Streets of America*

DISNEY'S ANIMAL KINGDOM
28 Festival of the Lion King | *Camp Minnie-Mickey*
Camp Minnie-Mickey Trails | *Camp Minnie-Mickey*
27 Kilimanjaro Safaris | *Africa*
26 Kali River Rapids | *Asia*
Mickey's Jammin' Parade | *Africa*
Boneyard | *DinoLand*

BLIZZARD BEACH
26 Teamboat Springs
Disney's Winter Summerland
Toboggan Racers
25 Downhill Double Dipper
24 Runoff Rapids
Melt-Away Bay

TYPHOON LAGOON
26 Typhoon Lagoon Surf Pool
25 Crush 'n' Gusher
24 Storm Slides
Humunga Kowabunga
22 Castaway Creek
Shark Reef

CHILD ADULT THRILL

Ratings & Symbols

Child Appeal, **Adult Appeal** and **Thrill** are rated on the Zagat 0 to 30 scale.

Surveyors' estimates of **Wait Time** are shown with reviews as Short, Moderate, Long and Very Long.

In the Parks

MAGIC KINGDOM

PARKWIDE

Backstage Magic   16 | 26 | 13
Tour | Duration: 7 hrs | Min age: 16 | Wait: n/a | Fastpass: No
"True Disneyphiles" tout this "behind-the-scenes tour" that explains "where, when, why and how" "the magic is made"; the "full-day" journey covers Magic Kingdom, Epcot and Hollywood Studios and includes "off-limits" areas like "utilidor" tunnels and "backstage ride entrances"; even fans wince at the $199 price tag (park admission not required), but most agree it's "worth" it and a "wonderful" "way to learn about the mouse."

Disney Dreams Come True Parade   28 | 23 | 15
Live Show | Duration: 20 min | Wait: n/a | Fastpass: No
Even some adults admit that this Magic Kingdom "tribute to Walt and his accomplishments" in parade form can "bring tears to the eyes"; though it "changes frequently", expect "all the trimmings" including "beautiful floats", a "wonderful theme song" and "favorite characters" from "all the big movies" ("bring on the princesses") who "acknowledge you regardless of your age"; just be sure to "secure a spot early" and "guard it."

Disney's Family Magic Tour   ∇ 24 | 20 | 14
Tour | Duration: 2.5 hrs | Min age: 3 | Wait: n/a | Fastpass: No
"A must for families with children", this "entertaining", Peter Pan-themed "treasure hunt" for ages three and up has folks "follow clues" to "rides, restaurants and picture spots" to "save the Magic Kingdom from being shut down" by Captain Hook; all "learn interesting facts" about the park, and kids "have a ball"; N.B. $27 plus park admission.

Disney's Keys to the Kingdom   8 | 28 | 13
Tour | Duration: 4.5 hrs | Min age: 16 | Wait: n/a | Fastpass: No
For "Disney freaks", going "behind the scenes" of the Magic Kingdom doesn't "ruin the magic", it "enhances it"; this "fascinating" tour takes guests "underneath the park" in the famed utilidors and to "backstage areas" that "most only speculate about"; fans soak up the "insider tips" and "WDW trivia" but say the "appeal varies greatly depending on the guide" and one's age; N.B. $60 plus park admission.

Disney's Magic Behind Our Steam Trains   ∇ 17 | 24 | 13
Tour | Duration: 3 hrs | Min age: 10 | Wait: n/a | Fastpass: No
"Train hobbyists" "love" this "excellent" and "informative" "close-up" tour of Magic Kingdom's WDW Railroad, which includes a stop at the

roundhouse and a ride on the rails before the park opens; it's an "enchanting" experience, so some would like to see the age limit dropped "so kids under 10" can enjoy it too; N.B. $40 plus park admission.

SpectroMagic Parade
28 | 27 | 17

Live Show | Duration: 20 min | Wait: n/a | Fastpass: No

"Memories are made" by this "stunning" "nighttime spectacular" – the "granddaddy of all WDW parades", it "blinks and burbles" its way down Main Street, U.S.A. with "beautifully detailed costumes", "infectious music" and more than 600,000 "intricately coordinated" "twinklers"; though a few nostalgists "miss the old Main Street Electrical Parade", more say this "gorgeous" "explosion of light" is "why you come to Disney" and makes for "the perfect end to a magical day."

VIP Tour Services - Magic Kingdom
20 | 25 | 17

Tour | Duration: n/a | Wait: n/a | Fastpass: No

Surveyors "can't say enough" about the "first-class service" on these exclusive (read: "expensive") outings at Magic Kingdom, Epcot, Hollywood Studios and DAK; custom itineraries, personal tour guides and "front row seating" for parades and shows please VIPers, as does the added perk of "meeting characters"; it's not cheap ($750 plus park admission) and many "never knew it existed", but splurgers swear it's "worth every penny" for the "best day ever."

☑ Wishes Nighttime Spectacular
29 | 29 | 22

Fireworks | Duration: 20 min | Wait: n/a | Fastpass: No

"Spectacular" indeed, the Magic Kingdom's "stunning" "story made out of fireworks" captures the No. 1 ranking for Child Appeal; narrated by Jiminy Cricket with appearances by Cinderella, Peter Pan, Ariel and Tinker Bell, the nightly display of "dazzling", "better-than-Fourth-of-July" "sky art" in front of "a fairy-tale castle" features "unique" "choreographed" pyrotechnic effects set to an "amazing musical score"; adults also admit to getting "emotional" reliving "childhood memories" – in sum, "to miss this would be to miss magic."

ADVENTURELAND

Enchanted Tiki Room: Under New Management
19 | 17 | 7

Animatronic Show | Duration: 9 min | Wait: Moderate | Fastpass: No

An Adventureland "favorite" for decades, this "campy" yet "sweet" animatronic bird show received "a modern update" not long ago with new music, "more wit and humor" and the addition of avian stars from *Aladdin* and *The Lion King*; still, vultures who want to "fire the new management" insist that "the enchantment is gone", having been replaced by "sarcasm" and "bantering" that's "for the birds."

Jungle Cruise
22 | 20 | 12

Boat Ride | Duration: 10 min | Wait: Long | Fastpass: Yes

The "stuck-in-1955" animatronics may look "fake" and the "skippers'" "shtick" may be "cheesy", but Adventureland's "comedic cruise", which opened with the Magic Kingdom in 1971, remains a "sentimental favorite"; though some say it's "outlived" its appeal since Animal Kingdom has "the real thing", kids "get a kick" out of the "surprises" "lurking" "around each corner" (water-spouting elephants, head-hunters), "especially at night", and even grown-ups who call it "outdated" say the "over-the-top puns" still make them "laugh . . . reluctantly."

Magic Carpets of Aladdin, The   25 | 13 | 13

Spinning/Orbiting Ride | Duration: 1 min 30 sec | Wait: Long | Fastpass: No

Partisans consider this "Aladdin-ized" Adventureland "version of Dumbo" a "better choice" than its pachydermal prototype in Fantasyland because it "fits more people" and the "wait is much shorter"; "it brings the same smiles" to little "pilots" who "tip" their "own carpet" "up and down" while keeping an eye out for the "hysterical" "spitting camels", yet "for some reason", kids still always seem to prefer "the elephants."

☒ Pirates of the Caribbean   25 | 26 | 18

Boat Ride | Duration: 10 min | Wait: Long | Fastpass: No

Considered WDW's "best dark ride" by many, Adventureland's indoor cruise is an "incredibly themed" "masterpiece", "right down to the smells emanating" from the "dank" "cavern" where "plundering" swashbucklers inhabit "elaborate" scenes and "cannonballs seem to whiz right by you"; the addition of "lifelike" audio-animatronic versions of Jack Sparrow and Barbossa from the 2004 film has made this "classic" even better, but while it's "boatloads of fun", it may "frighten" young ones.

Swiss Family Treehouse   17 | 14 | 7

Interactive Attraction | Duration: n/a | Wait: Short | Fastpass: No

"Kids today" might not know the Robinson family's story, but they'll "love" "climbing" and "swinging" in their "ultimate tree house" full of "clever little gadgets"; adults who "grew up watching" "one of Disney's greatest live action films" may wax "nostalgic" on the "almost never crowded" "self-tour", but dissenters say there's "enough walking" in the parks "without having to climb a tree."

FANTASYLAND

Ariel's Grotto   25 | 10 | 9

Interactive Attraction | Duration: n/a | Wait: Long | Fastpass: No

"Mermaid mavens" "love" the "individual attention" they get from the "elusive princess" who "signs autographs" and poses for "priceless" photos at this "enchanting" "character greet" in Fantasyland; a "cute", "interactive" "water playground" "helps pass the time" for the "little ones", but impatient adults say the "interminable wait" on line "with nothing to do" makes it a "real snoozer" ("only if your kids insist").

Cinderella's Golden Carrousel   26 | 16 | 9

Spinning/Orbiting Ride | Duration: 2 min | Wait: Moderate | Fastpass: No

Among "the most beautiful in the world" is how some carousel connoisseurs describe this "old-fashioned" "treasure" just outside Cinderella Castle in Fantasyland; "serene" and "fairy-tale-like", with "intricately carved" horses and "incredible" details, it's a "magical" "classic" that "never loses its charm whether you're five or 85", though for adults, the main appeal may be in "remembering" – and the "lack of a line."

Dream Along with Mickey

27 | 22 | 14

Live Show | Duration: 20 min | Wait: n/a | Fastpass: No
One of Disney's newest shows is also "one of its most magical" with "wonderful music" and "the best effects"; staged in front of Cinderella Castle in Fantasyland, the "well-choreographed" spectacle, starring Mickey, Minnie, "pirates and princesses", is enjoyable for both "boys and girls" and makes audiences of all ages "believe in dreams."

Dumbo the Flying Elephant

27 | 11 | 12

Spinning/Orbiting Ride | Duration: 2 min | Wait: Very long | Fastpass: No
"Obscenely long" lines and "maddening waits" can make this Fantasyland "staple" "a nightmare for adults" who don't understand "the allure of spinning elephants", but "the under-six set" finds this "simple" yet "magical" "carnival ride" where "they control how high they go" a "dream come true"; less jaded parents consider this "perfect intro to thrill rides" a "rite of passage" – as well as a "classic photo" op; tip: "go during a parade when lines may be shorter."

Fairytale Garden

▽ 23 | 15 | 9

Interactive Attraction | Duration: n/a | Wait: Moderate | Fastpass: No
Nestled against Cinderella Castle, this "whimsical", "charming" "outdoor theater" hosts Belle from *Beauty and the Beast,* who "reenacts" "the story of her life" by "casting characters" "from the audience"; adults say the "small setting" offers "plenty of interaction" but "not enough seats"; kids "love" "seeing a princess up close" but wish she'd "stay around" for photos and autographs.

"it's a small world"

25 | 18 | 8

Boat Ride | Duration: 10 min | Wait: Long | Fastpass: No
Originally conceived for the 1964–1965 World's Fair, this "timeless", "delightful" "little cruise" through the continents has become "crucial to the Disney World experience", not only for tots "mesmerized" by the "singing", "twirling" dolls in "colorful" "native" costumes, but also for "nostalgic" adults who want to "relive childhood memories"; a relatively recent (and "overdue") "face-lift" has "much improved" this Fantasyland "classic", yet for some, the most thrilling part is leaving that "darn" theme song behind.

Mad Tea Party

25 | 18 | 18

Spinning/Orbiting Ride | Duration: 2 min | Wait: Long | Fastpass: No
The Mad Hatter's un-birthday party as depicted in *Alice in Wonderland* gets another "Disney spin" at this "timeless" Fantasyland "family favorite" that sends guests "'round and 'round" in "colorful" "tea cups"; depending on "who's at the controls", the ride can be "slow and leisurely" or "frantic and nauseating" ("Dizzy World anyone?"), which amuses "rugrats" who "get a kick" out of watching the "Dramamine"-downing "over-30" crowd "turn green."

Many Adventures of Winnie the Pooh, The

27 | 15 | 11

Car/Tram Ride | Duration: 3 min 30 sec | Wait: Very long | Fastpass: Yes
"Pooh-lovers" of "all ages" "can't help but smile" during this "joyful", "adorable" Fantasyland "romp" that has them "bouncing", "floating" and "wading" through Hundred Acre Wood inside oversized "hunny

pots"; "amazing details" and special effects make "wide-eyed" younger visitors feel like they're actually "in the book", but some adults are "underwhelmed" by "unsophisticated sets", "no animatronics of note" and "horrific waits."

☑ Mickey's PhilharMagic | 27 | 27 | 17 |

Movie/Multimedia | Duration: 20 min | Wait: Long | Fastpass: Yes
Fantasyland's "must-see, -hear and -smell" "3-D" ("make that 4-D") adventure is so "realistic" kids and adults alike "reach out to touch" the screen; the "hilarious" "wild ride" through "classic" Disney films offers "masterfully executed" surprises "for all the senses", an "incredible" soundtrack and appearances by Simba, Aladdin and Ariel, leading some to call it Magic Kingdom's "most innovative creation in years."

Peter Pan's Flight | 27 | 19 | 14 |

Car/Tram Ride | Duration: 3 min | Wait: Very long | Fastpass: Yes
For kids – and adults who "don't want to grow up" – Fantasyland's "whimsical" "pirate ship" "flight" over an "exquisitely detailed" "London" is a "magical", "visually engaging" dark ride against which "all others are measured" ("you can actually see cars' headlights"); a "nostalgic" "classic", it makes "Pan fans" "tear up every time", but panners insist it needs "major TLC" and the "outrageous" lines for a glimpse of "Neverland" are "never worth the wait."

Pooh's Playful Spot | 26 | 11 | 10 |

Interactive Attraction | Duration: n/a | Wait: Short | Fastpass: No
A "fantastic" "addition" to Magic Kingdom, this "beautiful" Fantasyland playground lets "little ones" "run free" and "safely" "burn off some energy" while parents "take a breather"; kids "love" "exploring" the "tree house", "cooling off" in the "water area" and "meeting Tigger", but a few purists call it a "waste of space" and would rather see "a new E-ticket" attraction in the former "20,000 Leagues" site.

Snow White's Scary Adventures | 20 | 14 | 12 |

Car/Tram Ride | Duration: 3 min | Wait: Long | Fastpass: No
Spooked surveyors say the word "scary" in the name should tip off riders that this "slow-moving" Fantasyland "classic" "packed with nostalgia" is "no sweet ride"; while Snow White and the dwarfs make appearances, the "mean" "wicked witch" "keeps popping up" out of nowhere, so even though in true Disney fashion there's a "beautiful, happy ending", protective parents say it's "a little too dark" for "toddlers."

FRONTIERLAND

☑ Big Thunder Mountain Railroad | 26 | 27 | 24 |

Roller Coaster | Duration: 3 min 30 sec | Min ht: 40 | Wait: Very long | Fastpass: Yes
Frontierland's "twisty, turny, laugh-out-loud" "beginners' coaster" is a "family favorite" thanks to a "first-rate" red-rock mining theme ("look out for the geyser!") and drops that provide "adrenaline rushes" without upsetting "weak stomachs"; though swaggering sorts find it "kind of corny" and good for "wimps" given "no loops or big-ride thrills", even they admit it's a "classic" and the caboose is "an experience in itself"; tip: riding at night gives it a "whole different dimension."

Country Bear Jamboree

23 | 19 | 7

Animatronic Show | Duration: 17 min | Wait: Moderate | Fastpass: No

This "hokey" "hoedown"-cum-"family sing-along" in Frontierland is a Magic Kingdom "classic" that strikes most as a "beary fun" show and a smart place to "hibernate from heat or rain"; the "audio-animatronic" "musical adventure" features an ursine "jug band" performing "foot-stompin'" "country music", and though cynics say it needs a serious "revamp" ("next time I'll bring my hunting rifle"), mama and papa bears still get a "thrill" watching their cubs' "faces light up."

☑ Splash Mountain

27 | 28 | 26

Flume/Whitewater | Duration: 10 min | Min ht: 40 | Wait: Very long | Fastpass: Yes

Magic Kingdom's "happiest" ride is a "wonderful" flume "adventure" based on Disney's animated classic *Song of the South* that "tells the tale" of Br'er Rabbit on his search for the "laughin' place"; the "character-laden" lazy river journey meanders through "lavish indoor scenes" featuring more than 100 "adorable" animatronic "critters" and "delightful" music that will "stick in your head"; soggy surveyors say it's "always a scream – literally", especially the five-story "heckuva plunge" that leaves them "Zip-a-Dee-Doo"-damp, if not "gratuitously soaked."

Tom Sawyer Island

22 | 15 | 10

Interactive Attraction | Duration: n/a | Wait: Moderate | Fastpass: No

Visitors "make their own adventures" on this "cool little island" accessible only by "river raft"; kids love "running and romping" around the "beautiful oasis" in the middle of a lake in Frontierland, exploring "hidden caverns", "barrel bridges" and an "old fort" with a "pitch-black" escape tunnel; adults may find it a "peaceful" (if dull) "escape from the bustle of the park" but report that the "waiting to get back and forth" can be "a pain."

LIBERTY SQUARE

Hall of Presidents, The

10 | 23 | 6

Animatronic Show | Duration: 20 min | Wait: Moderate | Fastpass: No

You don't have to be a "history buff" to appreciate this "moving", "fascinating" theatrical presentation in Liberty Square that opens with a film on the U.S. Constitution and then presents a roll call of "incredibly lifelike", "detailed" audio-animatronic versions of U.S. presidents; admirers leave feeling "proud to be American", but kids who vote the show "a snoozer" will simply be "begging to leave."

☑ Haunted Mansion, The

23 | 26 | 19

Car/Tram Ride | Duration: 8 min | Wait: Long | Fastpass: Yes

"Spooked" surveyors swear this "Imagineer's triumph" in Liberty Square is an "E-ticket" "classic" born of "special-effects genius", which now has new polish following a post-Survey refurbishment; "creepy" "ghost hosts" usher guests into the "dead center" of a Victorian parlor then onto "doom buggies" where "dancing spirits", "hitchhiking ghosts" and an "infectious soundtrack" create a "hauntingly great" ride; though skeptics say it's "more funny than scary", believers call it MK's "cleverest" attraction with "attention to detail" that makes it "high on re-ridability" – and "too scary for preschoolers."

CHILD | ADULT | THRILL

Liberty Square Riverboat

`15` `18` `7`

Boat Ride | Duration: 17 min | Wait: Moderate | Fastpass: No
Weary travelers seeking a "relaxing" "getaway" from the "hustle and bustle of the park" will find it aboard Liberty Square's "beautiful" "old-fashioned" "paddleboat"; "slowly" "meandering down" the Rivers of America "around Tom Sawyer Island", adults feel like they've gone "back to another time" on the "old Miss", but kids may find it "boring" since "like an episode of *Seinfeld,* nothing happens."

MAIN STREET, U.S.A.

Walt Disney World Railroad

`23` `21` `10`

Train | Duration: 20 min | Wait: Moderate | Fastpass: No
Whether it's to "hop" "from one side of the park to the other" or to "get off your feet" and "experience" the "scenery" (which might include "real" deer or alligators), this "old-fashioned" "open-air" steam train is a "family-friendly treat"; the one-and-a-half-mile "circle" around Magic Kingdom – with stops in Frontierland, Mickey's Toontown and Main Street – goes at a "leisurely" pace, meaning it's "faster to walk if you're in a hurry"; tip: "ask to ride with the engineer."

MICKEY'S TOONTOWN FAIR

Barnstormer at Goofy's Wiseacre Farm, The

`28` `15` `19`

Roller Coaster | Duration: 1 min | Min ht: 35 | Wait: Long | Fastpass: No
Though primarily a "not too scary" "toe in the water" thrill ride for the "preschool set", Toontown Fair's "squeal"-inducing "kiddie coaster" has enough "twists and turns" to "pack a punch" for unsuspecting "preteens" and "some mothers"; parents like that "the whole family" can "enjoy" it together but warn "it's a tight squeeze" for grown-ups and little ones will insist on riding "over and over"; tip: "ask a cast member for a souvenir 'first-ride' card."

Donald's Boat

`23` `7` `8`

Interactive Attraction | Duration: n/a | Wait: Short/none | Fastpass: No
Only the "littlest guests" will be "entertained" by this "watery play area" centered around *Miss Daisy,* Donald's "cute" cartoonish boat in Mickey's Toontown Fair; for adults, the main appeal is the chance to "relax" while kids "run off energy" and/or "recharge" for more – "expect" them to "get soaked" and "be ready for battle" when it's time to go.

Judge's Tent

`27` `14` `12`

Interactive Attraction | Duration: n/a | Wait: Very long | Fastpass: No
"The quest" for a "personal picture with Mickey" "ends here" – "guaranteed" – since "The Boss" is "waiting here all day long" "with open arms" to "meet and greet" "thrilled" fans, whether "two years old" or "in their 40s"; the "indoor location", "old movies" playing and "other characters in the immediate area" make the "long wait" more "comfortable", but parents say "impatient" little ones still "get fidgety."

Mickey's Country House

`25` `14` `8`

Interactive Attraction | Duration: n/a | Wait: Moderate | Fastpass: No
"Take a peek inside" "the main mouse's house" on this "adorable" "walk-through" in Mickey's Toontown Fair; the five-room cottage is

CHILD | ADULT | THRILL

filled with "lots of cool details" but "not a lot of action" so while it's "perfect for little ones", "older kids will probably be bored"; tip: if the character greeting lines are too long at the end, you can "escape through the garage."

Minnie's Country House   26 | 13 | 9

Interactive Attraction | Duration: n/a | Wait: Moderate | Fastpass: No
"Little girls" "love" "seeing how Minnie lives" ("boy, she sure has her act together!") on this "cute" "walk-through" tour where kids can "touch and play with everything"; more "hands-on" than neighbor Mickey's manse, her "pink and frilly" "mouse house" invites "interaction" like "peeking into her fridge" and "listening to her answering machine", though impatient types say the "wait's too long for what it is."

Toontown Hall of Fame Tent   27 | 13 | 12

Interactive Attraction | Duration: n/a | Wait: Long | Fastpass: No
There's a "potpourri of characters" waiting to "meet and greet" "little ones" (and "children at heart") inside the colorful big top at Mickey's Toontown Fair; kids who "love" getting "zillions of photos" and "many autographs at once" think it's "the best part of any Disney trip", but weary parents complain about "long" lines full of "toddlers" in "meltdown" mode (and "their crabby adults").

TOMORROWLAND

Astro Orbiter   23 | 16 | 16

Spinning/Orbiting Ride | Duration: 2 min | Wait: Very long | Fastpass: No
Aimed at "very small children", this "dizzying" "Dumbo-style" "carnival ride" flies "up, down" and "around in circles", and acrophobes say it's "scarier than it looks" since it's perched on an "elevated platform" "several stories up" in Tomorrowland; though adults bemoan the "unbearable wait", the payoff is "spectacular" park views – plus they feel less "dorky" on a rocket ship than on a "flying elephant."

Z Buzz Lightyear's Space Ranger Spin   29 | 23 | 17

Car/Tram Ride | Duration: 4 min 30 sec | Wait: Long | Fastpass: Yes
One part "classic dark ride", one part "real-life video game", this "colorful" "interactive" attraction is "one of the best" for kids but also a "total blast for the whole family", bringing out the "competitive nature" in "all ages"; riders earn points by shooting targets with laser cannons, a "totally addictive" exercise that leaves some surveyors re-riding till their "thumbs are sore"; tip: "keep the blaster button depressed the whole time to score more points."

Carousel of Progress   13 | 22 | 7

Animatronic Show | Duration: 20 min | Wait: Moderate | Fastpass: No
Known among Disneyphiles as the park founder's "favorite", this World's Fair–turned–Tomorrowland "original" offers a "nostalgic", "entertaining look" at "the progress of technology" through "sweet" but "corny" vignettes; while this "historical treasure" (open only seasonally) strikes even fans as seriously "outdated", with animatronics that are "showing their age", those "inexplicably" drawn by its "gushing" "Disney-style optimism" and "infectious" theme song hope they never "pull the plug" on "Uncle Walt's baby."

Monsters, Inc. Laugh Floor

| - | - | - |

Interactive Attraction | Duration: 15 min | Wait; n/a | Fastpass: No

One of Magic Kingdom's newer attractions, this all-ages interactive video presentation in the 400-seat Tomorrowland theater stars Mike, the one-eyed hero from the eponymous animated film; high-tech features allow guests to text message jokes and yuk it up with the cartoon host in real time (à la Epcot's Turtle Talk with Crush) in an attempt to fuel the laugh-powered city of Monstropolis.

⚡ Space Mountain

| 23 | 28 | 27 |

Roller Coaster | Duration: 2 min 30 sec | Min ht: 44 | Wait: Very long | Fastpass: Yes

Disney's "classic" "rocket-ship"–themed coaster inside Tomorrowland's 180-ft.-tall "retro-futuristic" mountain "still gets the blood flowing" after more than 30 years with many "turns, drops, dips" and even "a bit of airtime" – riders "blast through space in complete darkness", and "not knowing which way you're going" only "adds to the thrill"; "nostalgic" Mountaineers who "loved it as a kid" "hope" this "WDW icon" "never changes" – but those who feel it "needs to be updated" should be pleased to hear that it's closing for refurbishment in early 2009.

Stitch's Great Escape!

| 17 | 13 | 12 |

Movie/Multimedia | Duration: 20 min | Min ht: 40 | Wait: Long | Fastpass: Yes

"Funny to some, scary to others", this "intense" "4-D experience" is full of "strange" "surprises" that leave visitors wondering "what's going to happen next?"; fans of the "love-hate attraction" praise its "impressive animatronics", but a "disjointed" storyline, lack of "Disney charm" and "gross" effects ("chili dog breath burped right in your face") leave "disgusted" surveyors swearing it "stinks – literally" (and suggesting "make your escape out of this line").

Tomorrowland Indy Speedway

| 26 | 16 | 14 |

Car/Tram Ride | Duration: 5 min | Min age: 1 | Wait: Very long | Fastpass: No

Drivers who've "been behind the wheel" of a real car might find "putting along" in a "go-cart" on "guide rails" at a whopping seven mph "pretty boring", but "little ones" who want to "feel like adults" "absolutely love" chauffeuring "mommy and daddy" around the twists and turns of Tomorrowland's "popular" miniature speedway; less jaded adults appreciate the "nostalgia" of the Disney classic but still fume about "smelly" exhaust and "tedious" lines; N.B. you must be at least 52 inches tall to ride alone.

Tomorrowland Transit Authority

| 16 | 20 | 7 |

Car/Tram Ride | Duration: 10 min | Wait: Short | Fastpass: No

"Nothing says relaxation" (or "napping toddler") like a "gentle", "breezy" mile-long tour through Tomorrowland aboard an elevated, open-air tram that's a "sentimental favorite" of many; traveling at just seven mph, this "underappreciated" ride (formerly known as the WEDway PeopleMover) offers "no thrills", but "sneak peeks" into Space Mountain while "great views" of the park make for a "surprisingly enjoyable" "breather."

EPCOT

PARKWIDE

Backstage Magic

16 | 26 | 13

Tour | Duration: 7 hrs | Min age: 16 | Wait: n/a | Fastpass: No
See review on page 20.

VIP Tour Services - Epcot

20 | 25 | 17

Tour | Duration: n/a | Wait: n/a | Fastpass: No
See review on page 21.

FUTURE WORLD

Behind the Seeds at Epcot

14 | 25 | 7

Tour | Duration: 1 hr | Wait: n/a | Fastpass: No
"Education with a Disney twist" is offered by this "surprisingly fascinating" tour of Future World's Land Pavilion greenhouses, where
knowledgeable guides explain the "impressive", "high-tech" aquacul-
ture that produces "Mickey-shape pumpkins" and other "strange
fruit"; adults appreciate the "gardening tips" and "project ideas" and
it can hold older kids' attention too, but "toddlers and preschoolers"
may find it "not terribly thrilling"; N.B. same-day reservations and
additional fee required.

Circle of Life, The

20 | 19 | 7

Movie/Multimedia | Duration: 20 min | Wait: Moderate |
Fastpass: No
Combining "adorable" *Lion King* characters with live action, this "touch-
ing", "eye-opening" Future World film puts "cautionary" environmental
lessons into a "palatable package" that's "humorous" and "entertaining"; "gorgeous scenes" and "astounding photography" engage
adults, and though some find it "preachy" and potentially "boring" for
"young children", most appreciate its "educational", "inspirational"
"message" ("I left wanting to recycle everything I saw!").

Dolphins in Depth

▽ 26 | 25 | 20

Tour | Duration: 3 hrs | Min age: 13 | Wait: n/a | Fastpass: No
A "fascinating" "educational" "adventure", Future World's "dolphin
research exhibition" allows visitors glimpses of normally off-limits areas ("food prep rooms, training tanks") then offers "face-to-face
time" "in the water" with the animals; it's "not a 'swim-with'
experience" – the mammals "come to you" only "if so inclined" – but
it's a "fantastic" opportunity that encourages "love and respect" for
the "beautiful creatures"; N.B. $150 per person, park admission not
included or required.

Epcot DiveQuest

▽ 20 | 27 | 23

Tour | Duration: 2.5 hrs | Min age: 10 | Wait: Moderate | Fastpass: No
"Swimming with the fishes" is "redefined" when guests (who shell out
150 clams) "get up close and personal" with sharks, turtles, rays and
60 other species in a six-million-gallon aquarium in the middle of
Future World; fans say the 40-minute dive is "the easiest and most fun
you'll ever do" with "top-notch" "theming" and "engaging" cast members, but the "best part" is "interacting" with family members "on the

other side of the glass"; P.S. you "must be a certified diver"; park admission not required.

Epcot Seas Aqua Tour

▽ 23 | 23 | 15

Tour | Duration: 3 hrs | Min age: 8 | Wait: Moderate | Fastpass: No
Some call it the "best behind-the-scenes tour in Epcot", though it's really "behind the glass" since you actually swim with "underwater life" in this "awesome" Future World tour; guests are given an "informative, educational" peek "backstage" at The Seas with Nemo & Friends before taking a 30-minute dip in the "beautiful aquarium"; N.B. ages 18 and younger must be accompanied by an adult; $115.

"Honey, I Shrunk the Audience"

24 | 22 | 17

Movie/Multimedia | Duration: 18 min | Wait: Long | Fastpass: Yes
There's "never a dull moment" at Future World's "hilarious" "4-D event" themed around the "Honey" film "franchise"; "incredible effects" that "you'll go home and tell your friends about" (e.g. "rats" "scurrying under your chair") offer "thrills that go beyond the screen"; still, while not wanting to "ruin the fun", some say the "realistic" effects can "freak out little kids" – and parents afraid of "slithering performers."

ImageWorks - The Kodak "What If" Labs

23 | 18 | 9

Interactive Attraction | Duration: 1 hr | Wait: Short | Fastpass: No
"Kids of all ages" "could spend hours" in this "cool" "technological playground" and "interactive lab" "conducting" "silly music" and "morphing" photos of themselves "into animals and flowers"; adults enjoy the "wacky pics" that can be "e-mailed to friends back home", but dissenters find this attraction, "reinvented" and refurbished not long ago, "cramped" and "not as good as it used to be."

Innoventions: The Road to Tomorrow

22 | 19 | 10

Interactive Attraction | Duration: 1-2 hrs | Wait: Short | Fastpass: No
"You could spend a whole day" exploring the "interactive" "innovations of tomorrow" occupying the two "museumlike" buildings that constitute this "often overlooked" Future World attraction; supporters say the "ever-changing displays" are "surprisingly cool" (citing the "robot race" and "e-mail booth" as standouts), but critics relegate it to a "rainy day", calling it a "walk-through advertisement" that's not "as cutting-edge as it was 10 years ago."

JAMMitors

23 | 24 | 12

Live Show | Duration: n/a | Wait: n/a | Fastpass: No
Looking like "janitors" "pushing metal trashcans around" the streets of Future World, this "wild and wacky troupe" becomes a "unique" band of "strolling percussionists" when they transform their receptacles into instruments; the "hilarious", "rocking" show, "a cross between *Blast* and *Stomp*", fuels "every child's dream" and "every parent's nightmare: playing drums on garbage cans."

Journey into Imagination with Figment

23 | 16 | 9

Car/Tram Ride | Duration: 6 min | Wait: Moderate | Fastpass: No
First-timers and kids find Future World's "slow-moving" dark ride that explores the "sights, sounds and smells of your imagination" "adorable" and "whimsical"; however, "disappointed" surveyors who remember the original version say the once "lovable" mascot has

become "a brat" in this "hokey" "revamp", suggesting it be renamed "*Lack* of Imagination."

Leave a Legacy   8 | 15 | 5

Exhibit | Duration: n/a | Wait: n/a | Fastpass: No

Surveyors are split on Future World's "mosaic landscape" comprised of one-inch tiles etched with photos and messages (i.e. "legacies") from guests who at one time were able to pay to "leave their mark for generations to come"; some "get a kick" out of "seeing their faces" on the "hulking monoliths" as a "reminder" of past visits, but others think the "creepy" monuments with "already-faded" images "look like tombstones" in an "ugly graveyard" that should be "torn down."

Living with the Land   14 | 22 | 7

Boat Ride | Duration: 13 min | Wait: Long | Fastpass: Yes

"Lettuce entertains you" in Future World's "educational" yet "enjoyable" boat ride that cruises through "amazingly detailed" ecosystems then moves to an "eye-opening" tour of a greenhouse featuring real "Mickey-shaped" "hydroponic" produce; though kids find some of the "practical" information "dull" and insiders insist it was "better when they had live" "narrators", there can nevertheless be a "surprisingly long wait" for this rather "tame" "time killer."

⚡ Mission: SPACE   21 | 27 | 28

Thrill Ride | Duration: 5 min 30 sec | Min ht: 44 | Wait: Long | Fastpass: Yes

"If you can handle it, there's nothing else like it" advise aficionados of Future World's "almost too thrilling" "space flight" simulator developed with NASA and Hewlett-Packard; the "centrifuge"-powered "rocket ship" reproduces an "all-too-real" "g-force" "sensation" that "exhilarates" some, "disorients" others ("barf bags are there for a reason"), and though a "nonspinning" "Green Team" option (added in 2006) draws "kudos" (and a 25 Thrill score) from those not up to the "hard-core" original, all should heed one respondent's rhyme: "if you're easily queasy, skip this trip"; tip: the attached Training Lab, an alternative "for those who can't ride", offers "exciting" "interactive" science experiences.

⚡ Seas with Nemo & Friends, The   27 | 19 | 12

Car/Tram Ride | Duration: 4 min | Wait: Long | Fastpass: No

Set in Epcot's former Living Seas space, this attraction "ingeniously intertwines" "colorful" aquariums and a *Nemo*-themed "dark ride" where guests board "clam-mobiles" and help search for the "beloved" ichthyoid; the "imaginative" animated effects "thrill" kids, and though "purists" say the "cutesy" "cartoon" "overlays" make the "real fish" look dull in contrast, overall most find it a "welcome change to a dated attraction" – even if it ignores what "the movie preaches": "fish don't like being in tanks!"

⚡ Soarin'   28 | 29 | 25

Simulator | Duration: 4 min | Min ht: 40 | Wait: Very long | Fastpass: Yes

Voted the Survey's Most Popular Attraction, Future World's "mindblowing", "breathtakingly beautiful" virtual hang-glider tour of California is "unlike any other ride"; combining IMAX technology, motion simulators and synchronized wind and scent machines, it's "so realistic" and "immersive" that "awestruck" guests are "convinced" they're actually flying; since this Epcot newcomer is also arguably the "smoothest, gentlest thrill ride ever created", it "appeals to all ages" and "raises the bar even for Disney"; tip: "get your Fastpass early in the day or you won't be riding."

Spaceship Earth 18 | 22 | 10

Car/Tram Ride | Duration: 14 min | Wait: Moderate | Fastpass: No
Future World's 18-story geodesic sphere (aka "the giant golf ball") is both Epcot's "iconic symbol" and home to this "underrated gem", designed in part by Ray Bradbury, that takes guests on an "educational" and "strangely soothing" journey through the "evolution of communication" from "cave paintings to computers"; thrill-seekers may call it a "dated" "snore", but even they say it's a "good place" to "cool off and nap on a hot afternoon" and admit "it wouldn't be Epcot without it."

☑ Test Track 26 | 28 | 26

Thrill Ride | Duration: 5 min | Min ht: 40 | Wait: Very long | Fastpass: Yes
Replicating a GM proving ground, this "exhilarating", "informative" "car test simulator" in Future World turns guests into "crash test dummies" as "cool" prototype vehicles are put through "realistic" maneuvers; lead-footed surveyors say the "real rush" is "blasting" "out of the lab" "through a wall" and "zipping" down a "high-banking" track at "a million miles an hour" (aka 65 mph), and though extreme riders say it isn't a "white-knuckler", it's still "fun for the family" – "when it's working"; tip: the "single rider line" can "cut your wait by more than half."

☑ Turtle Talk with Crush 29 | 22 | 14

Interactive Attraction | Duration: 13 min | Wait: Long | Fastpass: No
This "extremely clever" Future World relative newcomer, ranked the Survey's No. 2 for Child Appeal, turns into the "biggest surprise in WDW" when *Finding Nemo*'s "hilarious" animated "surfer dude" begins an "unscripted" "interactive conversation with the audience" in "real time"; kids "love" learning to "talk turtle" and are "entranced" when Crush speaks "specifically to them", while adults, who often "laugh harder than the three-year-olds", are equally "amazed" by the technology, with many wondering "how'd they do that?"

UnDISCOVERed Future World, The ▽ 10 | 22 | 9

Tour | Duration: 4 hrs | Min age: 16 | Wait: Short | Fastpass: No
Fans insist this "fascinating" exploration of the park's history from inception to its current incarnation is the "icing on the cake" at Epcot, allowing guests to sneak a peek at Future World's "behind-the-scenes" "technology" and "find out how the magic happens"; however, contrarians find this "for-adults" (16 and over) tour "not very futuristic" and contend it's better off left "undiscovered"; N.B. $49 plus park admission.

Universe of Energy: Ellen's Energy Adventure 19 | 22 | 12

Car/Tram Ride | Duration: 45 min | Wait: Moderate | Fastpass: No
The "fabulously funny" Ellen DeGeneres ("she *is* a source of energy") and Bill Nye the Science Guy manage to make the otherwise "boring" history of fossil fuels a "hoot" at this Future World attraction; fans insist there's more to this "exc-ellen-t", "innovative", "multisense experience"

"than meets the eye" (including an "unexpected" ride back in time), but critics cite "dated" "animatronics" and a trip so long that "coal can turn to diamonds" in the process; P.S. "beware the spitting dino!"

Yuletide Fantasy
`22` `26` `14`

Tour | Duration: 3.5 hrs | Min age: 16 | Wait: Short | Fastpass: No
It's only "offered a few months a year", but Epcot's "fabulous" "behind-the-scenes" tour of "holiday" displays and "Disney's version of Santa's workshop" is becoming a "tradition" with folks who feel it captures the "true spirit of Christmas fantasy"; fans insist the "charming" experience will "warm any Scrooge's heart", yet a few misers question whether the $69 price tag is "worth the money"; N.B. park admission is not included or required.

WORLD SHOWCASE

American Adventure, The
`13` `26` `7`

Exhibit | Duration: 26 min | Wait: Moderate | Fastpass: No
At the center of this "entertaining", "educational", "flag-waving" World Showcase pavilion is a "brilliantly executed" "multimedia" "journey" through American history that makes even repeat visitors "still cry at the end"; patriots also praise the pavilion's "fantastic" entertainment, "incredibly lifelike" animatronic versions of Ben Franklin and Mark Twain and some of the "most knowledgeable cast members" in WDW but fear revolt from kids, who may be too busy asking "is it over yet?" to notice; N.B. it was refurbished post-Survey.

Around the World at Epcot Segway Tour
`15` `28` `19`

Tour | Duration: 2 hrs | Min age: 16 | Wait: Moderate | Fastpass: No
A "must" for WDW groupies who "have seen and done it all", this "unique", two-hour guided tour has "even the klutziest" guests "zipping through" the World Showcase aboard Segway Human Transporters (aka "funky scooters") and learning "loads of Disney trivia" in the process; it costs an extra $95, but those who've shelled it out say "spend the money" because it's "truly remarkable" – and is one of the few "no-kids-allowed" options around; N.B. the Simply Segway Experience, an indoor primer course, is $35 for one hour.

British Invasion, The
`15` `26` `10`

Live Show | Duration: n/a | Wait: n/a | Fastpass: No
"Grab some fish 'n' chips" in the World Showcase's United Kingdom Pavilion and settle in to relive the Beatles "phenomenon" as this "feelgood" cover band pays "tribute" to the Fab Four; "baby boomers" swear this "lively" "blast from the past" sounds like "the real thing" ("yeah, yeah, yeah"), while "young kids" get into the act by "shaking their bottoms" – or "laughing at" "middle-aged" mommies "going wild all over again."

Canada Pavilion
`11` `21` `5`

Exhibit | Duration: n/a | Wait: n/a | Fastpass: No
More a "visual" attraction than a "real experience", the World Showcase version of "the Great White North" is "not that exciting", but its "authentic" architecture, "gorgeous" gardens and "fascinating" totem poles make for "great" photo ops; fans also point to its "engaging" cast

members, "inspiring", recently updated travelogue (*O Canada!*) and "must-eat" restaurant (Le Cellier Steakhouse) as more reasons it's worth "exploring."

China Pavilion
14 | 22 | 6

Exhibit | Duration: n/a | Wait: n/a | Fastpass: No

Surveyors have been "inspired" to visit the real thing after experiencing this "colorful", "storybook version" of China in World Showcase; "more for adults" than kids who "may get bored", the "intriguing" pavilion features "fabulous shopping" ("from expensive to kitschy"), "educational" exhibits and "entertaining" shows, and if some find it "stereotypical", the "amazing" architecture and "lovely" gardens make it worth "a look."

Dragon Legend Acrobats
25 | 25 | 15

Live Show | Duration: n/a | Wait: n/a | Fastpass: No

Seasoned surveyors say "animation and automation can't rival" these "incredible", "awe-inspiring" "young acrobats", who perform "breathtaking stunts" (like "folding themselves into trash cans") that skeptics swear "cannot be done"; fans say the "fabulous" show, staged in the China Pavilion courtyard in the World Showcase, leaves "children fascinated" and "adults amazed at how amazed they are."

France Pavilion
10 | 22 | 5

Exhibit | Duration: n/a | Wait: n/a | Fastpass: No

"*Oui, oui*", surveyors "love Paree" – or at least the World Showcase's "scrubbed clean" facsimile whose "beautifully realistic" belle epoque architecture (including a "mini–Eiffel Tower") and French-speaking cast members "take you away from a Florida theme park"; among the "charming" highlights are acrobats and mimes, "quaint shops", a "breathtaking" (if "extremely dated") Gallic-themed panoramic film and cuisine that some say is "among the best in Epcot."

Germany Pavilion
12 | 22 | 5

Exhibit | Duration: n/a | Wait: n/a | Fastpass: No

"Festive" "oompah-pah" bands, free-flowing "bier" and über-"friendly" German cast members contribute to the "great vibes" at the World Showcase's "charming" tribute to "old-world" Deutschland; fans laud the "interesting shops" (think gummi bears, Riesling, Hummels) and "authentic" "brats" and suds, though "no rides or shows" might cause *kinder* to "yawn"; N.B. book Biergarten reservations months in advance.

NEW Gran Fiesta Tour
- | - | -
Starring The Three Caballeros
(fka El Rio del Tiempo)

Boat Ride | Duration: 8 min | Wait: Short | Fastpass: Yes

World Showcase's "south-of-the-border" answer to 'it's a small world', this "slow-moving" indoor boat ride received a post-Survey blast of anatine animation with a new Donald Duck storyline, soundtrack and an overall spruce-up; Panchito and Jose Carioca, feathered friends from the namesake 1943 Disney classic, escort riders through a "colorful" "brochure of Mexico" in search of their *famoso amigo*; it can still be a "relaxing" way to "beat the heat" or await a restaurant reservation, even if some have felt it's "best enjoyed with a margarita."

ATTRACTIONS

CHILD ADULT THRILL

IllumiNations: Reflections of Earth
27 | 28 | 21

Fireworks | Duration: 13 min | Wait: n/a | Fastpass: No
"Much more than" fireworks, Epcot's "spectacular" "kiss goodnight" at
World Showcase Lagoon "chronicles the evolution of our planet" via a
"bedazzling" "extravaganza" incorporating lasers, water effects, "explosions" and curved LED screens on a floating, "spinning globe", all synchronized with "inspiring" music and narration; the "technical marvel"
offers "360-degree visual interest" while "embodying" "world community" themes that "appeal to all ages and cultures" – simply put,
surveyors say "it shouldn't be missed" "under any circumstances."

Impressions de France
9 | 23 | 6

Movie/Multimedia | Duration: 18 min | Wait: Moderate | Fastpass: No
"*C'est magnifique!*" gush Francophiles who call this "panorama" the
"best 'country' film" in World Showcase and "a feast for the eyes and
ears"; "breathtaking scenery" of "varied locales" such as the Eiffel
Tower, French Alps and Cannes combined with "hauntingly beautiful
music" "capture the soul of France" "without the plane ride and jet
lag"; still, some fans find it "dated" and warn it will "test the patience
of toddlers" ("puts my kids to sleep every time").

Italy Pavilion
11 | 22 | 5

Exhibit | Duration: n/a | Wait: n/a | Fastpass: No
Dining and shopping are the "main appeals" at this "visually stunning"
pavilion in the World Showcase featuring replicas of Venetian canals,
St. Mark's bell tower and Doge's Palace – "minus the pigeons"; the
amore-struck enjoy "authentic" cuisine and browse "beautiful fashions" at "genuine" Italian boutiques, but a "disappointed" faction find
no "reason to linger", insisting that a country with "such a heritage"
"needs more" "than expensive gift shops."

Japan Pavilion
14 | 23 | 6

Exhibit | Duration: n/a | Wait: n/a | Fastpass: No
Japanophiles laud the "lovely" "Zen gardens", "mesmerizing koi
ponds" and "authentic" architecture that give this "gorgeous" World
Showcase pavilion a "serene", "timeless" feel, and sybarites swear it
has the "best" dining and shopping options at Epcot; still, with "no
rides" or "movies" younger visitors will probably be "bored" unless
they're "making masks" or enjoying a treat from "the candy lady."

Kidcot Fun Stops presented by Sharpie
26 | 10 | 7

Interactive Attraction | Duration: n/a | Wait: Short | Fastpass: No
A combination "treasure hunt" and "arts and crafts project", these
"interactive" "pit stops" spread throughout Epcot have kids "collecting
charms", "coloring masks" and "learning without even realizing it"; parents say "whoever thought of" the "brilliant idea" "deserves a medal"
since the "little ones" "love" the "activities" and it keeps them "occupied
between shows", though it's of limited appeal to "teens and adults."

Maelstrom
20 | 21 | 15

Boat Ride | Duration: 5 min | Wait: Long | Fastpass: Yes
"The closest thing to a thrill ride" in World Showcase, this "insightful"
indoor cruise visits a 10th-century Viking village, "fanciful forest" and
modern-day oil rig with some "scary effects" and "surprises along the

way", plus a "fun twist at the end"; its "charming, old-fashioned appeal" and "couldn't-be-nicer" staff make it Epcot's "most underrated" attraction to some, even if the post-ride film's a "snooze"; tip: "in the morning you can usually walk right on."

Mariachi Cobre
15 | 23 | 9

Live Show | Duration: n/a | Wait: n/a | Fastpass: No
World Showcase visitors are "instantly transported" to Latin America upon hearing the "invigorating" mariachi music played by these "excellent" entertainers; the "perfect setting" enhances this "classic Mexican tradition" that's "adored" by adults, some of whom "schedule" their visits around performances – and fans insist "even kids will be captivated."

Matsuriza
19 | 22 | 9

Live Show | Duration: n/a | Wait: n/a | Fastpass: No
With an "intriguing" sound that "can be heard from 'countries' away", this "amazing" troupe of musicians performs traditional Japanese drumming – or Taiko – in World Showcase's Japan Pavilion; "children are fascinated" and it's "exciting for all ages" so it's "definitely worth a stop" if you're passing by.

Mexico Pavilion
16 | 23 | 7

Exhibit | Duration: n/a | Wait: n/a | Fastpass: No
Supporters say other World Showcase countries could "learn a thing or two" from this "colorful", "festive" "mini-city" encompassing a "relaxing" boat ride, "authentic" shopping ("if only bartering were possible") and "super" dining options "inside a pyramid" "temple"; though a few feel it could us some "updating", fans have *mucho amor* for its "Mexican-bazaar"-at-"twilight" atmosphere, "awesome" margaritas and "kid-friendly" vibe.

Miyuki
22 | 24 | 9

Live Show | Duration: n/a | Wait: n/a | Fastpass: No
In practicing the ancient tradition of Japanese candy-making, this "entertaining" and "skilled" confectionary artist "shapes" and "sculpts" taffylike rice dough into "fanciful animals", flowers and other "amazing" "take-home souvenirs" "right in front of your eyes"; her performances are "often overlooked", but fans say she's the "best sidewalk attraction in Epcot."

Morocco Pavilion
11 | 22 | 5

Exhibit | Duration: n/a | Wait: n/a | Fastpass: No
You might "forget you're in a theme park" as you "steep" yourself in "Moroccan life" at this often "overlooked" World Showcase pavilion with its "mysterious" "tapestry-draped" "bazaars" and "smell of exotic spices"; surveyors say the "land of Aladdin and Jasmine" boasts many "hidden treasures" – from "authentic" wares to "incredible" belly dancers to "free cultural tours" – though a few feel that the lack of a "ride/movie" makes it "dull" for "little ones."

MO'ROCKIN
16 | 23 | 9

Live Show | Duration: n/a | Wait: n/a | Fastpass: No
Their "unique" "mix of Middle Eastern music and rock" may sound "strange" to some, but these "entertaining" "pseudo-Moroccan" mu-

sicians prove that "different is what the World Showcase is all about"; the "lively" "Euro"-"party" "tunes" offer "something for the whole family": "babies love to dance", "moms enjoy the music" and "dads" "remain mesmerized" by the belly dancers.

Norway Pavilion
`14` `21` `7`

Exhibit | Duration: n/a | Wait: Short | Fastpass: No

This "enchanting" re-creation of a Norwegian village complete with "authentic" stave church and "big wood" "Viking ship" provides plenty of visual appeal; in addition to World Showcase's "only real action ride", it also features a "great koltbord", "interesting shopping" and a staff that "couldn't be nicer", though thrill-seekers may find the experience "not earth-shaking."

O Canada!
`12` `21` `7`

Movie/Multimedia | Duration: 18 min | Wait: Moderate | Fastpass: No

An "interesting", "informative" and recently updated (post-Survey) "tribute" to America's "neighbor to the north", this Canada Pavilion film combines "inspiring music" and "impressive" visuals of the country's wonders, both natural and man-made; shown in "breathtaking" CircleVision 360 with guests standing in the center of the theater, the presentation leaves some patrons "a little motion sick", others "yawning" and both wishing "there were seats."

Off Kilter
`18` `26` `11`

Live Show | Duration: n/a | Wait: n/a | Fastpass: No

Hailed by fans as "the best live act at Epcot", these "extraordinarily talented" "kilt-swinging" entertainers in World Showcase's Canada Pavilion fuse "traditional Celtic" with modern music to create a "unique" "upbeat" sound that has "kids and grandparents" "dancing" and "groupies" "singing along"; the band's "sense of humor" and "showmanship" have earned it a "huge following" of regulars (as well as dumbfounded converts who didn't know "bagpipes could rock").

Oktoberfest Musikanten
`18` `25` `8`

Live Show | Duration: n/a | Wait: Moderate | Fastpass: No

At the center of the "delightful" "Oktoberfest" atmosphere at the Biergarten Restaurant in World Showcase's Germany Pavilion is this "enthusiastic" "oompah-pah band" that performs "heartfelt" Deutschland "classics" suitable for "the whole family"; surveyors swear you'll be "surprised" at how much "fun" you'll have, especially "if you're willing to participate" ("polka, anyone?").

Pam Brody
▽ `14` `26` `10`

Live Show | Duration: n/a | Wait: Short | Fastpass: No

Fans of the "talented" British songbird/pianist in the floppy feathered hat say they "plan" their trips "around her performances" at the Rose and Crown Pub in the World Showcase and "wish she could be there every night"; a "wonderful entertainer", she has a vast and varied repertoire of songs (and anecdotes) and loves to "get the kids involved."

Reflections of China
`12` `22` `7`

Movie/Multimedia | Duration: 14 min | Wait: Moderate | Fastpass: No

This "soaring" 360-degree "surround film" in the World Showcase features "stunning visuals" of landmarks like the Great Wall and

Forbidden City and "insightful" glimpses into the "diverse" "facets of Chinese life"; surveyors say the "imagery and narration" may be "soothing", but having to stand the whole time is "killer on the legs", and kids who aren't into "educational" travelogues might "fall asleep on the floor."

Spirit of America Fife and Drum Corps — 18 | 23 | 8

Live Show | Duration: n/a | Wait: n/a | Fastpass: No
Americans will "want to wave a flag" while enjoying the "inspiring" "streetmosphere entertainment" of these "talented musicians" in "Colonial" garb who offer "a glimpse of 1776" in the World Showcase; surveyors salute the "moving", "living history event", calling it "more patriotic than the Fourth of July", even if a few say only "if you happen by."

United Kingdom Pavilion — 13 | 23 | 5

Exhibit | Duration: n/a | Wait: n/a | Fastpass: No
Even "without a ride or movie", there's still "a lot to see" in the World Showcase's "charming", "quaint" homage to Great Britain; the "lovely shops" (teas, toys, soccer) and "beautiful gardens" are "worth the walk around", and "Pooh and friends" are on hand to please kids, but most say it's the "fish 'n' chips" ("best this side of the pond") and "half-yards" "at the pub" that truly make for a "jolly good" time.

Voices of Liberty — 15 | 26 | 10

Live Show | Duration: n/a | Wait: Short | Fastpass: No
"Amazing voices" and "beautiful harmonies" put this "exceptional" "a cappella group" "in a category by itself"; "dressed in period outfits" and performing "with heartfelt patriotism" around the American Adventure in the World Showcase, the "engaging" "Colonial barbershop" choir gives "rapt audiences" a "musical history lesson" while eliciting "tears of pride" and "goosebumps" – or yawns from "bored teens."

World Showcase Players — 19 | 24 | 9

Live Show | Duration: n/a | Wait: n/a | Fastpass: No
This "hilarious" troupe of "improvisors" put their own "silly" twist on King Arthur's quest for the Holy Grail, which they reenact in the World Showcase's U.K. Pavilion; while surveyors like the "audience participation" aspect, they note that their "enjoyment" depends on which guests are "picked to fill the roles"; still, it's generally "entertaining", though parents say some of the material is "over children's heads."

DISNEY'S HOLLYWOOD STUDIOS

PARKWIDE

Backstage Magic — 16 | 26 | 13

Tour | Duration: 7 hrs | Min age: 16 | Wait: n/a | Fastpass: No
See review on page 20.

NEW Block Party Bash — - | - | -

Live Show | Duration: 30 min | Wait: n/a | Fastpass: No
Lip-syncing acrobats and live action characters from popular Disney-Pixar pics (Toy Story, The Incredibles) anchor this dynamic audience-participation party–cum–parade, a Hollywood Studios newcomer that

has guests of all ages singing, shouting and shaking their money makers; two-story floats mean the little ones can get views of the action from afar, and a soundtrack of revamped '70s and '80s dance hits means the 'rents will be rockin' too.

VIP Tour Services - Hollywood Studios   20 | 25 | 17
Tour | Duration: n/a | Wait: n/a | Fastpass: No
See review on page 21.

ANIMATION COURTYARD

Magic of Disney Animation, The   16 | 22 | 8
Live Show | Duration: 30 min | Wait: Moderate | Fastpass: No
Though insiders claim this "behind-the-scenes" peek at "old-fashioned" animation has "lost its luster" since it no longer features "real" "artists" in a "working studio" as in "past versions", supporters say it still offers "unexpected fun" plus "fascinating" "insight" into "the magic" (and lessons so you can "actually learn to draw"); however, some suggest there's "not enough" at this Animation Courtyard exhibit to "keep young ones interested."

◪ Playhouse Disney - Live on Stage!   29 | 12 | 12
Live Show | Duration: 25 min | Wait: Long | Fastpass: No
"Kids go crazy" when they see their "favorite" Disney Channel characters "come alive" in this "totally captivating and engaging" "sing-along"–cum–"dance party" in the Animation Courtyard; parents say the "adorable show" complete with "bubbles and streamers" is the "jewel" of Hollywood Studios for the "tot lot", but the "adult appeal is in watching them enjoy" since "uncomfortable" "floor" seating leads to "numb butts" and "aching joints"; N.B. following some post-Survey rejiggering, the show now features characters from *Handy Manny*, *Little Einsteins* and *My Friends Tigger and Pooh*.

Voyage of The Little Mermaid   28 | 19 | 11
Live Show | Duration: 17 min | Wait: Long | Fastpass: Yes
A "must-see" for "Mermaid fans" (read: "big and little girls"), this "truly magical" "journey under the sea" with "Ariel and her friends" in Animation Courtyard features a "unique" mixture of video, "peppy" "glow-in-the-dark" puppets, "spot-on" live actors and "nifty" special effects; "little kids" might find it "scary", but happy surveyors leave "humming the tunes" – and waking "sleepy" "dads, brothers and boyfriends."

ECHO LAKE

Indiana Jones Epic Stunt Spectacular!   23 | 25 | 19
Live Show | Duration: 30 min | Wait: Long | Fastpass: Yes
"Grab your Stetson and bull whip" for this "live action stunt show" based upon the movie franchise and featuring "audience participation" and re-creations so "intense" "you'll feel the heat of explosions on your face"; though "kids might not know who Indiana Jones is", the "impressive" "flames" and "crashes" still "entertain" "all ages", and a high "rewatchability" quotient pleases those jones-ing to learn "how they make the stunts look so real."

ATTRACTIONS

	CHILD	ADULT	THRILL

Sounds Dangerous - Starring Drew Carey | 11 | 14 | 7 |

Movie/Multimedia | Duration: 12 min | Wait: Moderate | Fastpass: No
Die-hard "Drew Carey fans" (and anyone "looking to get out of the heat") might appreciate this air-conditioned audio attraction in Echo Lake that demonstrates "how sound effects work in movies"; though many are immune to its charms ("poorly executed", a "waste of precious Disney time"), supporters insist the "entertaining" show "gets a bad rap"; P.S. "long periods" of "complete darkness" can "spook" kids.

Star Tours | 24 | 24 | 21 |

Thrill Ride | Duration: 7 min | Min ht: 40 | Wait: Long | Fastpass: Yes
Those "dreaming of being a Jedi" (or "bringing out their inner geek") will be "thrilled" with Echo Lake's "zany", "totally immersive" "intergalactic" "simulator ride" that "whips through the universe" and "the Death Star" with "cute droids" R2-D2 and C-3PO in tow; and if nemeses say the "aging" "adventure" is "as old as *Star Wars*" and in "dire need" of a "makeover", troopers insist Disney's first virtual attraction is still "amazing after all these years."

HOLLYWOOD BOULEVARD

Great Movie Ride, The | 16 | 24 | 12 |

Car/Tram Ride | Duration: 20 min | Wait: Long | Fastpass: No
Hidden inside a replica of Mann's Chinese Theatre on Hollywood Boulevard, this "laid-back" dark ride is often "overlooked" by thrill-seekers, but fans of classic films like *Casablanca* and *The Wizard of Oz* say it offers "silly, cheesy fun" with animatronic actors who are "more lifelike than the stars themselves"; "entertaining" "interactive" surprises put riders "in the movies", and though parts can be "scary for the little ones", overall it's a "restful", "cool" respite on a "hot day."

PIXAR PLACE

NEW Journey into Narnia: Prince Caspian | - | - | - |
(fka Journey into Narnia: Creating
The Lion, The Witch & The Wardrobe)

Interactive Attraction | Duration: 10 min | Wait: Moderate | Fastpass: No
Pegged to the release of Disney's second Chronicles of Narnia installment, *Prince Caspian,* this Pixar Place movie trailer/exhibition is set to open in early summer 2008; expect behind-the-scenes material from the movie, including original concept art, storyboards, props and costumes, a re-creation of Aslan's stone table chamber set made from the original molds – and even meet-and-greets with Prince Caspian himself.

Studio Backlot Tour | 18 | 22 | 14 |

Car/Tram Ride | Duration: 30 min | Wait: Long | Fastpass: No
Fans say this "interactive" "behind-the-scenes" walking and riding tour offers a "surprise"-filled look at the making of "movie magic", including stops at prop shops and Catastrophe Canyon, where a "stupendous" special effects display "gets the adrenaline flowing"; critics contend it's "not as interesting as it once was" and could benefit from a shot of "Botox", but at least it should put you "in the mood for a day at the Studio."

	CHILD	ADULT	THRILL

NEW Toy Story Mania!

-	-	-

Car/Tram Ride | Duration: 5 min 45 sec | Wait: n/a | Fastpass: Yes
Set to debut in spring 2008, this interactive newcomer (with a twin at Anaheim's California Adventure) is a combination dark ride and shooting gallery themed around Disney-Pixar's *Toy Story* franchise; guests don 3-D glasses and enter a world of midway-style games (hosted by Woody, Buzz and friends) where they score points by picking off balloons, aliens and barnyard animals; N.B. plans call for riders at the two different parks to compete with one another in real time.

Walt Disney: One Man's Dream

10	25	6

Interactive Attraction | Duration: 25 min | Wait: Short | Fastpass: No
"Disneyholics" say this "underrated", "mousebump"-inducing "tribute" to "the man behind the name" "should be mandatory" viewing since it displays "the seeds that grew into" the attractions that millions "enjoy today"; it's a "gold mine" of "Disneyana", from rare "archival footage" to a "replica of Walt's office", and though "fascinating" to "fanatics" who find it "moving", "ride fans" and "kids" will want to "move on."

STREETS OF AMERICA

"Honey, I Shrunk the Kids" Movie Set Adventure

26	13	13

Interactive Attraction | Duration: n/a | Wait: Short | Fastpass: No
Little ones "love" being transformed to "the size of ants" at this "brilliant" Streets of America "play area" where an oversized "spider's web", "giant LEGOs" and "large bugs" make kids "squeal with delight"; parents say the "photo"-friendly attraction helps the "two to eight" set "run off some steam" "safely" – "the only problem is getting them to leave."

Lights, Motors, Action! Extreme Stunt Show

25	27	23

Live Show | Duration: 25 min | Wait: Long | Fastpass: No
Direct from Disneyland Paris (hence the "French village" set), this "action-packed" Streets of America show "explodes" with "stunning" effects and "jaw-dropping" maneuvers involving cars, motorcycles and jet skis that keep fans "on the edge of their seats"; the "secrets behind the stunts" are revealed too, making it both "educational" and "thrilling"; tip: it "can be hot", so sit "high in the bleachers for shade."

Muppet Vision 3-D

27	23	13

Movie/Multimedia | Duration: 29 min | Wait: Moderate | Fastpass: No
The "zany antics" of "Kermit and the gang" rendered in "brilliant" "4-D" make for a "rip-roaring" good time at this Streets of America attraction that "captures the magic" of the original TV show and its "clever" "tongue-in-cheek" "shtick"; it might "look a bit dated compared to PhilharMagic", but the "entertaining" off-the-screen effects as well as "hidden" "adult humor" that "goes over the kids' heads" make this "good mid-afternoon cool down" a "perennial favorite."

SUNSET BOULEVARD

Beauty and the Beast - Live on Stage

27	24	11

Live Show | Duration: 30 min | Wait: Moderate | Fastpass: No
"Endearing" and "timeless", the "story of Belle and the Beast" comes to life "in front of you" in this "magical" musical production off Sunset

Boulevard that some call "better than the Broadway" version it inspired; the "concise", "feel-good" production – and its "awesome pre-show" featuring Four For a Dollar's "excellent a cappella" – will "leave you singing all day" and "make even the most beastly person crack a smile."

ⓩ Fantasmic!   27 | 27 | 21
Live Show | Duration: 26 min | Wait: Long | Fastpass: No
"Spell-binding" and "unforgettable", this nightly multimedia "spectacular" performed in a 6,900-seat amphitheater off Sunset Boulevard pits Mickey against infa-mouse "Disney villains" in a production blending live action and video ("amazingly" projected onto "walls of water") with "unbelievable" music, fire-spewing dragons, "fantastic" fireworks and other "mesmerizing" special effects; a "triumphant" finale leaves audiences "cheering", and though it can be "pretty scary" for "wee ones" (or "loud for grandparents"), most consider it a "don't-miss" "thrill"; tip: "book the dinner show package to eliminate the wait."

ⓩ Rock 'n' Roller Coaster Starring Aerosmith   22 | 29 | 29
Roller Coaster | Duration: 1 min 30 sec | Min ht: 48 | Wait: Very long | Fastpass: Yes
"Speed freaks" say "hold on tight" for the "stretch limo ride of your life", an "insane" yet "incredibly smooth" trip through the "dark heart of Hollywood" that some cruisers call "the best thrill at Disney" (aka "Space Mountain on 'roids"); if the "bone-jarring" "blastoff" (0 to 60 mph in under three seconds) doesn't "loosen your fillings", the "loops, dips and corkscrews" will, while "Aerosmith classics pound in your ears"; sure, the "long wait, short ride" aspect bothers some, but most say this "steel coaster" "truly rocks."

ⓩ Twilight Zone Tower of Terror, The   21 | 29 | 29
Thrill Ride | Duration: 5 min | Min ht: 40 | Wait: Very long | Fastpass: Yes
"A perfect combination of storytelling, technology" and "scream therapy", this "terrifically terrifying" 13-story "haunted"-elevator-gone-wild "free-falls" down a pitch-black shaft – and repeats the "heart in your throat", "pee in your pants" drop "over and over"; surveyors laud the Sunset Boulevard "wowser" as a "masterpiece of theming" with "meticulous details", "engaging" special effects and an all-too-real "feeling of impending doom" ("my son was so scared he bit me"), and repeat customers insist that the "randomized drop sequence" guarantees it's "never the same ride twice."

DISNEY'S ANIMAL KINGDOM

PARKWIDE

Backstage Safari   24 | 26 | 17
Tour | Duration: 3 hrs | Min age: 16 | Wait: n/a | Fastpass: No
For "a different kind of thrill", take this "educational" "family tour" offering an "amazing behind the scenes look" at Animal Kingdom, including visits to the veterinary hospital and elephant barn with "lots of little secrets revealed"; the "private" format allows for "up-close" "interactions" with "majestic" animals ("how often do you get to touch a black rhino?"), but "don't expect to pet everything you see"; N.B. $70 plus park admission.

VIP Tour Services - Disney's Animal Kingdom
20 | 25 | 17

Tour | Duration: n/a | Wait: n/a | Fastpass: No
See review on page 21.

AFRICA

Affection Section
24 | 14 | 9

Interactive Attraction | Duration: n/a | Wait: Short | Fastpass: No
"Basically a petting zoo", this "quiet", "clean" Africa attraction at Rafiki's Planet Watch caters to "young children" with hands-on opportunities to "interact" with goats, sheep, llamas and other "tame" "four-legged" friends; an "informative staff" that "knows the animals by name" and a "hand-washing station" are pluses, but "disappointed" adults cite "not enough variety" and have little affection for the "stinky" creatures.

Conservation Station
19 | 18 | 8

Interactive Attraction | Duration: n/a | Wait: Short | Fastpass: No
The "underrated gem of Animal Kingdom" is how fans describe this "informative" Africa experience consisting of a "narrated" "train ride" to a wildlife conservation station in Rafiki's Planet Watch; offering a look at things like food preparation areas and a veterinary clinic where you might "observe an operation in progress", it's considered "worthwhile" for "nature lovers", though a few feel the trek takes up "too much" of the day.

Habitat Habit!
▽ 20 | 19 | 13

Interactive Attraction | Duration: n/a | Wait: Moderate | Fastpass: No
"Slow down and learn something" by exploring this "cute", "informative" "walking trail"; located between Conservation Station and the Wildlife Express Train station, it features exhibits of endangered cotton-top tamarins, but the less-than-impressed question whether "two monkeys and a collection of preachy signs" constitutes an "attraction.'"

⧉ Kilimanjaro Safaris
27 | 28 | 19

Car/Tram Ride | Duration: 18 min | Wait: Very long | Fastpass: Yes
Take an "authentic" African "photo safari" "in the middle of Orlando" at the "centerpiece of the Animal Kingdom", a 100-acre "zoo on wheels" that fans say captures the "magic and wonder of nature"; while traversing the "bumpy" "plains" aboard open-air jeeps, guests get "up close and personal" with "freely roaming" elephants, rhinos and the like in their "'natural' habitats" (some "walk right up to the truck"), and though no guarantee of sightings makes it "hit-or-miss" for some, others say unpredictability is "part of the fun."

Mickey's Jammin' Jungle Parade
26 | 21 | 13

Live Show | Duration: 15 min | Wait: n/a | Fastpass: No
Animals, not surprisingly, are the main focus of Africa's "creative", "lively", "quirky" parade with "innovative floats", "crazy vehicles", "amazing costumes" and a "phenomenal beat" ("make room to dance!") that's "a welcome change to the usual"; fans say the "thrill is in the details" and the "up-close" "interaction" with cast members and "classic" characters from *The Lion King, Tarzan* and *The Jungle Book.*

	CHILD	ADULT	THRILL

Pangani Forest Exploration Trail | 21 | 23 | 11

Interactive Attraction | Duration: 20-25 min | Wait: Short/none | Fastpass: No
"Animal lovers won't be able to get enough" of Africa's "visually exciting" self-guided walking trail featuring hippos, meerkats, naked mole rats and exotic birds in "natural" "wildlife settings"; surveyors go especially ape for the "amazing" gorilla exhibit where "you'll swear they could just reach out and touch you", but beleaguered bipeds note there's "lots of walking" and the tour "can be boring if the animals aren't active and in view."

ASIA

❷ Expedition Everest | 24 | 29 | 29

Roller Coaster | Duration: 3 min | Min ht: 44 | Wait: Very long | Fastpass: Yes
Fans insist that calling this DAK "superstar" a ride is a "misnomer", since the "Matterhorn of the new millennium" – ranked No. 1 for Adult Appeal – is "an experience like no other" with an "excellent storyline", "fantastic" special effects ("the beast is awesome!") and "extraordinary thrills"; the "wicked", "unpredictable" indoor/outdoor coaster tops 50 mph, has an 80-ft. drop and "surprise direction changes" ("you must enjoy going backwards"), yet surveyors still manage to appreciate its "amazing attention to detail", even in the "spectacular queuing area", which makes the wait "half the fun."

Kali River Rapids | 26 | 26 | 23

Flume/Whitewater | Duration: 4 min 30 sec | Min ht: 38 | Wait: Very long | Fastpass: Yes
A "family favorite", this "refreshing" Asia land cruise with an "environmental message" starts with an "educational" slide show after which riders board circular "river rafts" that drift through an "elaborate, richly detailed" rainforest where "plummeting rapids", blazing fires and other riparian surprises await; it's "not for the dry at heart" – "even your sneakers" will "get thoroughly soaked" – but it's well "worth the wet"; tip: it's more fun at night "when you can't see the next turn."

Maharajah Jungle Trek | 21 | 24 | 11

Interactive Attraction | Duration: 20-30 min | Wait: Short | Fastpass: No
Wildlife fans "of all ages" "simply can't miss" Asia's "amazing" "wildlife exhibit" where "the thrill is in seeing" tigers, antelopes, deer, tapirs, komodo dragons and tropical birds; trekkers tag the "awe-inspiringly detailed" attraction as one of DAK's "overlooked gems" and say the "rare" Bengal felines and the walk-through exhibit where fruit bats "fly around the room" truly "steal the show."

CAMP MINNIE-MICKEY

Camp Minnie-Mickey Greetings Trails | 28 | 15 | 11

Interactive Attraction | Duration: n/a | Wait: Long | Fastpass: No
One of the "quicker ways" to "meet" "major characters" in the parks, Camp Minnie-Mickey's "must-do" "greeting spot" allows guests to get autographs and share "Kodak moments" with Disney heroes; kids "love" having "Mickey and friends" (who are "dressed in safari gear") "all in one spot", and adults appreciate the "nice, shady waiting area"; tip: "go when *The Lion King* show is running for shorter lines."

CHILD | ADULT | THRILL

☒ Festival of the Lion King

`28` `27` `16`

Live Show | Duration: 30 | Wait: Moderate | Fastpass: No

Expect a "roaringly good time" at this "visually stimulating", "Broadway-quality" stage show in Camp Minnie-Mickey that's teeming with "infectious" songs, "amazing" costumes and "nonstop action" (think "high-energy acrobatics", "larger than life" puppets and "mind-blowing" dancers); deemed WDW's "best live show" by some, it's performed in the round, resulting in an "intimate", "participatory" experience that fans insist is worth "planning your day around"; tip: arrive at least 30 minutes early to ensure seating.

Pocahontas and Her Forest Friends

`23` `13` `8`

Live Show | Duration: 12 | Wait: Moderate | Fastpass: No

"Kids are the center of attention" at Camp Minnie-Mickey's "cute" "interactive" show starring Pocahontas and her "amazing" "live" "animal friends" (including a rabbit, skunk, raccoon and snake); "little ones" may be "hypnotized" by the "front-row" experience, but "older ones" might be "bored to death" and unimpressed by "sets and props" they claim are "not up to Disney standards."

DINOLAND U.S.A.

Boneyard, The

`26` `8` `9`

Interactive Attraction | Duration: n/a | Wait: Short/none | Fastpass: No

In the center of DinoLand U.S.A., this dinosaur-themed "playground" encourages "young ones" to "run around" "to their heart's content" among "big climbing towers" and "slides of all sizes"; "gleeful" junior paleontologists can also "dig" to "unearth" fossils in the "bone" pit ("a large sandbox"), but while kids "love" it, parents may find it a "test in patience", both in "keeping track" of their kids and "getting them to leave."

☒ DINOSAUR

`21` `26` `25`

Thrill Ride | Duration: 3 min 30 sec | Min ht: 40 | Wait: Long | Fastpass: Yes

Travel 65 million years "back in time" to "save" "long-lost" creatures via this DinoLand U.S.A. ride (formerly known as Countdown to Extinction); aboard a "turbulent" motion simulator, passengers experience a "herky-jerky scramble in the dark" "rich in details and thrills", and while some find the jostling more "bone-jarring" than "spine-tingling", all agree the "prehistoric beasts" "around each corner" are so "realistic and threatening" "you'll swear" they could "gobble you up"; think twice about taking little ones – "I've seen *adults* cry."

Dino-Sue

`19` `16` `10`

Exhibit | Duration: n/a | Wait: Short | Fastpass: No

Standing guard in DinoLand U.S.A., this 13-ft.-tall, 40-ft.-long T. rex is a meticulous reproduction of the 67-million-year-old skeleton discovered by (and named for) paleontologist Sue Hendrickson; while there's "usually a great show going on around" the faux fossil, some surveyors say "it's just bones unless a cast member is there to answer questions."

Finding Nemo: The Musical

`-` `-` `-`

Live Show | Duration: 30 min | Wait: n/a | Fastpass: No

Explore the "incredible" undersea world of Marlin, Dory and Nemo in this lively DAK "Broadway-quality" stage show based on the Academy

Award-winning film; it's presented in DinoLand U.S.A.'s 1,500-seat Theater in the Wild, with "wonderful" dancers, acrobats, larger-than-life puppets and original songs, making it Disney's first musical production based on a non-musical film.

Primeval Whirl

25 | 21 | 21

Roller Coaster | Duration: 2 min 30 sec | Min ht: 48 | Wait: Long | Fastpass: Yes
"It's impossible not to giggle like a fool" riding DinoLand's "kooky", "colorful" "Wild Mouse Tilt-A-Whirl combination" that has cars (and heads) "constantly spinning" with "twists", "turns" and "steep drops" ("now I know how a Ping-Pong ball feels"); though the "jerky", "jarring" romp can be a "turnoff" to those "prone to headaches", some enthusiasts call the "silent but deadly" "midway-style" "thrill" WDW's "most underrated ride."

TriceraTop Spin

24 | 12 | 13

Spinning/Orbiting Ride | Duration: 1 min 30 sec | Wait: Moderate | Fastpass: No
"Preschoolers" find "unexpected fun" "controlling their dinosaurs" "up and down" in DinoLand U.S.A.'s "prehistoric version of Dumbo"; parents may find it a "blah" "carnival ride" with "no appeal for adults or teens", but unlike similar flying-in-circles attractions, DAK's version has "room for four" and "usually short waits."

DISCOVERY ISLAND

Discovery Island Trails

17 | 21 | 8

Interactive Attraction | Duration: n/a | Wait: Short/none | Fastpass: No
"Take time to explore" this "gorgeous" yet "little known" area of Discovery Island where pathways wrap around The Tree of Life and lead to a "wonderfully" "random collection of animals" (flamingos, macaws, deer and capybaras); adults say its "off-the-beaten-track" location makes it a "peaceful and quiet" "place to take a break", but children may "get bored quickly."

It's Tough to be a Bug!

25 | 24 | 18

Movie/Multimedia | Duration: 8 min | Wait: Long | Fastpass: Yes
"Creepy creatures" are the stars of Discovery Island's "extremely clever", "adorable" yet "intense" 3-D movie with "awesome" special effects that make audiences feel like they're "part of the action"; though some are bugged by simulated stings on their "backside" ("it actually hurts a bit!") and "potty humor" (they don't call them "stink bugs" for nothing), most get a buzz from seeing life "from a bug's point of view."

THE OASIS

Oasis Exhibits, The

∇ 15 | 19 | 7

Interactive Attraction | Duration: n/a | Wait: Short/none | Fastpass: No
Guests on a "stampede" to the "E-ticket" (read: "thrill") rides usually "breeze by" these "educational" exhibits at the Oasis near the park entrance; that's "too bad", fans say, since there are some "hidden gems" (deer, iguanas, flamingos) among the trees and vegetation, including some you might not see "in a regular zoo"; though children may "get bored" trying to find the creatures, odds are "they can't leave without learning something."

	CHILD	ADULT	THRILL

DISNEY'S BLIZZARD BEACH

Chairlift
23 | 21 | 13

Chair Lift | Duration: n/a | Min ht: 32 | Wait: Very long | Fastpass: No

In keeping with its "ski resort" theme, Blizzard Beach offers this "leisurely" way to ascend Mount Gushmore, "bypassing" its "steep" ramps and stairs; in addition to the "convenience" factor, the ride, which services Summit Plummet, Slush Gusher and Teamboat Springs, also affords "great views of the park" – though given "long lines", it may be "faster to walk."

Cross Country Creek
23 | 24 | 10

Pool | Duration: 15-20 min | Wait: Short | Fastpass: No

"Floating in an inner tube was never so relaxing" as on Blizzard Beach's "totally tubular" 3,100-ft.-long "lazy river" (especially since "you don't have to climb to do it"); the "slow" ride "bobbing along" a winding creek is "pleasant", and the occasional "spray" of "frigid" water ensures you'll stay "awake"; tip: when it's crowded, "it's much easier to get a tube down the creek a bit."

Disney's Winter Summerland Mini Golf
26 | 24 | 12

Mini Golf | Duration: 1 hr | Wait: Moderate | Fastpass: No

Located "just outside the gates of Blizzard Beach", this "enchanting" and "imaginative" pair of "Santa"-themed mini golf courses (in "winter and summer" versions) offers an "entertaining" "distraction" from "the parks and crowds"; swingers say "Christmas in July" is more "challenging", but both are "kid-friendly" and come with "surprises" and "great photo ops" that make them "better than Fantasia Gardens" for some; N.B. not included in Blizzard Beach admission: $9.75 for ages three-nine; $11.75 for 10 and over.

Downhill Double Dipper
25 | 25 | 23

Slide | Duration: n/a | Min ht: 48 | Wait: Long | Fastpass: No

It's a "race" to the finish line when tubers fly 230 feet down these "excellent" side-by-side "speed slides" at about 25 mph ("it's faster than it looks"); the "skiing" theme is "a blast", with graphics and an "enclosed" tunnel "adding to the excitement"; it's a "short" ride, but "adults and kids alike" "love it – repeatedly."

Melt-Away Bay
24 | 22 | 11

Pool | Duration: n/a | Wait: Short/none | Fastpass: No

Situated at the base of Mount Gushmore, this one-acre pool surrounded by its own "beautiful beach" is a "nice place to cool off" and "relax" after "walking" up and "sliding down mountains all day"; surveyors find "bobbing" on the undulating waters "calming" but say "if you want *real* waves, go to Typhoon Lagoon."

Runoff Rapids
24 | 25 | 22

Slide | Duration: n/a | Wait: Long | Fastpass: No

"Average thrill-seekers and novices alike" will "enjoy" the three "different" slides (one covered, two not) that make up this "cool" Blizzard Beach attraction; tubers can go it solo or with a friend ("riding together makes it even more fun"), but some say "having to carry your tube" up the "long set of stairs" "can take a toll."

Ski Patrol Training Camp
▽ | 27 | 11 | 15

Water Playground | Duration: n/a | Wait: Short | Fastpass: No
This Blizzard Beach multi-attraction complex is a "step up from the
kiddie park" with an agility course full of "floating chunks of ice", an
airborne ride that drops passengers off into a pool and a mogul run on
two-person inner tubes; preteens, in particular, "squeal with laughter
and delight", but for adults the "only appeal" is "taking a rest" while
the "little ones" are entertained.

Slush Gusher
23 | 25 | 24

Slide | Duration: n/a | Min ht: 48 | Wait: Long | Fastpass: No
"Daredevils unite" on "Summit Plummet's little brother", a "cool family ride" designed to resemble a snow-banked gully winding down
Blizzard Beach's Mount Gushmore; it's a "milder alternative" to its sibling's near-vertical drops, but at 90-ft. high the double-humped water
slide is "thrilling" enough to leave surveyors "holding on tight" – though
it "may be too fast for the little ones."

Snow Stormers
▽ | 25 | 24 | 22

Slide | Duration: n/a | Wait: Long | Fastpass: No
Lots of banks and sharp turns make these three parallel flumes feel
more like "ski runs" than waterslides; marked by slalom gates, the
"well-themed" Blizzard Beach attraction snakes down the side of
Mount Gushmore, and though it's "a long hike up to the top", it's
something "the whole family" can enjoy together.

⛷ Summit Plummet
19 | 28 | 29

Slide | Duration: 15 sec | Min ht: 48 | Wait: Very long |
Fastpass: No
"Bravo" cheer fans of the Survey's No. 1 Thrill, a free-fall slide (the
world's tallest and fastest) that sends daredevils plummeting down a
360-ft.-long "ski jump–style" chute from 120 feet atop Mount
Gushmore; the "almost 90 degree" "drop straight down" provides an
"awesome rush" that's "not for the faint of heart" and requires sliders
to "hold on to their trunks" in order to "maintain coverage" at speeds
of up to 55 mph; still, though "the bomb" (aka the "wedgie-maker") is
tough on "the bum", assenters insist it's the "absolute bestest" and
"worth every ouch"; tip: "be there when it opens" for the shortest wait.

⛷ Teamboat Springs
26 | 26 | 21

Slide | Duration: n/a | Wait: Long | Fastpass: No
"Thrilling enough for daredevils, yet tame enough for grannies", this
1,200-ft.-long group raft ride (one of the longest in the world) sloshes
guests along a series of waterfalls and rapids at speeds that are "faster
than you think"; up to six passengers can fit in one raft, making it a
"great ride the whole family can enjoy together."

Tike's Peak
▽ | 26 | 10 | 13

Water Playground | Duration: n/a | Max ht: 48 | Wait: Short |
Fastpass: No
Parents say this baby version of Blizzard Beach is "*the* place to set up
camp" for the day since the mini-Mount Gushmore, wee water cannons and "slow-moving", "toddler versions" of "adult" slides will keep
the "little sweeties" "busy" for hours while older kids "do the grown-

up thing"; the "swim diaper" crowd also "has a blast" just "sitting and splashing in the water" ("they won't want to leave").

Toboggan Racers

26 | 25 | 21

Slide | Duration: n/a | Wait: Long | Fastpass: No
The "race aspect is what really sells" this Blizzard Beach "favorite", where up to eight guests "get ready, set" then lunge headfirst down a 250-ft. waterslide in individual chutes; "uncomplicated fun" "for groups and families", the ride is especially "exciting" for "kids competing with parents" (though "sledding" experts maintain "weight does wonders with gravity").

DISNEY'S TYPHOON LAGOON

Bay Slides

▽ 22 | 23 | 21

Slide | Duration: 1 min | Wait: Moderate | Fastpass: No
Designed for tiny thrill-seekers (only guests 60" and under can ride), these pint-sized slides send little ones swooshing down mild flumes into a quiet corner of the surf pool; though "shorter" than the ones at Blizzard Beach, they can be "lots of fun", providing a "moderate thrill for moderate wait times."

Castaway Creek

22 | 26 | 10

Pool | Duration: 20-35 min | Wait: Short | Fastpass: No
"Grab a tube" and "float along" Typhoon Lagoon's "tranquil" lazy river; while it's "not intended to be anything but relaxing", the 2,100-ft.-long "drift around the park" with "beautiful foliage" does offer a few surprises, namely, "periodic sprays" of water; the trip takes about 30 minutes but there are exits along the route, which comes in handy when the "slow" going gets "boring" for the kids.

⧖ Crush 'n' Gusher

25 | 27 | 26

Slide | Duration: n/a | Min ht: 48 | Wait: Long | Fastpass: No
Set in a Disneyfied "abandoned fruit plantation", Typhoon Lagoon's "inventive take on waterslides" sends tubers down (and up) one of three fast-moving series of flumes – the Banana Blaster, Coconut Crusher and Pineapple Plunger – each featuring more than 400 feet of "awesome" dips and turns offering "good airtime" opportunities; "the bumps" can be "tough on the behind", but that doesn't bother aquanauts who consider this "thrilling" "water coaster" one of the "best" wet rides around.

Gangplank Falls

▽ 24 | 24 | 21

Slide | Duration: n/a | Wait: Long | Fastpass: No
Typhoon Lagoon's family-friendly water rapids ride enables up to five guests to pile into an oversized inner tube and take the plunge together; like Keelhaul and Mayday falls, the trek down Mount Mayday features waterfalls, caves and interesting scenery.

⧖ Humunga Kowabunga

24 | 27 | 27

Slide | Duration: n/a | Min ht: 48 | Wait: Long | Fastpass: No
"Cowabungaaaa, dude!" shout enthusiasts aboard Typhoon Lagoon's top-ranked thrill ride, a pair of side-by-side speed slides that send guests zooming 30 mph down a 214-ft.-long flume, through caverns and off a 51-ft. drop; though some say it "seems to be scarier for

adults than kids", most admit it's "fun" but warn that the landing can be "painful" – "you *will* get a wedgie", as well as "bragging rights for the rest of the trip."

Keelhaul Falls

▽ 23 | 24 | 20

Slide | Duration: n/a | Wait: Long | Fastpass: No

Similar to Mayday Falls, this Typhoon Lagoon rapids ride snakes down the side of a mountain sending guests, who travel in large individual inner tubes, on a wet and wild tropical adventure; because there's no height requirement, small children can be part of the family fun.

Ketchakiddee Creek

▽ 27 | 12 | 14

Water Playground | Duration: n/a | Wait: Short/none | Fastpass: No

Half-pints "play for hours" in Typhoon Lagoon's aqua-playground designed for both "swimmers and non-swimmers" with "shallow creeks", "mini-waterslides" and an interactive tugboat with water cannons; it's "perfect for toddlers" who like to "dig in the sand", and some parents even find it "fun to join in" too; N.B. under 48" only; adult supervision required.

Mayday Falls

▽ 23 | 24 | 20

Slide | Duration: n/a | Wait: Long | Fastpass: No

The longest of Typhoon Lagoon's three whitewater rides sends tubers sloshing and spinning down Mount Mayday through caves and waterfalls in the shadow of the shipwrecked shrimper Miss Tilly; like Keelhaul Falls, guests ride solo and there's no height requirement.

Sandy White Beach

▽ 23 | 26 | 9

Beach | Duration: n/a | Wait: Short | Fastpass: No

Guests looking to "relax" and "enjoy the sun" will find the "always clean" powdery shores surrounding the Surf Pool a "nice" escape; "building a castle" "in the sand" or nodding off in a hammock between two palm trees is what vacations are all about for some, but activists ask, "who wants to play on the beach when there's so much else to do?"

Shark Reef

22 | 26 | 20

Pool | Duration: 5 min | Wait: Long | Fastpass: No

"Shark lovers" will eat up Typhoon Lagoon's "exciting" but "safe" opportunity to watch "real" bonnetheads, leopard sharks and other "sea creatures" "up close" and "underwater"; after a brief snorkeling lesson, guests swim with the "ocean life" through a coral reef – "makes you want to get scuba certified" say those who call it the next best thing to diving "in the tropics", albeit with "extremely cold" saltwater; N.B. there's a land-based observation area for less daring types.

Storm Slides

24 | 23 | 22

Slide | Duration: 35 sec | Min ht: 60 | Wait: Long | Fastpass: No

Slides with names like Jib Jammer, Rudder Buster and Stern Burner constitute this Typhoon Lagoon attraction, considered "lots of fun" but relatively tame compared to the show-stealing Humunga Kowabunga; still, the "basic waterslides" that "whoosh" riders through the 300-ft.-long tubes into caves and waterfalls at more than 20 mph are not without thrills, prompting the less adventurous to say "never again."

⊡ Typhoon Lagoon Surf Pool | 26 | 27 | 23 |

Pool | Duration: n/a | Wait: Short/none | Fastpass: No

The centerpiece of Disney's 56-acre water playground, this three-million-gallon surf pool, one of the world's largest, churns out "unbelievable six-ft. waves" about every 90 seconds, bringing hundreds of other "screaming" swimmers hurtling toward you "at rapid speeds"; surveyors swear it's "the ocean without the salt and sand", and it's why some "select Typhoon Lagoon over Blizzard Beach", but even fans warn "you better hold on" to the "little ones."

At the Resorts

MAGIC KINGDOM AREA

Parasailing | ▽ 18 | 28 | 28 |

Disney's Contemporary Resort | 4600 N. World Dr.

Parasailing | Duration: 7-10 min | Wait: Moderate | Fastpass: No

This is no virtual parasailing "experience": you really *are* "soaring" 450 feet above Seven Seas Lagoon "strapped" on a "giant kite" with "the wind in your hair"; surveyors say the trip, which departs from the Contemporary Resort, is "peaceful" and "gentle" and the guides "patient and reassuring", and while few dispute the "phenomenal" "views", some say the price tag ($95 single, $160 tandem) is "far too expensive" considering "the length" of the trip.

⊡ Richard Petty Driving Experience | 16 | 24 | 24 |

Walt Disney World Speedway | 3450 N. World Dr.

NASCAR Racing | Duration: n/a | Wait: Long | Fastpass: No

"Adrenaline junkies" and "NASCAR enthusiasts" call this "speed-tacular" stock car training experience the "ultimate thrill ride"; after "suiting up" and "learning the ropes", Winston Cup wannabes "zip around" Walt Disney World Speedway's mile-long track "with a professional driver" or "pay the big bucks" and "drive themselves" at speeds up to 145 mph in a "safe environment"; though most say "way over my budget" (up to $1,384), wheel fanatics feel "it's worth every penny."

Sea Raycer Speedboats | 22 | 24 | 21 |

Disney's Contemporary Resort | 4601 N. World Dr.

Boat Ride | Duration: n/a | Wait: Short | Fastpass: No

"Zipping" around "Disney World waterways" aboard a "tiny" "watermouse" is a "blast", but what truly makes this experience "see"-worthy are "spectacular, one-of-a-kind views", especially of the Magic Kingdom; the two-passenger speedboats are rented by the half-hour at various spots throughout WDW for about $30; guests must be at least 12 years old and five feet tall to drive.

Wide World of Sports Complex | 16 | 24 | 11 |

800 Victory Way

Sports Venue | Duration: n/a | Wait: n/a | Fastpass: No

The main attraction at this "huge" athletic facility is "Champion Stadium" where the Atlanta Braves hold spring training ("fans love getting up close and personal" since "there's not a bad seat in the house"), but the "gorgeous" 220-acre complex also hosts "a multi-

"tude" of other sports including tennis, soccer and basketball; naturally, it's of greatest interest to "participants" and those who know them; N.B. open only for scheduled events.

EPCOT AREA

Fantasia Gardens and Fairways Mini Golf | 23 | 23 | 10 |

1205 Epcot Resort Blvd.
Mini Golf | Duration: n/a | Wait: Moderate | Fastpass: No
Swingers looking to "slow down" "after a long day of heat and crowds" can "choose between" these two distinctly different Epcot Area mini golf courses; the "adorable" Gardens, featuring "memorable scenes" from *Fantasia*, is "fun for all ages" with "diverse holes" and "innovative challenges"; the "more adult" Fairways (par 61), which includes "hills, valleys, sand traps and water", can be "frustrating" and, some say, "almost too hard to be fun"; N.B. $9.75 for ages three–nine; $11.75 for 10 and over.

Downtown Disney

WEST SIDE

Cirque du Soleil La Nouba | 24 | 29 | 22 |

1478 E. Buena Vista Dr.
Live Show | Duration: 1.5 hrs | Wait: n/a | Fastpass: No
"Mind-blowingly breathtaking" typifies reactions to this "acrobatic" "feast for the eyes and ears" set in a futuristic big-top at Downtown Disney; more than 70 performers pull off "amazing acts of physical strength" and grace that will have you "on the edge of your seat" thinking you're "in a dream" and wondering "how do people do that with their bodies?"; though it's "very expensive" ($70–$122), most consider it a "must-see", especially for Cirque first-timers.

DisneyQuest Indoor Interactive Theme Park | 27 | 22 | 19 |

1478 E. Buena Vista Dr.
Arcade | Duration: n/a | Wait: Moderate | Fastpass: No
"Video gamers" say this Downtown Disney "arcade on steroids" is the "ultimate electronic theme park" with five floors of high-tech "interactive" "experiences" including an "amazing" "create-your-own roller coaster" simulator and a "virtual" "pirate adventure" that's "worth the price of admission alone", plus "retro" faves like Asteroids; it's "great for evenings and rainy days", though detractors note that "thrills vary" and the "noise" and crowds can lead to "sensory overload."

DINING

Dining

With hundreds of dining options, there's something for most every palate at WDW. And except for the no-alcohol-allowed Magic Kingdom, all areas offer cocktails, beer and wine (the widest wine selections are in Epcot's World Showcase restaurants). Dress at most table-service restaurants is casual (only **Victoria & Albert's** requires a jacket for men). With three days' notice, table-service restaurants can accommodate special dietary requests (e.g. vegetarian, gluten-free, even kosher, which is delivered from off-site). Tipping is the usual 15–20%, though in some cases gratuities are included if you've purchased a **Magic Your Way** package dining plan.

IN THE PARKS: While the parks have no shortage of fast food, you can also eat healthfully, with fresh fruit and salads widely available. Epcot's 11 World Showcase pavilions offer glimpses of other cultures as well as tastes of their cuisines: bratwurst in Germany, chicken tagine in Morocco, sushi in Japan. Many of Epcot's sit-down restaurants have walk-up window versions too, where you can sample some of the same food at lower prices – and without a reservation.

AT THE RESORTS: The lower-cost WDW resorts have food courts offering a variety of dishes and budget options. If you're looking to splurge, top-rated resort picks include the aforementioned Victoria & Albert's; **Jiko** in the Animal Kingdom Lodge; and the **California Grill** at Contemporary Resort. Only "Deluxe" resorts offer 24-hour room service, but there's pizza delivery at the "Value" resorts and the Disney Vacation Club resorts. A few resorts have 24-hour counter-service eateries, including the Grand Floridian, the Contemporary and the Polynesian.

DOWNTOWN DISNEY AND BOARDWALK: From fresh seafood at **Fulton's Crab House** to kids' favorites like **Rainforest Cafe,** Downtown Disney has a panoply of dining options. Open for lunch and dinner, restaurants stretch from Downtown Disney Marketplace to Pleasure Island and West Side, and there are plenty of late-night options too, including **Planet Hollywood, Bongos Cuban Cafe, Raglan Road** and **House of Blues.** Disney's BoardWalk options range from the likes of **ESPN Club** to high-end **Flying Fish Cafe.**

CELEB CHEFS: Todd English (**Todd English's bluezoo** at the Walt Disney World Dolphin) and Wolfgang Puck (**Wolfgang Puck Cafe** at Downtown Disney) have brought some star wattage to WDW dining, as have a few non-culinary celebs: singer Gloria Estefan (**Bongos Cuban Cafe** at Downtown Disney) and football coaching legend Don Shula (**Shula's Steak House** at the Dolphin resort).

BOOK IT: Reservations for most WDW full-service dining options can be made by calling 407-939-3463 up to 180 days in advance. Some restaurants now impose penalties for no-shows and will charge your credit card a cancellation fee, so be sure to ask when calling. If you can't get a reservation, try just showing up – early or late – and you may find an empty table or just a short wait.

Top Food

MAGIC KINGDOM

22 Main Street Bakery | *Main Street*
   Plaza Ice Cream | *Main Street*
20 Liberty Tree | *Liberty Square*
   Enchanted Grove | *Fantasyland*
   Plaza Restaurant | *Main Street*

EPCOT

23 Boulangerie Pâtisserie | *World Showcase*
   Le Cellier Steak | *World Showcase*
22 Tokyo Dining | *World Showcase*
   Teppan Edo | *World Showcase*
   Tangierine | *World Showcase*

DISNEY'S HOLLYWOOD STUDIOS

22 Hollywood Brown Derby | *Hollywood Boulevard*
20 Mama Melrose's | *Streets of America*
19 Toluca Turkey | *Sunset Boulevard*
   50's Prime Time | *Echo Lake*
   Starring Rolls | *Sunset Boulevard*

DISNEY'S ANIMAL KINGDOM

21 Tusker House | *Africa*
   Flame Tree BBQ | *Discovery Island*
   Harambe Fruit Market | *Africa*
17 Rainforest Cafe | *The Oasis*
   Pizzafari | *Discovery Island*

DOWNTOWN DISNEY

23 Ghirardelli | *Marketplace*
22 Earl of Sandwich | *Marketplace*
   Raglan Road | *Pleasure Island*
21 Fulton's Crab House | *Pleasure Island*
   Portobello Yacht Club | *Pleasure Island*

RESORT AREAS

27 Victoria & Albert's | *Grand Floridian, Magic Kingdom Area*
26 California Grill | *Contemporary Resort, Magic Kingdom Area*
25 Jiko/Cooking Place | *Animal Kingdom Lodge, Animal Kingdom Area*
24 Boma | *Animal Kingdom Lodge, Animal Kingdom Area*
   Yachtsman Steak | *Yacht Club Resort, Epcot Area*

Ratings & Symbols

Food, Decor and **Service** are rated on the Zagat 0 to 30 scale.

Cost reflects our surveyors' estimate of the price of dinner with one drink and tip and is a benchmark only. For places without ratings, cost is shown as follows:

| ⌐| $25 and below   ᴱ| $41 to $65

ᴹ| $26 to $40   ⱽᴱ| $66 or more

◑ serves after 11 PM

B, L, D, S show Breakfast, Lunch, Dinner or Snacks are served.

In the Parks

MAGIC KINGDOM

ADVENTURELAND

El Pirata Y El Perico Restaurant *Mexican*   17 | 16 | 15 | $11
Counter service | L, S
Pirate or not, you'll have to "fight the hordes" at this Adventureland outpost, the MK's only – and therefore "crowded" – Mexican, where the taco-centric bill of fare strikes mateys as "tasty and substantial"; critics squawk the "almost never open" spot leaves something "to be desired", but "reasonable prices" suit "hungry" swabs "on a budget."

FANTASYLAND

Enchanted Grove *Ice Cream*   20 | 14 | 16 | $8
Counter service | S
"Most pass by" this "hidden" "snack stand" in Fantasyland near the Mad Hatter's Tea Party, but "true fans" know it as a "delightful" find; while it offers a variety of "quick", "refreshing" "treats" – ice creams, slushies – insiders insist the soft-serve swirls are "the best."

Pinocchio Village Haus *American*   16 | 17 | 15 | $11
Counter service | L, D, S
Decked out with murals of its nosy namesake, this "cute" Fantasyland haus offers "fairly inexpensive", "typical" "fast food", including pizza and "Figaro fries" loaded with bacon and cheese; skeptics sniff "same old stuff" but even they'd agree it's good for "watching the 'it's a small world' boats go by", hence it's often "packed", making seating "hard to find."

FRONTIERLAND

Pecos Bill Café *American*   18 | 17 | 15 | $11
Counter service | L, D, S
One of the park's original eateries, this Wild West–theme "dine-and-dash" near Splash Mountain in Frontierland "gets the job done" for pardners who cite "*delicioso*" burgers, hot dogs and such; "limited" options irk some and critics take aim at "standard Disney

| | FOOD | DECOR | SERVICE | COST |

food", but insiders suggest "doctoring up" your victuals at the "fabulous fixin's bar."

LIBERTY SQUARE

Columbia Harbour House *American/Seafood*   19 | 17 | 16 | $12
Counter service | L, D, S

"Tucked away" in Liberty Square yet within earshot of the Haunted Mansion's "howls", this "better-than-average" "nautical New England-theme" counter-service eatery emphasizes seafood and "healthy" American fare with vegetarian options; though contrarians find the menu "boring" and the "dark", wood-laden interior "dreary", compromisers contend that any "dieter's oasis" that also offers "good fast food" equals a "family favorite."

Liberty Tree Tavern *American*   20 | 21 | 21 | $25
Table service | Reservations: Required | L, D

Across from the riverboat landing in Liberty Square, this popular "blast from the past" filled with "charming" 18th-century "period furnishings" serves a "good-value" à la carte lunch but specializes in "down-home" "Thanksgiving-style" character-dining dinners; its "hefty portions" of "carved meats" and other "standard" American fare are more than enough to "share with your fellow revolutionaries", and if the place "hasn't changed since the 1970s", it still makes folks "feel at home."

MAIN STREET, U.S.A.

Casey's Corner *Hot Dogs*   18 | 18 | 17 | $10
Counter service | L, D, S

A "must" "if your idea of nirvana is a hot dog" at a ballpark, this counter-service cafe on Main Street, U.S.A. "hits a home run" with its "belly-busting" franks, corn dog nuggets and "old-fashioned" baseball-theme setting complete with a "ragtime" piano player outside and "vintage" sports cartoons inside; it gets "annoyingly crowded", but "fast" service and "enjoyable" castle views "while waiting for the parade or fireworks" are pluses.

Main Street Bakery *Bakery*   22 | 17 | 19 | $8
Counter service | S

The "sweet" "aroma" wafting from this "convenient" stop on the east side of Main Street, U.S.A. can make it "hard to pass up" the treats it produces, including the "ooiest, gooiest" cinnamon rolls "the size of one's head", "magically delicious" cupcakes, coffees and other "yummy" "parade food" – just beware "slow-moving" lines "longer than those at Space Mountain."

Plaza Ice Cream Parlor *Ice Cream*   22 | 18 | 18 | $9
Counter service | S

Cone-oisseurs say a "prime location" on Main Street, U.S.A. and "generous servings" of "delicious" "hand-scooped" ice cream (try the "waffle-bowl sundaes") make this "old-fashioned parlor" "perfect" for a "little pick-me-up"; "efficient" servers "dressed in vintage" costumes make the "long lines" "move quickly", which placates "hot, cranky" kids "waiting for the parade or fireworks to begin."

	FOOD	DECOR	SERVICE	COST

Plaza Restaurant, The *American*
20 | 19 | 20 | $18

Table service | Reservations: Required | L, D

"Very large" sandwiches and burgers plus milkshakes "beyond com-pare" sate surveyors at this "overlooked" "getaway" with "Victorian-style" decor and "quaint" "gazebo seating" on a side lane in Main Street, U.S.A.; sure, some fault "slow" service and find prices "a little high" for "nothing fancy" American fare, but most consider it a "sweet" "retreat from the din."

Tony's Town Square Restaurant *Italian*
17 | 21 | 20 | $27

Table service | Reservations: Required | L, D

Amici say "generous servings" of "solid" red-sauce "Italian classics" are reasons to frequent this "cute, quaint" glass-enclosed patio on Main Street, U.S.A. where you can "dine with Lady and the Tramp"; though a few feel it's "fallen in quality", most agree it's a "handy, if not totally dandy" spot to "share some spaghetti" – just don't "push meat-balls to your girlfriend with your nose."

TOMORROWLAND

Auntie Gravity's Galactic Goodies *Ice Cream*
∇ 18 | 13 | 16 | $9

Counter service | S

"On a hot day" sweet tooths can't resist the pull of this Tomorrowland "quick stop" serving ice-cream sundaes and soda-fountain treats; ser-vice can be "slow" but "there are always seats", and if some find the experience rather earthbound, kinder kin say Auntie's "out-of-this-world" fruit smoothies are "the best at WDW."

Cosmic Ray's Starlight Cafe *American*
16 | 15 | 14 | $12

Counter service | Reservations: Required | L, D, S

With a "hilarious" animatronic "alien lounge singer" performing "cringe-worthy" "renditions of classic hits", it's no surprise that "kids love" this "manic" counter-service American in Tomorrowland; it of-fers "good variety" (burgers, salads, even "kosher" options) and the "large portions can easily be shared", but more worldly sorts yawn over "passable" quality, "stuck-in-the-past" decor and an "annoying" setup with "separate lines" for different kinds of food.

Lunching Pad, The *American*
15 | 12 | 13 | $11

Counter service | S

"Addictive", "fall-off-the-bone-delicious" turkey legs are the highlight at this walk-up window near Tomorrowland's Astro-Orbiter; most consider it fine for a "quick bite", with "plentiful" seating and a "great variety" of American fare that's decent "for the price", but dissenters liken it to "a school cafeteria" complete with "inefficient" service and "pre-fab" chow.

Tomorrowland Terrace Noodle Station *Asian*
13 | 10 | 13 | $11

Counter service | L, D, S

This "reasonable" quick-service option with "great views of Cinderella Castle" near the entrance to Tomorrowland dishes up "Disneyfied Asian" ("noodle bowls", teriyaki chicken) plus American standards like chicken nuggets; given that it's seasonal it is not always open, which is fine by critics who knock "bland" fare "from Planet Blech."

| | FOOD | DECOR | SERVICE | COST |

EPCOT

FUTURE WORLD

Coral Reef Restaurant *Seafood* | 19 | 25 | 20 | $37 |
Table service | Reservations: Required | Serves alcohol | L, D
Both "children and adults are mesmerized" by this "over-the-top",
"under-the-sea" tiered dining room in the Living Seas Pavilion, where
"floor-to-ceiling" windows look into a "spectacular" five-million gallon
aquarium; most find the fin fare "fresh" and "surprisingly good", if "a
bit pricey", and though sensitive souls say that it can be "a little odd"
to "watch Nemo swim by while you eat his cousin" for dinner, the setting "awes" and "entertains", especially when "Mickey's in the tank."

Electric Umbrella *American* | 16 | 14 | 15 | $11 |
Counter service | Serves alcohol | L, D, S
"If you don't like the international cuisine" inundating Epcot, there's
always this "basic" American "fallback" at Innoventions in Future
World, offering burgers, wraps and a few "healthier items"; it's strictly
"no-frills" with "not much by way of decor", but ample patio seating
means "plenty of room."

WORLD SHOWCASE

Biergarten Restaurant *German* | 21 | 19 | 23 | $19 |
Table service | Reservations: Required | Serves alcohol | L, D
Sommerfest *German*
Counter service | Serves alcohol | L, D, S
"Traditional oompah entertainment" is "a hoot" for "the whole family" at
this "busy", "noisy" Germany Pavilion dining hall, offering an "all-you-
can-eat buffet" with "a wide selection" of "authentic" wurst, schnitzel,
sauerbraten and salads, plus "huge" amounts of beer; "bring a crowd" to
fill a whole table, or expect "family-style seating" beside "strangers" –
either way, it delivers "good value" and is especially "great for lunch";
N.B. Sommerfest, a like-themed alfresco counter-service eatery at the
entrance, serves à la carte bratwurst, beer, wine and desserts.

Bistro de Paris Restaurant *French* | 22 | 22 | 21 | $41 |
Table service | Serves alcohol | D
Amis insist "you can't beat" the "imaginative", "well-presented" fare
"that would hold its own in a major city" at this "quaint, romantic"
World Showcase France Pavilion bistro that's "calmer than its downstairs counterpart" (Chefs de France); servers are "charming" and you
can "watch the fireworks" from its "inviting" château-like setting, so
though a few fault "limited" choices, overall it merits an "ooh-la-la."

Boulangerie Pâtisserie *Bakery* | 23 | 17 | 18 | $11 |
Counter service | Serves alcohol | L, D, S
"Don't miss" this "adorable" if "crowded" patisserie set in a "mock-up
of a quaint Parisian alleyway" near the back of Epcot's France Pavilion;
"delectable" tarts and the "best Napoleon outside Paris" "hit the
sweet spot", while savory cheese plates and *très bien* ham croissants
also please; most say it's "worth" braving the "long lines", even if
some find the "genuine French" 'tude a bit "rude."

Chefs de France Restaurant *French*

22 | 22 | 21 | $40

Table service | Serves alcohol | L, D

Francophiles say this "unpretentious but perfectly French" "upscale" "favorite" in World Showcase's France Pavilion will make you "forget you're in Florida" with its "enchanting" bistro atmosphere and "terrific views" of World Showcase; "delicious", "well-presented" fare and "formal" but "friendly" service add allure, and if snootier swells sniff "ersatz Gallic", defenders declare it "the next best thing" to Paris – "and cleaner"; P.S. the prix fixe lunch is a "terrific deal."

Kringla Bakeri Og Kafe *Norwegian*

22 | 15 | 19 | $9

Counter service | Serves alcohol | L, S

"Perfect for a light lunch" or "late-evening dessert" "before watching IllumiNations", this counter-service bakery at Epcot's Norway Pavilion doles out "wonderful", "flaky-crust" pastries, "Scandinavian-style" gourmet sandwiches and more; "cute", "cheery" servers enhance the experience, though some kringe at the "cramped" confines; N.B. beer, wine and coffee liqueurs also available.

⚡ Le Cellier Steakhouse *Canadian/Steak*

23 | 21 | 23 | $41

Table service | Reservations: Required | Serves alcohol | L, D

"Reserve months in advance" if you want to enjoy this Canadian steakhouse "gem" "hidden under" Canada Pavilion; "high-quality" meats, "incredible" cheddar cheese soup and "regional breads" that add "cultural flair" explain its popularity, and if some find the "dark" setting "dungeonlike", others call it "cozy" with a "friendly" staff that adds to the "warm atmosphere" – and "you probably won't take your eyes off the food" anyway.

Lotus Blossom Cafe *Chinese*

15 | 14 | 17 | $14

Counter service | Serves alcohol | L, D, S

"Crispy egg rolls" and a "polite" staff earn nods, but overall this "cafeteria-style" "fast-food" Chinese behind Nine Dragons restaurant in the China Pavilion draws middling marks; some declare it "satisfying" for a "quick bite" "on a budget", while others shrug it off as "uninspired."

Nine Dragons Restaurant *Chinese*

19 | 21 | 20 | $28

Table service | Serves alcohol | L, D

The "beautiful" decor (Oriental rugs, mahogany accents) earns praise at this "upscale" China Pavilion eatery, as do "caring" staffers (though some are so "authentic" they can be "difficult to understand"); fans insist "even General Tso would approve" of the "fragrant" fare, including "wonderful dim sum" "served family-style", but an unimpressed minority lets out a "yawn" over "pricey" eats on par with "your local take-out joint."

Restaurant Marrakesh *Moroccan*

20 | 23 | 21 | $33

Table service | Serves alcohol | L, D

It's "easy to believe" you've "been transported to Casablanca" say admirers of this "wonderfully exotic", relatively "undiscovered" Moroccan "secret" in Epcot's Morocco Pavilion; though some sophisticates cite "dumbed-down" eats, most find the food "tasty", the service "warm and gracious", and the tile-laden room "beautiful" – especially when the "lovely" belly dancers shake their thing (they're "child-friendly" to boot).

	FOOD	DECOR	SERVICE	COST

Rose & Crown Pub & Dining Room *British* | 20 | 21 | 22 | $28

Table service | Reservations: Required | Serves alcohol | L, D

"All jokes aside about English cuisine", Anglophiles insist this "authentic" pub inside Epcot's United Kingdom Pavilion offers "surprisingly good" fish 'n' chips and other "traditional" eats; a "top-notch" suds selection and "friendly" service help keep it "lively", and though less loyal subjects say it's "unfortunately" "English" (read: "bland"), most agree the view of IllumiNations from the patio makes it "worth" a stop.

San Angel Inn Restaurante *Mexican* | 19 | 23 | 19 | $25

Table service | Reservations: Required | Serves alcohol | L, D, S

You're "sitting inside" but "you'll swear" you're at an "outdoor cantina" at this "romantic" Mexico Pavilion *restaurante* with "outstanding" decor incorporating an "Aztec pyramid", "steaming volcano", "starry sky" and 'riverfront' views of the pavilion's Gran Fiesta Tour boat ride; some find the "permanent twilight" too "dark", but "delicious sangria" and "killer" margaritas lighten the mood and "improve" the "pretty good" food; P.S. some say the "chow's better and cheaper" at the counter outside.

Sunshine Season Food Fair *Eclectic* | 20 | 14 | 16 | $13

Counter service | Serves alcohol | B, L, D, S

This "inexpensive" "healthy oasis" inside Future World in Epcot's Land Pavilion offers "fast" counter service and a "large variety" of "fresh, well-prepared" Eclectic fare (including "wonderful" soups) that suits groups of hungry eaters "who all want something different"; despite complaints that the "cavernous", "crowded" space has a "confusing layout" and "awful acoustics", boosters say it's among WDW's "best" food courts.

Tangierine Cafe *Moroccan* | 22 | 19 | 18 | $15

Counter service | Serves alcohol | L, D, S

At this "quicker" counter-service version of the Morocco Pavilion's Restaurant Marrakesh, surveyors find some of the same "flavorful" dishes "without the wait" ("or the half-naked" dancers); the "interesting" variety ranges from "tasty" couscous to "delicious" baklava, and though service can be "slow" and the decor's minmal, fans deem it "one of Disney's best ethnic" options.

Teppan Edo *Japanese* | 22 | - | 22 | $34
(fka Teppanyaki Dining Rooms)

Table service | Reservations: Required | Serves alcohol | L, D

A 2007 makeover brought a new name and a stylish, black-and-red interior (that spills over into World Showcase's chicest bathrooms) to this "entertaining", "interactive" eatery in Epcot's Japan Pavilion; "excellent" "teppan grill" fare (including "melt-in-your-mouth steaks") is prepared by "fabulous" "showmen"-chefs who "juggle" "ingredients with aplomb"; purists might moan "glorified Benihana", but defenders declare it "fun" for kids both "little and big"; N.B. beepers allow you to explore the area while waiting for a table.

Tokyo Dining *Japanese* | 22 | - | 22 | $27
(fka Tempura Kiku)

Table service | Reservations: Required | Serves alcohol | L, D

Sleek, dark-wood Asian looks, solicitous servers and expansive, second-floor views of a torii gate rising from World Showcase Lagoon give this Japan Pavilion tempura and sushi specialist an upscale flair; numerous sakes and wines offered by the glass or bottle, as well as a selection of specialty cocktails – including some based on shochu, a traditional vodkalike spirit – are holdovers from Matsu No Ma, the bar that shared the space in its previous incarnation.

NEW Tutto Italia *Italian*

| - | - | - | M |

Table service | Serves alcohol | L, D

Situated in the shadow of St. Mark's Campanile in World Showcase's Italy Pavilion this popular pasta purveyor (formerly Alfredo's) proffers a straightforward selection of appetizers, salads, meats and *contorni* served by bow-tied *amici* straight from the old country; a dark, clubby interior of chandeliers and Mediterranean murals provides a cool respite, as does the potent house *margherita,* made with Limoncello and grappa; N.B. alfresco seating is first come, first served.

Yakitori House *Japanese*

| 19 | 18 | 18 | $19 |

Counter service | Serves alcohol | L, D, S

"Tasty teriyaki" and "surprisingly good sushi rolls" are among the "modern-day" Japanese "fast-food" offerings at this "out-of-the-way" counter-service eatery in Japan Pavilion; it's a reliable "standby, early or late", and most report "fast service", "even during the lunch rush", plus you can dine "under lanterns" on the "secluded" garden patio complete with a "koi pond."

Yorkshire County Fish Shop *English*

| 22 | 12 | 17 | $11 |

Counter service | Serves alcohol | L, D, S

This "bargain" "walk-up window" beside the United Kingdom Pavilion's Rose & Crown pub is "always a winner for" a "quick" hit of fish 'n' chips ("better than in London" insist addicts) served with the requisite "Bass Ale to wash it down"; "long queues" testify to its popularity, and though it could use "more seating" – and some decor – you can dine "on the terrace next door, overlooking the lagoon."

DISNEY'S HOLLYWOOD STUDIOS

ECHO LAKE

Z 50's Prime Time Cafe *American*

| 19 | 25 | 23 | $24 |

Table service | Reservations: Required | Serves alcohol | L, D

"The theme's the thing" at this "must" for "kitsch" lovers that's like "eating at The Beav's house"; expect "standard '50s" American "comfort food" served in a "mom's kitchen" setting (black-and-white TVs, Formica counters) with "hilarious" "role-playing" servers who "pick on you", albeit "in a fun Disney way"; even those who find the fare merely "adequate" agree that "entertainment" is the reason to come.

Sci-Fi Dine-In Theater Restaurant *American*

| 15 | 25 | 20 | $23 |

Table service | Reservations: Required | Serves alcohol | L, D

An "out-of-this-world atmosphere" pulls "nostalgic boomers" to this "pseudo-drive-in" with "eat-in" convertibles, "car hops on skates" and a "giant screen" playing "cheesy sci-fi movie trailers" under a "twinkling sky"; "light-up ice cubes" wow kids, but as for the "limited" (and some say "mundane" and rather "pricey") American fare, surveyors advise "keep it simple."

Studio Catering Co. *Mediterranean*   ▽ 16 | 15 | 16 | $15

Counter service | Serves alcohol | L, D, S

This unassuming counter-service Mediterranean in Echo Lake serves "sandwiches, cold beer" and less predictable park fare like Greek salads and chicken Caesar wraps; "not many people find it", thus it benefits from short lines, but "don't expect to have much to look at while eating."

HOLLYWOOD BOULEVARD

ABC Commissary *Eclectic*   14 | 13 | 14 | $12

Counter service | Serves alcohol | B, L, D, S

This Hollywood Boulevard cafeteria is appreciated for its "varied" Eclectic choices that go "beyond burgers" (e.g. Cuban sandwiches) and for being "one of the few Hollywood Studios eateries open for breakfast"; lines can be "long" but there's TV "paraphernalia" and "theme songs" for diversion ("thank goodness I love *Lost*"), plus "outdoor, shaded seating" – though to cold-hearted critics who cite "lackluster" quality, the a/c inside is the "only redeeming feature."

Hollywood & Vine *American*   18 | 16 | 19 | $27

Table service | Reservations: Required | Serves alcohol | B, L, D

Dinner at this Hollywood Boulevard faux diner is a "quick, fun" affair, with "basic", "nothing fancy" buffet fare that fans deem a "very good deal", especially when you get it "as part of the Fantasmic! package" (though "early entry to the show is better" than the eats); Playhouse Disney character dining at lunch and breakfast helps draw attention away from the neon-heavy decor, which some call a "tad tacky."

⊡ Hollywood Brown Derby, The *American*   22 | 23 | 22 | $39

Table service | Reservations: Required | Serves alcohol | L, D

At this "stunning", "incredibly detailed re-creation" of the bygone LA institution, celebrity caricatures and formal, "attentive" service conjure up the "Old Hollywood of the '30s and '40s"; "classy" and "clubby", it offers "excellent" California-accented fare, including a "truly remarkable" Cobb salad, "fork-tender" steaks and "decadent" grapefruit cake, and though a few question whether it's worth the cost, most roar approval.

STREETS OF AMERICA

Backlot Express *American*   16 | 15 | 15 | $11

Counter service | Serves alcohol | L, D, S

"Near several fun attractions" in Streets of America, this "convenient" stop for a "relatively painless" "quick bite" offers a "covered" outdoor seating area adorned with "props from stage productions"; sure, the menu doesn't venture far beyond "standard burgers and fries" and there's "no a/c", but most report it delivers "decent" fare at a "fair" price.

Mama Melrose's Ristorante Italiano *Italian*   20 | 21 | 21 | $26

Table service | Reservations: Required | Serves alcohol | L, D

"A little off the beaten path" and "often overlooked" (it's near the Muppets), this Italian resembles a "real" "red-sauce joint", with "celebrity photos" on brick walls and red-and-white checked curtains; if the fare "doesn't wow", supporters say "it doesn't disappoint" either, and most agree it's a "decent" choice for something "between a signature restaurant and a burger", especially at lunch; P.S. the "Fantasmic! dinner package is definitely worthwhile."

Toy Story Pizza Planet *Pizza*

13 | 17 | 14 | $11

Counter service | L, D, S

Looking "just like Pizza Planet" from the namesake blockbuster, this "busy" counter-service joint "with a big arcade in the middle" is "WDW's version of Chuck E. Cheese's"; despite reports of "painfully slow" service and pies "comparable to frozen", most allow it's an "affordable" place to fill up the kids, "if you can tolerate the chaos."

SUNSET BOULEVARD

Rosie's All-American Cafe *American*

▽ 15 | 14 | 14 | $15

Counter service | Serves alcohol | L, D

This walk-up window on Sunset Boulevard is "decent" for "a quick bite", as long as you're looking for "typical Disney fast food", in this case a fairly "good assortment" including burgers, fries and other American standards; "outdoor seating at covered picnic tables" is a plus.

Starring Rolls Cafe *Sandwiches*

19 | 14 | 17 | $8

Counter service | Serves alcohol | B, L, D, S

"Don't blink or you'll miss" this "cute" "little" counter-service spot "tucked away on Sunset Boulevard" next to the Brown Derby, where cinnamon rolls and other pastries make for a "quick and convenient breakfast" and lunchtime features gourmet-ish sandwiches that please even "picky mothers-in-law"; P.S. some report getting the Derby's "excellent grapefruit cake" here, even though it's not on the menu.

Toluca Turkey Leg Cart *American*

19 | 9 | 14 | $9

Counter service | Serves alcohol | L, D

There's "no dignified way" to eat this walk-up stand's "messy", "mouthwatering" smoked "turkey-zilla legs" that reviewers warn will "bring out the animal in you"; while sightings of "cavemanlike parkgoers" "gnawing meat off a bone" provoke a "go figure" or two, converts contend "everyone who eats one raves"; there's cold beer to boot.

DISNEY'S ANIMAL KINGDOM

AFRICA

Harambe Fruit Market *Health Food*

21 | 17 | 17 | $7

Counter service | S

It's "nice to be able to get fruit" "instead of ice cream or sweets" say surveyors of this "walk-up" thatched kiosk in Africa; it also offers cheese plates and other "refreshing" snacks, along with "awesome frozen lemonades", leading some to label it one of WDW's "healthiest" options.

Tusker House
Restaurant & Bakery *African/American*

21 | 18 | 17 | $14

Table service | Reservations: Required | Serves alcohol | L, D

Considered one of the "best in the parks" if looking for "healthy fare amid so much" "junk food", this dining hall serves African-accented American fare the likes of "tasty" rotisserie meats, stews, salads and vegetarian items, which can be washed down with "excellent house beer"; there's "lots of air-conditioned seating" plus outside tables with thatched roofs that provide "shady" views of "awesome" acrobatic performances.

ASIA

NEW Yak & Yeti Restaurant *Pan-Asian* — | — | — | M

Table service | Serves alcohol | L, D

Tucked behind a two-story, cobalt-blue facade is this expansive new Pan-Asian, Animal Kingdom's only table service eatery, where favorites include potstickers, stir-fries and grilled meats; exposed beams, chandeliers and oriental *objets* create an appropriately exotic atmosphere, and a small downstairs bar boasts international beers, sakes and specialty drinks; N.B. the attached Local Food Café, a lower-priced, counter-service option, offers a limited menu in an outdoor market setting.

DISCOVERY ISLAND

Flame Tree Barbecue *BBQ* 21 | 16 | 15 | $13

Counter service | Serves alcohol | L, D, S

"Delicious" chicken and "tender", "smoky" ribs are among the "hearty", "surprisingly good" eats at this walk-up BBQ counter on Discovery Island; entrees come with veggies "not fries", which pleases those seeking "healthier" options, and though the queue for 'cue is "quite long", "shaded" outdoor seating with "breathtaking" views of Mount Everest provides a "serene" "break from the parks."

Pizzafari *Pizza* 17 | 19 | 17 | $12

Counter service | Serves alcohol | B, L, D, S

This "cafeteria-style" Italian has its many dining rooms (and bathrooms) "funkily" and "creatively" covered with "beautiful" African scenes that make it "a favorite with kids"; though the personal pizzas may merely "get the job done", "lots of seating", "decent prices" and the option of "eating outside" make it one of DAK's better "little quick-stop" places.

THE OASIS

Rainforest Cafe – Animal Kingdom *American* 17 | 24 | 17 | $25

Table service | Serves alcohol | L, D

"Adorable" animatronics – "animal noises, thunderstorms" – create a "jungle" "fantasy come true" at these chain links in Animal Kingdom and Downtown Disney Marketplace; though "little ones" might find the hubbub "intimidating" and grown-ups gripe "you pay for the decor" given "standard" American fare and "coin-flip" service, it's "fun", if not fine, dining; P.S. expect "huge portions" and "lines as long as the Amazon."

At the Resorts

MAGIC KINGDOM AREA

Z Artist Point *Pacific NW* 24 | 23 | 23 | $47

Disney's Wilderness Lodge | 901 Timberline Dr.
Table service | Reservations: Required | Serves alcohol | D

For a "quiet" "grown-up dinner", try this "hidden jewel" at Wilderness Lodge, where "lots of woods" and "beautiful ceiling murals" make for a lodgelike feel that "perfectly replicates the rustic Northwest"; the menu follows suit with an "unmatched selection of game" and "wonderful" cedar-plank salmon, all enhanced by "outstanding" service and an "extensive" wine list; if some find it "pricey" and say "not for kids", most feel it's "worth every penny" to enjoy "Yellowstone without the cold."

⊠ California Grill *Californian* | 26 | 25 | 24 | $50
Disney's Contemporary Resort | 4600 N. World Dr., 15th fl.
Table service | Reservations: Required | Serves alcohol | D
Ranked No. 1 for Popularity and No. 2 for Food, this "special-occasion" "crown jewel" "high atop" the Contemporary Resort provides "scrumptious", "attractively presented" Californian fare, from "cut-with-a-fork" filet mignon to "awesome" sushi, made even better by "thoughtful" service and "panoramic views" that alone are "worth the price" – "time it right and catch the fireworks" from your table or out "on the catwalk" overlooking "Mouseland"; grousers grumble about "noise", "underdressed diners" and "lots of kids", but hey, "it *is* Disney"; P.S. "reservations are a must."

Capt. Cook's ❶ *American* | 15 | 13 | 16 | $11
Disney's Polynesian Resort | 1600 Seven Seas Dr.
Counter service | Serves alcohol | B, L, D, S
"If you're marooned at the Poly" you can always "grab a snack" or enjoy a "quiet break" (complete with beer or wine) at this 24-hour quick-service American providing made-to-order burgers and sandwiches by day and "prepackaged" selections at night; the "touch-screen self-serve" check-out should please those who find the staff "slow"; N.B. the above Decor score may not reflect a post-Survey remodel.

Cítricos *Mediterranean* | 23 | 23 | 23 | $49
Disney's Grand Floridian Resort | 4401 Grand Floridian Way
Table service | Reservations: Required | Serves alcohol | D
When you're "not dressed for Victoria & Albert's" but still want a "classy" yet "laid-back" atmosphere, insiders say head to this oft-"overlooked" "must-do" on the second floor of the Grand Floridian; the "imaginative" Mediterranean fare is "delicious" if "expensive", service is "exceptional" and the "sophisticated" setting with "sweeping lagoon views" is "quiet" enough for "conversation", so though a few feel it promises "more than is delivered", most label it "excellent" overall.

Garden View Lounge *British* | ▽ 23 | 23 | 24 | $28
Disney's Grand Floridian Resort & Spa | 4401 Floridian Way
Table service | Reservations: Required | Serves alcohol | L, S
The "delightful" British "high tea" presented in this "enchanting", "window-filled" lounge in the Grand Floridian Resort strikes admirers as the "epitome of elegance and excellence"; "take your time" to "enjoy" the "delicious" sandwiches served in this "proper" yet "surprisingly kid-friendly" space, where costumed servers and "beautiful", "Victorian" decor "transport you to another time and place."

Gasparilla Grill & Games ❶ *American* | ▽ 15 | 11 | 14 | $13
Disney's Grand Floridian Resort & Spa | 4401 Floridian Way
Counter service | Serves alcohol | B, L, D
Near an arcade that's "nice for young ones", this 24-hour take-out window at the Grand Floridian offers a "large selection" of American

standbys, from pizza to burgers; though the decor's dismissable, you can eat "on the porch for beautiful views" of the "castle in the distance"; in short, if you "don't expect too much" it'll do "when everything else is closed."

Grand Floridian Cafe *American*   21 | 21 | 21 | $28

Disney's Grand Floridian Resort & Spa | 4401 Floridian Way
Table service | Serves alcohol | B, L, D

Pragmatists say this "cute", "cheery" alternative at the Grand Floridian offers the "same high-quality" fare found at the rest of the resort for "a fraction of the cost"; sure, the American menu "could be more diverse", but it offers "good, simple" salads, sandwiches and prime rib dinners and well-priced "mini-desserts"; "lovely" pool views add atmosphere, though some prefer to "bring it to the room."

Kona Cafe *Hawaiian*   23 | 19 | 22 | $25

Disney's Polynesian Resort | 1600 Seven Seas Dr.
Table service | Reservations: Required | Serves alcohol | B, L, D

The Hawaiian-influenced cuisine at the Polynesian Resort's atrium eatery offers "something for everyone", including "tasty" breakfast options (macadamia pancakes, "Tonga toast"), but it's particularly noted for its "outstanding desserts"; "generally good" service, an "away-from-the-mobs" second-floor location and a "plain"-but-pleasant "tropical" setting with views of a "lush waterfall" please most, yet fail to sway a few skeptics who say "don't make a special trip."

Narcoossee's *Seafood*   22 | 22 | 22 | $49

Disney's Grand Floridian Resort | 4401 Grand Floridian Way
Table service | Serves alcohol | D

"Enticing" "Floribbean"-style seafood "seduces" supporters at the Grand Floridian's "posh" octagonal "pavilion" on "the edge of Seven Seas Lagoon", where the "breathtaking" views of "Cinderella Castle" and nightly fireworks feel like a "private show"; an extensive wine list and "smooth" service are pluses, and if a few feel it's "overrated" ("good but not stellar"), more recommend it for a "romantic getaway from the kids."

'Ohana *Hawaiian*   21 | 22 | 22 | $32

Disney's Polynesian Resort | 1600 Seven Seas Dr.
Table service | Reservations: Required | Serves alcohol | D

Satiated surveyors say "come hungry" to the Polynesian Resort's Hawaiian-themed "one-price-fills-all" "carnivore's delight" where "huge skewers" of "delicious" meats are served "family" (read: "'ohana") style "fresh from a flaming fire pit"; it's "not for the vegan" (even if there is a vegetarian platter on the menu) and it's all a bit "too much" for some ("bring earplugs" and "Alka-Seltzer"), but "attentive" service and bounteous "coconut cocktails" placate pouters; P.S. "raucous" "character breakfasts" feature Lilo and Stitch.

Roaring Fork ❶ *American*   17 | 15 | 17 | $16

Disney's Wilderness Lodge | 901 Timberline Dr.
Counter service | Serves alcohol | B, L, D, S

Though no one's exactly roaring with excitement, most regard this counter-service spot in the National Park–inspired Wilderness Lodge near Magic Kingdom as a "solid" option for "basic" American eats (some would say "glorified fast food"); crowds, noise and "limited options" are downsides, but it's "adequate for the price", has "entertaining staffers" and is open late (midnight).

Sandtrap Bar & Grill *American* ∇ 23 | 19 | 24 | $18

Disney's Osprey Ridge Golf Course | 3451 Golf View Dr.
Table service | Serves alcohol | B, L

"Please don't tell anyone" about this "hidden" "escape" at Osprey Ridge Golf Course – it's lacking "crowds", and devotees (including "many Disney employees") "like it that way"; "whether you're a golfer or not", fans say swing by for "good" if predictable American standards served by a "gracious staff", plus "nice views" of the greens – in sum, "sanity."

Trail's End Restaurant *American* 19 | 19 | 20 | $23

Disney's Fort Wilderness Resort & Campground | 4510 N. Ft. Wilderness Trail
Table service | Reservations: Required | Serves alcohol | B, L, D

"Decent" "homestyle" buffet fare – including "typically Southern" breakfasts (grits, sausage gravy, biscuits) – is the draw at this "friendly" "rustic cabin" in Pioneer Hall at the Fort Wilderness Resort; adventurers call it a "hidden gem" that's "worth the schlep" for "gluttony at a good price", with "many kids' selections" to boot; P.S. you "can wander" hundreds of acres of horseback and hiking paths "before or after a meal."

⦿ Victoria & Albert's *American* 27 | 27 | 27 | VE

Disney's Grand Floridian Resort | 4401 Grand Floridian Way
Table service | Reservations: Required | Serves alcohol | D

Ranking No. 1 for Food, Decor and Service, this "divine" New American in the Grand Floridian offers a "magical", "civilized escape from the fray" thanks to its "inventive, yet accessible" prix fixe–only cuisine, "magnificent" wines, "impeccable, choreographed" service and "truly exquisite" atmosphere complete with "lovely" harp music; sure, it may be "ungodly expensive" – $125 for six courses – but believers beg "leave the kids" (no children under 10 allowed) and "hock the car" since this is one place that "lives up to its exemplary reputation"; N.B. reserve well ahead; jackets required.

Whispering Canyon Cafe *American/BBQ* 21 | 22 | 23 | $25

Disney's Wilderness Lodge | 901 Timberline Dr.
Table service | Reservations: Required | Serves alcohol | B, L, D

"Tasty, hearty" "all-you-can-eat" American "campfire" and BBQ fare takes a back seat to the waiters' "rowdy cowboy" "hijinks" at this "hootin', hollerin'" "spectacle" at the Wilderness Lodge; "you may be the brunt of the joke" ("don't ask for ketchup!") but the "country-bumpkin" shtick is "always entertaining"; if you "embarrass easily" or want a "quiet", "fancy" meal "go someplace else" – otherwise "bring earplugs" 'cuz there's "nothing whispering about it."

EPCOT AREA

Beach Club Marketplace *American* 18 | 15 | 17 | $13

Disney's Beach Club Resort | 1800 Epcot Resort Blvd.
Counter service | Serves alcohol | B, L, D, S

Breakfasts that are "just enough to start your engines for a long day at the park" can be had at this counter-service American joint inside the

Atlantic Wear and Wardrobe Emporium at Disney's Beach Club Resort; there are also "grab-and-go" "pre-fab" sandwiches and salads "for taking to the pool" plus "yummy gelato" – just expect to sacrifice "selection" for "convenience."

Beaches & Cream Soda Shop *American* | 21 | 21 | 20 | $14 |

Disney's Beach Club Resort | 1800 Epcot Resort Blvd.
Table service | Serves alcohol | L, D, S

"Bring your appetite and stretchy pants" to this "fun, old-fashioned soda shop", where the burgers are "good, juicy and messy", the onion rings "greasy and delicious" and the sundaes and malts "fabulous" – check out the "attention-grabbing" kitchen sink, "a family-sized" "monster" involving "a full can of whipped cream" and "every topping imaginable"; it's as "cramped" as it is "cute", so some suggest "get it to go."

Big River Grille & Brewing Works ❷ *American* | 17 | 15 | 17 | $22 |

Disney's BoardWalk | 2101 N. Epcot Resort Blvd.
Table service | Serves alcohol | L, D

"Right on the BoardWalk", this "beer lover's Shangri-La" features housemade Gordon Biersch microbrews "you can't find anywhere else on Disney property" as well as burgers, sandwiches and other "typical bar fare" that's "plain" but "hearty" – and often served with a side of "noise"; big copper brewing tanks are on display inside, while patio seating offers "fabulous views" of "people and boats" cruising by.

Cape May Cafe *American* | 20 | 20 | 21 | $29 |

Disney's Beach Club Resort | 1800 Epcot Resort Blvd.
Table service | Reservations: Required | Serves alcohol | D

"Even landlubbers" can find something to love at this dinner buffet at the Beach Club serving "tons" of "fresh, flavorful" clams, shrimp, chowder and other American "treats", including barbecue ribs, mac 'n' cheese and hot dogs; maybe "it's not gourmet", but "you won't leave hungry" and the "clam bake" decor evokes a pleasant case of "south Jersey" nostalgia; N.B. no lunch; breakfast is character dining only and features Goofy and friends "dressed for the shore."

Captain's Grille *American* | 19 | 17 | 20 | $25 |
(fka Yacht Club Galley)

Disney's Yacht Club Resort | 1700 Epcot Resort Blvd.
Table service | Reservations: Required | Serves alcohol | B, L, D

It sails under a new moniker these days, but this American eatery a "short walk from Epcot" at the dignified Yacht Club Resort remains largely "undiscovered" – i.e. there's "never a long wait"; mates say it offers a "quiet alternative" to character breakfasts and also find it "inviting" for lunch and dinner, with "cute" nautical decor and service that passes muster, but a less-impressed few find it "just ok."

ESPN Club ❷ *American* | 16 | 20 | 17 | $22 |

Disney's BoardWalk | 2101 N. Epcot Resort Blvd.
Table service | Serves alcohol | L, D, S

It's "every sports fan's dream" to "gorge on fried foods and an ice cold one" while watching games on a "gazillion TVs", and that's what this action-addict's "oasis" delivers; though the unaddicted say the "typical" bar fare is "not amazing", the setting's "ho-hum" and you can forget about "having a conversation", to "total fanatics" it's "heaven."

	FOOD	DECOR	SERVICE	COST

☑ Flying Fish Cafe *Seafood*   `24` `23` `22` `$46`

Disney's BoardWalk Resort | 2101 N. Epcot Resort Blvd.
Table service | Serves alcohol | D

A "sea star" "right on the BoardWalk", this "favorite" flies high thanks to "expertly prepared", "amazingly fresh" fish (e.g. "to-die-for potato-crusted red snapper") served in a "whimsical", "underwater-themed" dining room where you "watch the chefs in action"; there are "great steaks" too, plus a "knowledgeable" staff that "aims to please", so even if some complain that it's "noisy" and "pricey", most think it's "worth every cent" to enjoy this "grown-up oasis."

Fresh Mediterranean Market *Mediterranean* ▽ `21` `17` `17` `$23`

Walt Disney World Dolphin | 1500 Epcot Resort Blvd.
Table service | Serves alcohol | B, L

"True to its name, everything here is fresh" say boosters of this buffet in the lower level of the Dolphin with an open kitchen and brightly colored tiled walls; "made-to-order" breakfasts include "awesome French toast", "tasty, huge" omelets and pancakes, while lunch features "unusual", "different-every-day" Mediterranean-inspired dishes; P.S. there's "good wine at low prices" too.

Garden Grove Cafe *American*   ▽ `19` `18` `16` `$17`

Walt Disney World Swan | 1500 Epcot Resort Blvd.
Table service | Serves alcohol | B, L

After a remodel not too long ago, this airy cafe at the Swan resort offers a "huge", "good-value" breakfast buffet plus standard-issue American lunch fare (dinner and weekend breakfasts are character dining only) in an indoor gazebo-like space, themed after the Central Park Gardens, with a 25-ft. oak tree at its center; service can be "a bit slow", but the many choices make it "easy to please everyone."

Il Mulino New York *Italian*   `-` `-` `-` `E`

Walt Disney World Swan | 1500 Epcot Resort Blvd.
Table service | Reservations: Required | Serves alcohol | D

This Swan resort link of the acclaimed New York City–based chain serves hearty specialties from Italy's Abruzzi region – including meat and fish preparations, pastas, wood-fired pizzas and salads – in an upscale-but-casual contemporary setting with wood plank floors and brick walls; an international wine list with more than 250 selections pleases oenophiles, and complimentary antipasti accompany each meal.

Kimonos ☻ *Japanese*   `21` `19` `20` `$33`

Walt Disney World Swan | 1500 Epcot Resort Blvd.
Table service | Serves alcohol | D

"Fresh", "excellent" sushi is the draw at this swank and "not particularly Disneyfied" Japanese in the lobby of the Swan resort; "gracious" service and "perfect" cocktails also please, and if you can't carry a tune for "fun" nightly karaoke, be sure to "carry a big wallet" since some say it's "pricey for what you get"; P.S. it's "great for a nightcap."

Old Port Royale Food Court *American*   `16` `17` `16` `$13`

Disney's Caribbean Beach Resort | 900 Cayman Way
Counter service | Serves alcohol | B, L, D, S

"If you can survive the crowds" at this colorful cafeteria-cum-market at Caribbean Beach Resort, surveyors say you'll find a "decent selec-

	FOOD	DECOR	SERVICE	COST

tion and quality" as far "as food courts go"; the "varied" American menu "caters to all ages" and "tastes" (Mickey waffles are a fave), and while most agree service "could be better", overall it's deemed "ok" for "families on a budget."

Shula's Steak House *Steak* — 23 | 20 | 22 | $61

Walt Disney World Dolphin | 1500 Epcot Resort Blvd.
Table service | Reservations: Required | Serves alcohol | D

Jumbo photos celebrating Dolphins coach Don Shula's perfect season plus menus printed on "signed" pigskins set the tone at this "masculine", "clubby" steakhouse chain link located in – you guessed it – the WDW Dolphin; "huge hunks" of "excellent" "red meat" come with "football-size baked potatoes" and "huge prices" to match, but "big spenders" say the "fantastic" 500-bottle wine list and "attentive" service help make it "well worth the cost."

Shutter's at Old Port Royale *American* — ▽ 16 | 16 | 17 | $24

Disney's Caribbean Beach Resort | 900 Cayman Way
Table service | Reservations: Required | Serves alcohol | D

This casual Caribbean Beach Resort spot serves a "limited" menu of American cuisine with island accents that draws mixed reviews ("surprisingly good" vs. "nuttin' special") in an atmosphere that's also debated ("cafeterialike" vs. "delightful"); while some suggest "don't bother if you're not staying here", others say order the "good rum drinks" and "you won't care about anything else."

Spoodles ● *Mediterranean* — 20 | 20 | 20 | $31

Disney's BoardWalk | 2101 N. Epcot Resort Blvd.
Table service | Reservations: Required | Serves alcohol | B, D

Overlooking Disney's BoardWalk, this Mediterranean with a decided "country feel" – think "farmhouse" chairs, wooden tables, Fiestaware plates – has a "limited" but generally "good" menu, with special praise going to the flatbread and dips; "delicious" sangria, an "excellent" wine list and "engaging" service are pluses, and though the "huge", "open-kitchen" space can be "noisy", some like its "high-energy" vibe.

☒ Todd English's bluezoo *Seafood* — 24 | 26 | 23 | $53

Walt Disney World Dolphin | 1500 Epcot Resort Blvd.
Table service | Reservations: Required | Serves alcohol | D

"Everyone feels like one of the beautiful people" sipping "the best martinis" to a "techno beat" in Todd English's "trendy" seafooder at the Dolphin, where Jeffrey Beers' "sleek, sophisticated" interior draws a "wow", as does the "cutting-edge" kitchen that "magically marries flavors" in "creative" preparations of the "freshest fish"; add in "knowledgeable" servers who "bend over backward" and admirers say "you can't go wrong" here – but "you can go broke."

☒ Yachtsman Steakhouse *Steak* — 24 | 22 | 23 | $52

Disney's Yacht Club Resort | 1700 Epcot Resort Blvd.
Table service | Reservations: Required | Serves alcohol | D

"Great aged beef" is the lure at this "understated, elegant" surf 'n' turfer inside Disney's Yacht Club, where diners get to choose their cuts; an "excellent wine list", "sumptuous" sides and "wide assortment of desserts" help keep things shipshape, as does the subtly nautical decor and service that "makes you feel like royalty" (tabs are royal too).

| | FOOD | DECOR | SERVICE | COST |

DISNEY'S ANIMAL KINGDOM AREA

☑ Boma – Flavors of Africa *African* | 24 | 24 | 22 | $33 |

Disney's Animal Kingdom Lodge | 2901 Osceola Pkwy.
Table service | Reservations: Required | Serves alcohol | B, D

A "safari for the senses", this "amazing", "bountiful" "all-you-can-eat buffet" in Animal Kingdom Lodge mingles "exotic", "African-inspired" dishes with more "Americanized" options for "less adventurous diners"; the "incredible array" extends to a "delirious" dessert selection and an "exceptional" South African wine list, all served in a thatch-laden lobby locale with "delightful decor" that's "kid-friendly without being childish" – in other words, "top-notch Disney."

End Zone Food Court ◑ *American*   ▽ | 18 | 16 | 17 | $12 |

Disney's All-Star Sports Resort | 1800 W. Buena Vista Dr.
Counter service | Serves alcohol | B, L, D, S

Wall-sized pictures of athletes and cartoons on TV provide the backdrop at this quick-service American food court/mini-mart in the All-Star Sports Resort, boasting a large seating area and beverage bar; while there's a "good selection" of eats including "fresh fruit, salads", burgers, pizzas and bakery items, it's more "convenient" than special, with "reasonable" prices and "quick-moving lines" scoring extra points.

Everything Pop
Shopping & Dining ◑ *American* | 18 | 16 | 15 | $12 |

Disney's Pop Century Resort | 1050 Century Dr.
Counter service | Serves alcohol | B, L, D, S

This "junk food paradise" in Pop Century Resort supplies "a good variety" of American "favorites" like chicken noodle soup and "TV dinner" specials, plus some "wacky twists" ("tie-dyed cheesecake", "Twinkie tiramisu"); it's "hectic" at "peak times" and the unimpressed find it simply "standard", but night owls like that it's open till midnight.

Intermission Food Court ◑ *American*   ▽ | 19 | 16 | 16 | $13 |

Disney's All-Star Music Resort | 1800 W. Buena Vista Dr.
Counter service | Serves alcohol | B, L, D, S

The All-Star Music Resort's food court/convenience market is fine for "a quick meal" on the go, dispensing "standard" but "good" American fare including "very kid-friendly" items (burgers, hot dogs, pizza) as well as made-to-order salads and bakery items; though respondents tolerate the "cheesy"-yet-"cute" musical decor (life-size cutouts of famous performers), "apathetic" service has some singing the blues; P.S. it's "loud and crazy" at peak times.

☑ Jiko – The Cooking Place *African* | 25 | 25 | 25 | $48 |

Disney's Animal Kingdom Lodge | 2901 Osceola Pkwy.
Table service | Reservations: Required | Serves alcohol | D

It might be "off the beaten path" at Animal Kingdom Lodge, but admirers of this "jewel" consider it "worth the travel" (and the "splurge") to enjoy one of the "most interesting" meals at WDW; its "fabulous" "African-fusion" cuisine is "an adventure for the taste buds", and the "fantastic" staff (rated No. 2 for Service) "takes time to explain" it; throw in a "first-class" South African wine selection ("reputed to be the largest in the U.S.") and a "classy", "exotic" interior and it's no wonder most "leave roaring for more."

	FOOD	DECOR	SERVICE	COST

Mara, The *Eclectic*

| 16 | 13 | 14 | $14 |

Disney's Animal Kingdom Lodge | 2901 Osceola Pkwy.
Counter service | Serves alcohol | B, L, D, S

Sporting bright river scenes painted on the walls, this small and "generally quiet" Animal Kingdom Lodge food court offers "lots of choices" that go beyond basics to include Eclectic "surprises" like "pepper pot soup" in a "bread bowl", hummus and, for dessert, Zebra Domes, which fans call "worth a trip to Disney by themselves"; there are also sandwiches, salads and other "quick" to-go items.

World Premiere Food Court ● *American*

| ▽ 18 | 15 | 16 | $12 |

Disney's All-Star Movies Resort | 1800 W. Buena Vista Dr.
Counter service | Serves alcohol | B, L, D, S

The All-Star Movies Resort's only eatery is a "utilitarian cafeteria"/ convenience market inside Cinema Hall with five stations, each named after a classic movie palace; admirers applaud options like "good fruit and salads", pizza, burgers and baked goods, while bashers boo the "same boring food" served by "cast members" who need coaching.

DOWNTOWN DISNEY AREA

Artist's Palette, The *American*

| 19 | 17 | 18 | $16 |

Disney's Saratoga Springs Resort & Spa | 1960 Broadway
Counter service | Serves alcohol | B, L, D

Expect "filling" panini sandwiches, flatbread pizzas and "lots of vegetarian options" at this "quick-service" American "buffeteria" at Disney's Saratoga Springs Resort that's also a "well-stocked convenience store"; "easels on the tables" that "keep kids busy while you wait" make "slow" service palatable, and though a few fear it's "overpriced" or yawn "nothing stands out", they admit "nothing truly disappoints" either.

Boatwright's Dining Hall *Southern*

| 20 | 19 | 19 | $23 |

Disney's Port Orleans Resort - Riverside | 1251 Riverside Dr.
Table service | Serves alcohol | B, D

For the look and flavor of the "rustic Deep South" head to this "favorite" at Port Orleans Riverside offering a "must-do" breakfast (sweet-potato pancakes, banana French toast) and "yummy" Bayou Bloody Marys and jambalaya at dinner; service can be "slow", but that doesn't faze fans who say it provides the "most" chow "for the least money."

Maya Grill *Nuevo Latino*

| 20 | 19 | 18 | $29 |

Disney's Coronado Springs Resort | 1000 W. Buena Vista Dr.
Table service | Serves alcohol | B, D

"Tasty" margaritas and "reasonably priced" steak and seafood star at this Nuevo Latino in the Coronado Springs Resort near Animal Kingdom; though sluggish service takes some knocks and a few surveyors are less than impressed ("ordinary"), most appreciate its "excellent variety", with special praise going to the "well-worth-the-cost" breakfast buffet offering "all you can eat" of "everything you can imagine."

Olivia's Cafe *American*

| 19 | 19 | 20 | $24 |

Disney's Old Key West Resort | 1510 N. Cove Rd.
Table service | Serves alcohol | B, L, D

Old Key West Resort's "unassuming" coffee shop – "WDW's version of a dive" – offers "basic" American fare in "fun, light" islandy surroundings; somewhat "hidden", it's popular with "laid-back" vacationers (and "Disney suits" at lunch), and its breakfasts are a hit with kids; still, the "friendly" servers' "Key West speed" "can be a problem" if in a hurry.

Pepper Market *Eclectic*

19 | 18 | 16 | $17

Disney's Coronado Springs Resort | 1000 W. Buena Vista Dr.
Counter service | Serves alcohol | B, L, D

With "fun, lively" Mexican decor, this "festive" Coronado Springs "cafeteria-style" eatery offers "huge portions" of "cooked-to-order" Eclectic dishes from a "terrific selection" that fans say will "please everyone in the family"; not so pleasing are a "slow" staff, a "confusing" layout and mandatory gratuity for "what is essentially self-service", but overall it strikes most as a definite "step above fast food."

NEW Riverside Mill Food Court ◑ *American*

- | - | - | I

Disney's Port Orleans Resort - Riverside | 1251 Riverside Dr.
Counter service | Serves alcohol | B, L, D, S

A massive blue barn with rough-hewn timbers and a three-story red waterwheel fronting the Sassagoula River provides a rustic setting for a riparian repast at Disney's Port Orleans Resort - Riverside; quick-service counters offer Cajun-accented American salads, sandwiches, pizzas and pastas for lunch and dinner, an on-site bakery satiates sweet tooths and a short-order grill serves up breakfast standards; N.B. grab a table outside overlooking the marina for a break from the maddening crowds.

Sassagoula Floatworks & Food Factory ◑ *American*

17 | 19 | 17 | $13

Disney's Port Orleans Resort - French Quarter | 2201 Orleans Dr.
Counter service | Serves alcohol | B, L, D, S

Beignets "almost as good as in New Orleans" are standouts at this "easy-to-use" counter-service eatery in the lobby of Port Orleans French Quarter, where "cool Mardi Gras decor" matches the "loud, festive" vibe; the likes of burgers, salads and pizzas are on offer too, and though a few lament a "limited selection", it's "handy" for a "low-budget" bite.

NEW Turf Club Bar & Grill *American*

- | - | - | M

Disney's Saratoga Springs Resort & Spa | 1960 Broadway
Table service | Serves alcohol | L, D

Expect peppercorn-crusted tuna, NY strip steaks and other Traditional American favorites at this links-side newcomer at Saratoga Springs Resort, where an equestrian theme runs from the jockey jerseys gracing the walls to the Preakness Cosmo cocktail; dine inside at wooden tables, at the clubby bar or outside on a roomy covered patio overlooking the manicured greens and, in the distance, the shops of Downtown Disney.

Downtown Disney

MARKETPLACE

Cap'n Jack's Restaurant *Seafood*

16 | 16 | 17 | $29

1780 E. Buena Vista Dr.
Table service | Reservations: Required | Serves alcohol | L, D

The "amazing" water views earn more consistent praise than the food at this Village Lake–front seafooder at Downtown Disney Marketplace;

though it can be a pleasant "respite" with a "great deck for drinks", mutineers cite "slow" service and "disappointing" dishes, contending there are "better choices in the area."

Earl of Sandwich *Sandwiches*

22	14	17	$11

1780 E. Buena Vista Dr.
Counter service | B, L, D, S

"Inventive" "gourmet" sandwiches at "affordable" prices explain why this Downtown Disney Marketplace spot is "always packed"; though some find the atmosphere "austere" and suggest "the Earl needs more servants" to combat "long lines", most are willing to wait for what some call "the best value on WDW property."

Ghirardelli Soda Fountain & Chocolate Shop *Dessert*

23	16	16	$10

1710 E. Buena Vista Dr.
Counter service | S

For a "decadent ending" to a "day at the parks" head to this "chocoholics' paradise" at Downtown Disney Marketplace, where "outrageously delicious" sundaes, "fabulously thick" shakes and other "heavenly concoctions" pack plenty of "calories for your buck"; though it's a "complete madhouse" with "plain" decor and "slow" service, addicts insist it's "worth the lines" and suggest "get it to go"; P.S. sugar-free options "score points with diabetics."

Rainforest Cafe – Downtown Disney *American*

17	24	17	$25

1800 E. Buena Vista Dr.
Table service | Serves alcohol | L, D
See review on page 65.

Wolfgang Puck Express – Marketplace *Californian*

21	13	16	$17

1780 E. Buena Vista Dr.
Counter service | B, L, D, S

In-a-hurry parkgoers looking for "fresh", "on-the-go" fare that "doesn't taste like fast food" stop by this "upscale" "order-at-the-counter" chain link at Downtown Disney Marketplace, which provides a "quick Wolfgang fix" when there's no time for the nearby full-service Wolfgang Puck Café; fans wolf down its "great variety" of "tasty" Californian eats including pizzas, sandwiches and salads, even if some find it "pricey" with "hit-or-miss" service.

PLEASURE ISLAND

Fulton's Crab House *Seafood*

21	20	20	$44

1670 E. Buena Vista Dr.
Table service | Serves alcohol | L, D

Fans say this "quaint" "riverboat replica" at Downtown Disney Pleasure Island provides an "excellent" selection of "fresh", "well-prepared" seafood (including lobster bisque that "makes you want to lick the bowl") plus "attentive" service in a "cozy" nautical setting with "nice water views"; critics crab that it's "seen better days", citing "frayed around the edges" decor and "inconsistent" eats at "high prices", but "big crowds" prove they're outvoted.

Portobello Yacht Club *Italian*

| 21 | 20 | 21 | $39 |

1650 E. Buena Vista Dr.
Table service | Serves alcohol | L, D

By most accounts, this "taste of Italy" on Pleasure Island is indeed a pleasure thanks to "consistently good" *cucina* with a "modern twist" and "charming" servers who "know their wines"; complaints are mostly mild ("nothing unusual", "expensive"), and the fact that you can dine inside amid "relaxing" yacht-club decor or on a patio overlooking Lake Buena Vista are more reasons why admirers call it a "secret gem."

Raglan Road Irish Pub & Restaurant ● *Irish*

| 22 | 24 | 21 | $30 |

1640 E. Buena Vista Dr.
Table service | Serves alcohol | D

"Gourmet Irish cuisine" is not an oxymoron – fans swear "it exists" at this "authentic pub" in Downtown Disney serving "delicious" fare "with flair" that's a "nice change from park food"; it "feels like Dublin" too thanks to a "fantastic" ("albeit deafening") band, "comely" dancers, "courteous service" and arguably the "best beer choices at WDW"; P.S. the "electric atmosphere" at night is "not kid-friendly."

WEST SIDE

Bongos Cuban Cafe ● *Cuban*

| 18 | 19 | 17 | $30 |

1498 E. Buena Vista Dr.
Table service | Serves alcohol | L, D

"Step into Havana" at singer Gloria Estefan's "hip, happening" cantina at Downtown Disney's West Side, where "basic but good" Cuban fare is paired with *"caliente* cocktails" including "killer mojitos"; "snazzy, tropical" decor and "rockin'" (maybe "too loud") music creates an "electric" atmosphere, and if *críticos* say it's "nowhere near authentic" and cite "lacking" service, amigos insist it's a still a "blast."

FoodQuest/Wonderland Cafe *American*

| 20 | 16 | 16 | $19 |

1478 E. Buena Vista Dr.
Counter service | Serves alcohol | L, D, S

Expect "ridiculously" "large" portions of the "best cheesecake around" – as well as a "never-ending menu" of pizza, salads and wraps and other Americana – at this "simple" spin-off of the "famous" Cheesecake Factory chain inside DisneyQuest (admission required) at Downtown Disney's West Side; "difficult" seating and decor that "could look more magical" rankle some, but the "solid", "reasonably priced" eats keep most satisfied.

House of Blues ● *Southern*

| 20 | 22 | 19 | $27 |

1478 E. Buena Vista Dr.
Table service | Serves alcohol | B, L, D

"Belushi would be proud" of this "down-home" Downtown Disney nightclub-cum–Southern eatery that fans find "more sophisticated" than other "gimmicky" joints; its "pure fun" vibe and "inspirational" Sunday gospel brunch draw kudos, as do "friendly" servers, "strong" yet "reasonably priced" cocktails and "cornbread to die for"; still, skeptics who knock "long" waits and "humdrum Cajun" fare say "stick to the music, dudes."

	FOOD	DECOR	SERVICE	COST

Planet Hollywood ◗ *American*   13 | 20 | 15 | $25

1506 E. Buena Vista Dr.
Table service | Serves alcohol | L, D

"Cheesy-but-cool" pop-culture decor is the main claim to fame of this "gimmicky" chain eatery–cum–Hollywood prop "museum", set in a planet-shaped structure anchoring Downtown Disney's West Side; critics who pan its "mass-market" American eats and "disinterested" service declare it "so '80s" and "so over", but tell that to the "crowds" who keep the atmo-sphere "crazy" and "loud" (the nightly DJ helps too).

Wetzel's Pretzels *Bakery*   18 | 10 | 17 | $7

1478 E. Buena Vista Dr.
Counter service | Serves alcohol | S

"Fresh", "piping hot" pretzels are the claim to fame of this take-out place at Downtown Disney's West Side; "kids love" the pretzel dogs ("great for running around with") and "low-fat" options please the adult folk who call it good for a "snack on the go", even if twisted cynics note "you could get this at the mall."

Wolfgang Puck Café *Californian*   21 | 19 | 18 | $34

1482 E. Buena Vista Dr.
Table service | Serves alcohol | L, D

Experience a "bit of California in Florida" at this "Puck empire" outpost in Downtown Disney's West Side where the "good variety" includes "fresh, creative" "wood-fired pizzas", sushi and salads; service can be "inattentive" and some insist "Wolfy can do better", but "long waits" (eat at the bar to avoid them) and "incredible" noise (outside seating can be quieter) prove they're outvoted; P.S. it's "worth climbing the stairs" to the upper-level "fine-dining area."

CHARACTER DINING
& DINNER SHOWS

Character Dining & Dinner Shows

Character dining assures little ones a first-person encounter (as well as a hug, kiss and photo op) with costumed versions of animated Disney stars. The meal is often centered around an activity or theme – such as princesses or dinosaurs – and characters stop by each table for face time with guests. The focus is usually on the experience rather than the fare, which is either family-style or buffet; the cost averages about $25–$30 for adults and $13 ages three–nine (gratuity not included). Those that take place in Cinderella Castle cost about $10 more per ticket, while the **My Disney Girl's Perfectly Princess Tea Party,** which includes jewelry and a doll, costs $250 for one adult and one child. WDW's two dinner shows – **Hoop-Dee-Doo Revue** at Fort Wilderness and **Disney's Spirit of Aloha** at the Polynesian – cost $25–$30 for kids and $50–$60 for adults (gratuity included).

IN THE PARKS: The current hot tickets are meals at Cinderella's Royal Table in Magic Kingdom's Cinderella Castle. It's almost impossible to get a reservation, but other more accessible Magic Kingdom options include **Goofy's Liberate Your Appetite** dinner at Liberty Tree Tavern, and the breakfast, lunch or dinner **Buffet with Character** at the Crystal Palace. Highlights in other parks include **Princess Storybook Dining** at Akershus in Epcot's Norway Pavilion; the relatively new **Playhouse Disney's Play 'n' Dine at Hollywood & Vine** at Hollywood Studios; and, for Donald Duck fans, **Donald's Safari Breakfast** in Animal Kingdom.

AT THE RESORTS: For face time with the mouse, try **Chef Mickey's** at the Contemporary Resort. **'Ohana** at Disney's Polynesian Resort features Lilo, Stitch, Mickey and Pluto. At 1900 Park Fare at Disney's Grand Floridian, you'll find Mary Poppins and friends for breakfast, Cinderella for dinner.

BOOK IT: You can make Character Dining reservations up to 180 days ahead by calling 407-939-3463. For last-minute reservations, a good bet is the sprawling Cape May Cafe at Disney's Beach Club Resort, where Goofy and pals move table to table.

Top Entertainment

25	Hoop-Dee-Doo	*Fort Wilderness Resort, Magic Kingdom Area*
24	Chef Mickey's	*Contemporary Resort, Magic Kingdom Area*
	Playhouse Disney	*Hollywood Studios, Hollywood Boulevard*
23	Once Upon a Time	*Magic Kingdom, Fantasyland*
	Buffet at Crystal Palace	*Magic Kingdom, Main Street*

Top Value

26	Playhouse Disney	*Hollywood Studios, Hollywood Boulevard*
22	Goofy's Liberate Your Appetite	*Magic Kingdom, Liberty Square*
	Hoop-Dee-Doo	*Fort Wilderness Resort, Magic Kingdom Area*
21	Chef Mickey's	*Contemporary Resort, Magic Kingdom Area*
20	Supercalifragilistic Breakfast	*Grand Floridian, Magic Kingdom Area*

FOOD | SERVICE | ENTERT. | VALUE

Ratings & Symbols

Food, Service, Entertainment and **Value** are rated on the Zagat 0 to 30 scale.

Buffet with Character at
The Crystal Palace, A *American*

| 22 | 22 | 23 | 20 |

Magic Kingdom, Main Street, U.S.A.

"Hip, hip Pooh-ray!" shout fans when "Tigger, Eeyore and Piglet" lead a "playful" parade through The Crystal Palace that makes kids' "eyes sparkle" during breakfast, lunch and dinner at this "cheery" spot in the "middle of Magic Kingdom"; though a few pooh-pooh it as "too big and busy" and say "the experience varies" with the "crowd level", most report "excellent" character access, "attentive" service and American fare that's "better" than at some other character dining options.

⚡ Chef Mickey's Fun Time Buffet at
Chef Mickey's *American*

| 22 | 22 | 24 | 21 |

Magic Kingdom Area | Disney's Contemporary Resort | 4600 N. World Dr.

"Dance, sing and swing your napkin over your head" at this American in the Contemporary Resort, where "no child is overlooked" by the "awesome" cast at what fans call one of WDW's "best" character meals; "Mickey-shaped" waffles and a "multitude" of breakfast options are replaced by prime rib and "wonderful" Parmesan mashed potatoes later in the day, and though it's "too loud" for some, most enjoy the "party atmosphere" where kids "from 1 to 101" "don't have to be quiet"; P.S. expect "an added 'wow' when the monorail" swooshes overhead.

Chip 'n' Dale's Harvest Feast at
The Garden Grill Restaurant *American*

| 21 | 22 | 22 | 20 |

Epcot, Future World

"Extremely fresh" fruits and vegetables, grown in the on-site greenhouse, plus "heaping platters" of meat, potatoes and other American fare are served family-style for lunch and dinner at "one of Walt Disney World's best-kept secrets", where the round, "slowly rotating" room offers "constantly changing" views of Living With the Land in Epcot's Future World; there's "plenty for all, something for everyone", especially boys who find "the princess meals not 'manly' enough" and like the fact that "Chip and Dale don't leave you with lipstick kisses."

Cinderella's Happily Ever After Dinner
at 1900 Park Fare *American*

| 22 | 23 | 22 | 20 |

(fka Cinderella's Gala Feast at 1900 Park Fare)

Magic Kingdom Area | Disney's Grand Floridian Resort & Spa | 4401 Floridian Way

"One of the rare occasions to meet Prince Charming", this "little-and-big-girl's-dream-come-true" is a "must" for "any princess"; fans laud "upper-end" breakfast offerings and "quite good" American buffet fare at dinner, all served in an "elegant" yet "cheery" room while Cinderella, her royal beau, stepmother and stepsisters "sign books" and pose for "pictures with the kids"; a few find it "expensive" and warn "boys might not like" all the girlie goings-on, but most folks "leave full and happy."

CHARACTER DINING & DINNER SHOWS

	FOOD	SERVICE	ENTERT.	VALUE

Disney's Spirit of Aloha Dinner Show *Hawaiian* | 19 | 21 | 22 | 18 |

Magic Kingdom Area | Disney's Polynesian Resort | 1600 Seven Seas Dr.
Happy haoles hail this Polynesian luau for being "as good as anything in Hawaii" with "fun fire dancing" and "better-than-expected" "theme-appropriate" family-style fare served in an open-air pavilion; those not in the spirit give the heave-ho to the "Don Ho–type" shtick, claiming it lacks the "quality" of "other Disney shows", but others suggest "doing it once" for a "change of pace"; N.B. held Tuesday–Saturday at 5:15 and 8 PM.

NEW Donald's Safari Breakfast at | - | - | - | - |
Tusker House Restaurant *African/American*

Disney's Animal Kingdom, Africa
The namesake quack and his pals Mickey, Goofy – and occasionally even the missus, Daisy – promise a taste of adventure at this sprawling quick-service eatery in Harambe Marketplace on the outskirts of Africa; vintage safari photos, lanternesque lighting and ersatz animal heads create an exotic setting, while chutneys, porridge and yam casserole lend the standard buffet fare a shot of Colonial/African flair.

Fairytale Lunch at | 21 | 24 | 21 | 16 |
Cinderella's Royal Table, A *American*

Magic Kingdom, Fantasyland
"You're eating in the castle, for goodness' sake!" say surveyors smitten by the chance to dine "with princesses" for a "special-occasion" breakfast, lunch or dinner; the American fare is "up to par", and though skeptical stepsisters scoff there are "not many choices" and "entertainment is limited to Cinderella in a chair", kinder souls say "excellent" service, an "impressive" show and a location in the "epicenter of magic" make it "worth" it, "especially for little girls."

Garden Grove Cafe *American* | - | - | - | - |

Epcot Area | Walt Disney World Swan | 1500 Epcot Resort Blvd.
This "pleasant surprise" in the Swan resort offers solid "family fun" in the form of classic American breakfasts (weekends only) and dinners, hosted by Pluto and Goofy, which are enjoyed under the boughs of a dramatic 25-ft. oak tree; a short boat ride from the World Showcase entrance to Epcot, it serves as a low-key, typically less-crowded alternative to more high-profile character meals.

Goofy's Beach Club Breakfast at | 20 | 21 | 21 | 19 |
Cape May Cafe *American*

Epcot Area | Disney's Beach Club Resort | 1800 Epcot Resort Blvd.
You'll find breakfast "basics" "done well" at this "blessedly low-key", "less-frequented" option at the Beach Club Resort, where Goofy, Minnie Mouse, Chip and Dale start the day "dressed for the shore" in "cute", "old-fashioned suits"; though foodies might wish for more "specially prepared" items, at least the characters are "more accessible" than at the larger "mainstream" eat-and-greets, making for good "value."

Goofy's Liberate Your Appetite at | 23 | 24 | 23 | 22 |
Liberty Tree Tavern *American*

Magic Kingdom, Liberty Square
Minnie, Goofy, Pluto and friends "sporting Colonial-style duds" host this "surprisingly tasty" "Thanksgiving feast", featuring "old-

fashioned" "stick-to-your-ribs" American fare (a "great substitute for quickie park food") served family-style in a "cozy" Colonial tavern setting; a "helpful", "friendly" staff, "plentiful" portions and characters who "spend lots of time interacting with guests" add up to a Magic Kingdom "winner"; P.S. "when you're done, catch the parade right outside."

❷ Hoop-Dee-Doo Musical Revue *American* `22` `24` `25` `22`

Magic Kingdom Area | Disney's Fort Wilderness Resort & Campground | 4510 N. Ft. Wilderness Trail

"Buckets" of American "country food and corny songs" make for "a hootin', hollerin' good time" at this "classic Disney" "must-see" at Fort Wilderness Campground; surveyors say it offers the "best entertainment" among dinner shows, citing "talented actors", "great audience interaction", "top-notch" service and "lots of humor" to "make you smile" ("unlimited wine and beer" helps too); though a few city slickers find fault ("overpriced", "not for dieters"), most call it a "must-do" – "again and again"; N.B. held nightly at 5, 7:15 and 9:30 PM.

Mickey's Backyard BBQ *American* `21` `22` `22` `20`

Magic Kingdom Area | Disney's Fort Wilderness Resort & Campground | 4510 N. Ft. Wilderness Trail

A "sleeper" among character meals, this BBQ bash held at Fort Wilderness Campground "feels like a large family gathering"; the "cowboy-themed evening" includes line dancing "with characters" to a country band ("children love it") and an "unending" American buffet, and if a few find the eats "nothing outstanding" and question the cost, more say it delivers "great entertainment value"; N.B. offered Thursdays and Saturdays, March–December only.

My Disney Girl's ▽ `15` `24` `25` `15`
Perfectly Princess Tea Party *Tearoom*

Magic Kingdom Area | Disney's Grand Floridian Resort & Spa | 4401 Floridian Way

"Disney magic at its finest" describes this "delightful" "mother-daughter" tea held at the "beautiful" Grand Floridian, where "incredible" hosts Rose Petal and Aurora help create "priceless memories"; sure, the "food could be better", but the "extras" – including a doll, bracelet and a tiara to take home – "make up for it", and though you might "need to take out a second mortgage" ($250 for one child and one adult), it's "worth every penny" since "your little princess will remember it forever."

'Ohana's Best Friends Breakfast `21` `22` `23` `20`
featuring Lilo & Stitch *American*

Magic Kingdom Area | Disney's Polynesian Resort | 1600 Seven Seas Dr.

Start your day with a "conga-line" parade at this "Polynesian retreat", where Mickey and pals come "dressed Hawaiian" and Stitch is "up to his usual pranks"; the breakfast "basics" served family-style are "bountiful and delicious" (though some wish there were more choices), "kids love" "dancing the hula" with characters who "take time for pictures and hugs", and parents ("grandparents" too) "enjoy watching the little ones" and the "beautiful" Seven Seas Lagoon, making this an "intergenerational" "favorite."

	FOOD	SERVICE	ENTERT.	VALUE

Once Upon a Time Breakfast at | 19 | 22 | 23 | 17
Cinderella's Royal Table *American*

Magic Kingdom, Fantasyland

"Dreams really do come true" for "little girls looking for princesses" at this "regal" American breakfast where "lovely" Cinderella and friends are "patient" and "gracious"; though even fans admit it's "pricey", the pre-plated meal is "not the best" and reservations can be "extraordinarily difficult" to secure, believers insist it's "more than worth it" "when you see the look on your child's face."

Z Playhouse Disney's Play 'n' Dine at | 19 | 23 | 24 | 22
Hollywood & Vine *American*

Disney's Hollywood Studios, Hollywood Boulevard

"The preschool set" "goes crazy" for "adorable characters" who engage them in "constant dancing and songs" at this "yet to be discovered" relative newcomer to Hollywood Studios' Hollywood & Vine; maybe the American breakfast and lunch buffet fare is "not the best", but fans feel the "awesome" cast makes for some of the "most entertaining", "good-value" character dining around – and it doesn't take a "Little Einstein" to figure out it's a "great way to eat breakfast inside Hollywood Studios before the park opens."

Princess Storybook Dining at | 18 | 20 | 23 | 18
Akershus Royal Banquet Hall *Norwegian*

Epcot, World Showcase

"Royalty roams the room" at this World Showcase "great place to meet princesses" "in their finest" who "tell stories", "play games" and offer "many hugs" while "spending as much time as each child needs"; lunch and dinner feature "diverse, interesting" Norwegian fare like *kjottkake* (meatballs), venison and salmon, but some feel the American-style breakfast buffet is more kid-friendly – and a "nice alternative" to the "pricier" Cinderella Castle breakfast.

Supercalifragilistic Breakfast at | 22 | 22 | 22 | 20
1900 Park Fare *American*

Magic Kingdom Area | Disney's Grand Floridian Resort & Spa | 4401 Floridian Way

Start your day amid the "charming cacophony" created by Mary Poppins, Alice, Mad Hatter, Pooh and company at this "upper-end" breakfast buffet – one of WDW's "best" say fans – at the Grand Floridian; the "excellent" choices are served in a "bright, airy", "beautiful" space, and though some say the "big, noisy room" "just doesn't feel magical", realists focus on the food and advise you "won't need lunch" after this meal; P.S. easy "monorail access" is a plus.

Wonderland Tea Party at | ▽ 19 | 23 | 24 | 21
1900 Park Fare *Tearoom*

Magic Kingdom Area | Disney's Grand Floridian Resort & Spa | 4401 Floridian Way

Parents aren't permitted to partake of this pint-size tea party featuring Alice, Mad Hatter and a "wonderful" staff, but the kids "all seem to have a great time" playing games and singing songs; guests enjoy PBJ sandwiches, decorate-your-own cupcakes and "tea" (which looks a lot like apple juice) while grown-ups take a pager and wander for an hour.

NIGHTLIFE

Nightlife

IN THE PARKS: Except in the no-alcohol Magic Kingdom, you can imbibe in all of WDW's theme parks. Options include Epcot's World Showcase, where partiers can globe-trot (margaritas in Mexico, sake in Japan, etc.); Hollywood Studios' **Tune-In Lounge,** serving kitschy cocktails amid Tinseltown trappings; and the **Dawa Bar** at Animal Kingdom, where you can relax with African wine, beer or rum punch.

AT THE RESORTS: All the resorts have a lounge of some kind. At the posh end is the Grand Floridian's **Mizner's Lounge,** featuring single-malts and live entertainment, while at the bare-bones end there are the All-Star resorts' pool bars. South African wines are spotlighted at the **Cape Town Lounge** in Disney's Animal Kingdom Lodge, while the Contemporary Resort's **California Grill** and **Outer Rim** lounges offer lovely views. Children are allowed in all resort bars if accompanied by parents, except at Pleasure Island, where clubgoers must be 21 (though at **Adventurers Club** and **Comedy Warehouse,** those 18-20 are allowed if accompanied by someone 21 or older).

THE BOARDWALK: For post-fireworks nightlife, the BoardWalk offers the likes of **Atlantic Dance Hall's** nightly DJ Dance Party; **ESPN Club's** suds and sports; and **Jellyrolls'** dueling pianos and sing-alongs.

DOWNTOWN DISNEY: WDW's premier nightlife area is Downtown Disney, both Pleasure Island and West Side. Pleasure Island is a villagelike collection of themed clubs including the Survey's Most Popular nightspot, **Adventurers Club.** Pleasure Club-goers pay admission of $11.67 for a single club or $23.38 for a multiclub ticket. Next to Pleasure Island (and with no admission charge) is **Raglan Road,** featuring music most nights. Downtown Disney West Side offers concerts at **House of Blues** and salsa at **Bongos Cuban Cafe.** For alcohol-free family fun, there's **Cirque du Soleil** and **DisneyQuest** (see Attractions), plus an AMC multiplex.

COST CONTROL: Uniform pricing for cocktails and beer was instituted at WDW post-Survey; cost codes may not reflect this change.

Top Appeal

25	Raglan Road	*Downtown Disney, Pleasure Island*
	Adventurers Club	*Downtown Disney, Pleasure Island*
24	Narcoossee's	*Grand Floridian, Magic Kingdom Area*
	Comedy Warehouse	*Downtown Disney, Pleasure Island*
	Jellyrolls	*BoardWalk, Epcot Area*

Top Decor

26	Adventurers Club	*Downtown Disney, Pleasure Island*
25	Raglan Road	*Downtown Disney, Pleasure Island*
24	Victoria Falls	*Animal Kingdom Lodge, Animal Kingdom Area*
	Tune-In Lounge	*Hollywood Studios, Echo Lake*
	Magic Mushroom Bar	*Downtown Disney, Marketplace*

Ratings & Symbols

Appeal, Decor and **Service** are rated on the Zagat 0 to 30 scale.

Cost reflects surveyors' estimated price of each nightlife venue's price range:

I Inexpensive
M Moderate
E Expensive
VE Very Expensive

In the Parks

EPCOT

WORLD SHOWCASE

Rose & Crown Pub | 24 | 23 | 22 | M |

It's "back to jolly ol' England" at this London pub facsimile with "authentic" decor, "traditional food", an occasional pianist and "gracious" "native British" staffers; pop in for "a cold pint" and you'll be "cheek by jowl" with a "convivial" crowd, so "be prepared to stand"; P.S. for diners, the waterside patio is "one of the great seats" for viewing IllumiNations.

DISNEY'S HOLLYWOOD STUDIOS

ECHO LAKE

Tune-In Lounge | 22 | 24 | 23 | M |

"Talk about kitschy!": this "amazing" "little bar adjoining the 50's Prime Time Cafe" boasts "retro" "details" like vintage TVs, "drinks from 'dad's liquor cabinet'" and service with some "comedy" attuned to "the good ol' days"; it's "cool" after the "hubbub" of Hollywood Studios, but it "gets crowded" with diners "waiting to be seated" next door.

DISNEY'S ANIMAL KINGDOM

AFRICA

Dawa Bar | - | 23 | 22 | M |

Go native in the Animal Kingdom's Harambe Village at this "wonderful little" thatched bar that's been Imagineered into a shady bush break for a "nice cool" brew or "African wine"; the open-air site next to Tusker House is "welcome" "on a hot day" and a "super place" to catch the safari parade, musicians and "fantastic acrobats" who periodically swing by.

At the Resorts

MAGIC KINGDOM AREA

California Grill Lounge | 24 | 23 | 23 | E |

Disney's Contemporary Resort | 4600 N. World Dr.
A "high-end" hangout in the California Grill on the Contemporary's 15th floor, this more "modern", "less themed" lounge is "a must" for "at least

one drink" to take in the "amazing views of Magic Kingdom" and the "nightly fireworks show"; it's "pricey" and "gets packed", but those "wishing on a star" for "stellar" service and an "excellent wine list" "feel very pampered" here; P.S. the eatery's "first-rate" fare is also available.

Crockett's Tavern

19	20	20	M

Disney's Fort Wilderness Resort & Campground | 4510 N. Ft. Wilderness Trail

Drink to "bygone days" at this "rustic" bar "in the heart of Fort Wilderness" campground in the back of the log cabin that also houses the "family-oriented" Trail's End canteen; settlers say it's a "peaceful" place to decamp over hooch and a light menu to stave off "the munchies" while "waiting for the Hoop-De-Doo" dinner show to start next door.

Garden View Lounge

22	21	21	E

Disney's Grand Floridian Resort & Spa | 4401 Floridian Way

"Lovely for a spot of tea", this "very elegant" lounge "off the cavernous lobby of the Grand Floridian" also serves classy cocktails in its flowery, sunlit environs; reservations are advised for the Brit-style "full tea", whose "tasty and well-presented" light dishes and "excellent service" ensure a "special mother-daughter afternoon"; P.S. "your princess" is welcome, but the pace may be too leisurely to keep younger ones entertained for long.

Mizner's Lounge

▽ 22	21	22	E

Disney's Grand Floridian Resort & Spa | 4401 Floridian Way

"You'll forget you're in the House of Mouse" at this stylishly "clubby" hotel lounge overlooking the Grand Floridian's gardens, whose "luxurious" frills do justice to the Jazz Age architect it's named for; "attentive but unobtrusive" servers pouring sippable ports and brandies ensure "you're a regular on your second visit", and the "fine" "nightly band music" feels so genteel many only wish it "went later."

Narcoossee's

24	22	24	E

Disney's Grand Floridian Resort & Spa | 4401 Floridian Way

A "refined retreat from the chaotic World", this seafooder/lounge occupies an eight-sided "waterfront" pavilion "behind the Grand Floridian" with an "amazing" "view of the Magic Kingdom" over the lagoon; admirers coo over its "peaceful" setting, "full bar", "attentive-not-intrusive" service and "delicious" dining, calling it an "irresistible" place to "catch the fireworks" or "the Electrical Light Pageant"; N.B. the broad wine list has many half-bottle options.

Outer Rim Lounge

21	21	21	M

Disney's Contemporary Resort | 4600 N. World Dr.

"Have a beer and watch the monorail" run the Contemporary Resort's perimeter at this fourth-floor "alcove" lounge, where staffers are "willing and able" to help you "unwind" (they might even "create new drinks on the fly"); those out of sorts with "dated" decor à la *That '70s Show* or "all the commotion at Chef Mickey's" nearby can turn their attention to the "big windows" offering a "great view of Bay Lake."

Tambu Lounge

-	-	-	M

Disney's Polynesian Resort | 1600 Seven Seas Dr.

True to its islandy surroundings on the second floor of the Polynesian's Great Ceremonial House, this bamboo- and idol-embellished lounge specializes in tiki-tastic concoctions like Blue Hawaiians, mai tais and deadly Zombies; subdued by day, it's more active come early evening as families drift in to ease back on wicker with something sweet and fruity before a luau at neighboring 'Ohana.

Territory Lounge

| 19 | 19 | 20 | M |

Disney's Wilderness Lodge | 901 Timberline Dr.

Explorers who light out for this "rustic watering hole" in the Wilderness Lodge "feel that they're in a National Park" embellished with "little Disneyfied" touches like "a map on the ceiling" (in case you "happen to be lying down" at night's end); the "energetic staff" plies microbrews, "Northwest vineyard" wines and house cocktails, and standard bar food comes with the territory.

EPCOT AREA

Ale and Compass

| 18 | 18 | 19 | E |

Disney's Yacht Club Resort | 1700 Epcot Resort Blvd.

The lobby breakfast nook at Disney's Yacht Club morphs into this "maritime-themed" "drinking" bar in the evening, a "quick stop for a libation" and "minimal appetizers" "after a long day in the park"; it attracts a "mostly adult" crew gearing up for dinner, few of whom threaten mutiny if there's "nothing exciting" on the horizon here.

Atlantic Dance Hall

| 18 | 20 | 19 | M |

Disney's BoardWalk | 2101 N. Epcot Resort Blvd.

"A bit of time travel" on the BoardWalk, this "1930s"-style mockup evokes a "supper club from back in the day", but while some "love the location and decor", nostalgists preferred it "when they had live music and swing competitions" instead of "hip-hop and rock hits"; let-down partiers report "junior high dance" flashbacks with "only a few brave couples" on the floor, suggesting that an "identity crisis" explains why it's "underutilized."

Belle Vue Room

| 22 | 21 | 21 | E |

Disney's BoardWalk | 2101 N. Epcot Resort Blvd.

"Tucked away" in the BoardWalk Inn, this "cozy" lounge is a "secret" "flop stop" where those in-the-know "wind down" "in solitude" diverted by a "game library" of "classics" ("Scrabble and Connect Four") as antique radios replay oldie shows; service is "always friendly", and the patio with a "people-watching" vue is "a plus in nice weather."

Crew's Cup

∇ | 23 | 23 | 24 | M |

Disney's Yacht Club Resort | 1700 Epcot Resort Blvd.

It takes "just a handful of folks" to make this "lovely little" rowing-themed pub in the Yacht Club runneth over, but the "dark", "oaky" atmosphere is "charming" and "restful" when you're thirsty for a "schooner" or two; sure, space is "tight" at times, but all hands are "friendly", there's "tasty bar food" on offer and it's always a "cozy" berth "for a nightcap."

ESPN Club

| 21 | 21 | 19 | M |

Disney's BoardWalk | 2101 N. Epcot Resort Blvd.

"Hang out with the boys" at this BoardWalk "husband's paradise" broadcasting "all types of sports" on "TVs everywhere", from the "giant screen" with "stadium-style seating" to sets "in the restroom" ("gotta love it"); spoilsports say the "loud and crowded" conditions lead to "sensory overload" plus "spotty" service and "long waits", but most call it a winner for "wings and beer", macho "memorabilia" and watching "the big game" with "no Mickey Mousing."

Jellyrolls
24 | 19 | 21 | M

Disney's BoardWalk | 2101 N. Epcot Resort Blvd.

"What a blast!": the "good times" are always "rolling" at this "interactive" "dueling-pianos bar" on the BoardWalk, "a definite favorite" where a pair of "talented" keyboardists lead "sing-alongs" to standards and "requests" ranging from "oldies" to "Garth Brooks to AC/DC"; once the crowd starts to "unwind" and get "more vocal", it's bound to be "rocking till closing time"; N.B. 21 and over only.

Kimonos
23 | 21 | 22 | E

Walt Disney World Swan | 1500 Epcot Resort Blvd.

"Sushi, sake and karaoke" are the draws at the Swan hotel's "stylish" Japanese restaurant/bar, where a display of the namesake garb up on the teak walls oversees a nightly songfest that's even more "entertaining" when "conventioneers are in town"; "service is quick" and the drinks are "strong", a plus when it takes a swig of "liquid courage" to "get up on stage" "and let yourself go."

Lobby Court Lounge
- | - | - | M

Walt Disney World Swan | 1500 Epcot Resort Blvd.

Dispensing coffee and pastries by day, the bright and open "lobby bar at the Swan" serves evening desserts and drinks in the "transitional" space between the hotel's entrance and parkside exit; it's convenient for a "nightcap on the way to your room", but some lobby for a better setup since the "no-man's-land" locale "has no real appeal."

Martha's Vineyard
∇ 22 | 21 | 19 | M

Disney's Beach Club Resort | 1800 Epcot Resort Blvd.

For a "respite" "after a long day at Epcot", the Beach Club Resort's lounge is a "quiet place to relax" amid breezy pastels and wicker furniture before "dinner at the Cape May Cafe"; the libations include the likes of the Blue Glow-Tini, which can be enjoyed with bar bites like spinach dip with chips and Buffalo chicken strips.

Shula's Steak House Lounge
21 | 20 | 20 | E

Walt Disney World Dolphin | 1500 Epcot Resort Blvd.

Appropriately located in the Dolphin, the bar at this football-themed chain meatery is an "upscale" spot for "grown-ups" to touch down amid dark wood, leather and gridiron mementos; scoring with "super service" and an impressive vino list, it's a "serene" "retreat" for "top-notch everything" – but low rollers warn that's "including the prices"; N.B. puffers prize the smoking lounge and its select cigar menu.

DISNEY'S ANIMAL KINGDOM AREA

Cape Town Lounge & Wine Bar
21 | 22 | 21 | M

Disney's Animal Kingdom Lodge | 2901 Osceola Pkwy.

Wander "off the beaten path" to discover a wide selection of South African wines at this loungey neighbor to Jiko at the Animal Kingdom Lodge; the "very knowledgeable" barkeeps "go out of their way" to oblige if you'd like to sample a vintage "before buying the bottle"; N.B. the adjacent Cape Town Wine room can accommodate up to 40 guests for private events.

NEW Rix Lounge
| - | - | - | M |

Disney's Coronado Springs Resort | 1000 W. Buena Vista Dr.
Late-night revelers flock to this casbah-chic newcomer that brings a splash of South Beach to WDW with its blown-glass light fixtures, red-velvet banquettes with satin throw pillows and gauzy sheers flowing from double-height ceilings; a nightly DJ mingles oldies with current hits, and an upscale menu of martinis, champagnes and tableside bottle service (starting at $200 a pop) belies its location inside the moderately priced Coronado Springs Resort.

Victoria Falls
| 23 | 24 | 22 | M |

Disney's Animal Kingdom Lodge | 2901 Osceola Pkwy.
Lounge fans fall for this "upscale" "favorite" in the Animal Kingdom Lodge's "amazing lobby", a "lovely" patch of Africana sporting safari-style earth tones and "comfortable" leather chairs; the locale "overlooking Boma" is "a little noisy" but still "delightful" for "drinks and conversation", and the "waterfall in the background" is extra "relaxing" after sampling the "world-class" "choice of spirits" and wine list highlighting South African labels.

DOWNTOWN DISNEY AREA

River Roost
▽ | 24 | 21 | 23 | M |

Disney's Port Orleans Resort - Riverside | 1251 Riverside Dr.
Decked out with club chairs, a fireplace, chandeliers and TVs tuned to sports, this lounge in the Port Orleans Riverside offers a place to roost in Southern comfort while you "wait for a table at Boatwright's" next door; a menu of appetizers complements Dixie drinks like Hurricanes and Mississippi Mudslides, and "piano-playing Bob" Jackson's ivory tickling is a "wonderful treat" "for all ages."

Turf Club Lounge
| 19 | 22 | 18 | E |

Disney's Saratoga Springs Resort & Spa | 1960 Broadway
Outfitted with overstuffed chairs and equestrian gear, this lounge at the Saratoga Springs provides some "quiet" turf near the eponymous eatery; it's a "comfortable", "uncrowded" haven where "families are welcome", "a pool table invites" and a "friendly staff" serves a "small" menu plus cocktails and nonalcoholic treats like Blackberry Lemonade, but action-seekers may feel the pace "needs improvement."

Downtown Disney

MARKETPLACE

Cap'n Jack's Restaurant
| 18 | 18 | 19 | E |

1780 E. Buena Vista Dr.
With a pierside mooring "out of the mayhem" in Downtown Disney's Marketplace, this "quaint" seafood shack is "one of the original venues" from 1975 and still supplies its signature strawberry margaritas; supporters salute the chance to hoist a few and "enjoy the water views",

though the fin fare-filled menu works best "for lunch" given "limited selections at dinner."

Magic Mushroom Bar at the Rainforest Cafe   21 | 24 | 20 | E
1800 E. Buena Vista Dr.

With "all that grows in the rainforest" as backdrop, the bar at this chain eatery in Downtown Disney's Marketplace (head for the erupting volcano) has "great visual style", capped by a huge mushroom canopy; the "aquariums", animatronic fauna, simulated thunderstorms and Homo sapien "families" "packed" into the restaurant will keep "your child interested" while you make the "pretty strong" "margaritas" magically disappear.

PLEASURE ISLAND

☒ Adventurers Club   25 | 26 | 22 | M
1590 E. Buena Vista Dr.

Anyone who's "dreamed of going on a safari or wearing a pith helmet" is in for "zany fun" at this ultra-"quirky combination" of theater, "improv" and "variety show" on Pleasure Island, a "wacky send-up" of a "1930s" explorer's club where "eccentric" "world travelers" share "tall tales" and the audience "takes the oath" and becomes "part of the show"; with "talking masks, hidden passageways" and "outrageous" getups, it's "truly unique" and promises "a new adventure" "every time you go."

BET SoundStage Club   17 | 18 | 17 | M
1590 E. Buena Vista Dr.

"Dress to impress" and get ready to "shake your money maker" at Black Entertainment Television's double-decker Pleasure Island showcase, where "up-to-date" sets of "the best in hip-hop and R&B" plus "large-screen" "music videos" keep the dance floor bumpin'; if you're betting on "great beats" and a "diverse group", "this is the club for you."

☒ Comedy Warehouse   24 | 21 | 20 | M
1590 E. Buena Vista Dr.

"On a good night", this Pleasure Island laugh factory produces "loads of fun" with "rather short" sets of "hilarious improv" from "quick-on-their-feet" jesters, so "be prepared to participate" in an "all-ad lib" format that guarantees it's "never the same show twice"; the "PG" routines are kept "Disney clean" so you can "take the kids", but fans who fancy "more adult humor" can try the "looser" (and more crowded) later gigs.

☒ 8 TRAX   21 | 18 | 18 | M
1590 E. Buena Vista Dr.

"Dig out the polyester" and "hustle" over to "shake it old-school style" at Pleasure Island's "always busy", "cheesy-on-purpose" disco "flashback", spinning the "gr8" "'70s and '80s" dance trax "everyone loves"; some are bummed at "throwback" decor that "could use an overhaul", but "plenty of neon" and a *Saturday Night Fever* floor are all the "mid-30s" crowd needs to break out the "boogie shoes" and "cut loose" "like a fool."

	APPEAL	DECOR	SERVICE	COST

NEW Fuego by Sosa Cigars
– | – | – | M

1502 E. Buena Vista Dr.

One of the few free-standing structures on Pleasure Island, this stogie stand-cum-night spot offers dozens of smokes and spirits in an airy, loft-style space with banquette seating and vintage photos of hand-rollers gracing the walls; patio tables out back provide a refuge for respiration, and a display case up front offers a small selection of cutters and other puffer's paraphernalia.

Mannequins Dance Palace
21 | 20 | 17 | M

1590 E. Buena Vista Dr.

"The party crowd" keeps this "high-energy" multilevel danceland alive "into the night", grooving to "body-thumping" "trance" and "techno" amid "pulsing lights, mirrors and smoke machines" that "add to the frenzy" of what some call the "best club on Pleasure Island"; the signature "revolving dance floor" "makes people-watching easy", but it "can be tricky", so "don't drink too much" from the "huge bar"; P.S. Thursday is the unofficial gay night, but "alternative lifestyles" are always represented.

Motion
19 | 17 | 17 | M

1650 E. Buena Vista Dr.

Some "visual shortcomings" in the "warehouse" layout may leave critics unmoved, but DJs spinning "a great mix" of "Top 40 dance hits" and "smokin' hip-hop" matched "with videos" on the "giant screen" make this Pleasure Island "hot spot" "a must-do" for "twenty-somethings" and their friends looking to "groove"; clubbers who "try to party too early" may find things in slow motion, but it "gets really happening after midnight."

Portobello Yacht Club Lounge
21 | 21 | 20 | E

1650 E. Buena Vista Dr.

A "first-class" berth in Downtown Disney, this "relaxing" Italian restaurant/bar sees its crowd mushroom as the Pleasure Island set arrives to start the evening with "excellent martinis", "sangria"-like *vino con frutta* or wine from a noteworthy list; a few may find it "stuffy" and "expensive", but most are grateful for a shipshape "escape" in the "midst of the chaos."

☑ Raglan Road Irish Pub & Restaurant
25 | 25 | 23 | M

1640 E. Buena Vista Dr.

Doublin' for a saloon "in Ireland itself", this "terrific" Pleasure Island option "keeps one's spirits (and glass) raised" with four bars "imported" from the Auld Country, a "fabulous beer selection" and "genuine" grub like shepherd's pie that "takes pub fare to a new level"; 'tis a "personable" spot to "tip one back" and "not feel rushed", and the "traditional" "Irish band and step dancers" keep things "loud" and lively "late into the night."

Stone Crab Lounge
20 | 20 | 18 | E

Fulton's Crab House | 1670 E. Buena Vista Dr.

Occupying a quaint paddleboat along with Fulton's Crab House in Downtown Disney, this popular lounge is an "excellent" "place to hang out" "away from the crowds" while waiting for a table to open up in the restaurant; given the sizable wine list, fresh oyster bar and romantic views of the lake, customers who land here are anything but crabby.

WEST SIDE

Bongos Cuban Cafe

| 20 | 21 | 19 | E |

1478 E. Buena Vista Dr.

"The rhythm is gonna get you" at this "energetic" "Gloria Estafan-owned" eatery in Downtown Disney's West Side, which drums up support with its "'50s" Havana stylings, "tasty" tropical drinks ("try the mojitos") and "live salsa" that keeps the dance floor "packed"; sí, it's "pricey" and the "traditional Cuban-style cooking" is "not the best", but it's so "high on atmosphere" night owls "love it."

House of Blues Concert Hall

| 23 | 21 | 19 | E |

1478 E. Buena Vista Dr.

Lose your blues at this "upbeat" concert venue, bar and eatery with easy access from Downtown Disney's West Side; it offers a "fantastic" chance to catch an "excellent selection" of live "musical acts" "up-close and personal" since there's "not a bad seat in the house", and the "New Orleans" juke-joint decor (and "creative" down-home cookin') suits everything from R&B to hard rock; P.S. Sunday's two gospel brunches have true believers testifying they "can't wait to do it again."

SHOPPING

Shopping

Whether your tastes run to imported silk Moroccan rugs and Mikimoto pearl necklaces or custom Crocs beach sandals (with mouse-ear-shape holes) and monogrammed Mickey Mouse ears, you can find it in WDW's many shops.

IN THE PARKS: The biggest retailer in Magic Kingdom is the usually super-busy **Emporium** on Main Street, U.S.A. carrying all kinds of Disneyana. At Epcot, those in search of merchandise beyond typical Disney souvenirs can go on a veritable global spree in World Showcase's trove of appealing stores: you'll find Mexican piñatas, imported sweaters in Norway, silk dresses in China, cuckoo clocks in Germany, silk scarves in Italy, pearls in Japan and more. Disney's Hollywood Studios finds include animation cels and celebrity memorabilia in stores like **Sid Cahuenga's One of a Kind** and **Animation Gallery,** while Disney's Animal Kingdom offers traditional African wares and nature-theme gifts in shops such as **Mombasa Marketplace** and **Island Mercantile.**

AT THE RESORTS: Resort shop offerings are homogenized and consist mostly of vacation-appropriate sundries (sun block, toiletries) and standard Disney souvenirs. For upscale resort clothing try Disney's Grand Floridian Resort & Spa, and for a big selection of swimsuits check out both the Polynesian Resort and the **Beach Club Marketplace** at the Beach Club Resort.

DOWNTOWN DISNEY AND BOARDWALK: For one-stop shopping, head to **World of Disney Store** at Downtown Disney Marketplace, a 51,000-sq.-ft. retail behemoth stocking every "souven-ear" imaginable – clothing, jewelry, books, DVDs, housewares and more, all with Disney logos. WOD's newest addition is the extravagant **Bibbidi Bobbidi Boutique** for girls ages three and up, whose parents fork out between $35 and $175 to have their "little princesses" done up in princess attire, complete with hair and makeup. There are about 14 more shops at the Marketplace, including non-Disney standouts such as the venerable **Arribas Brothers** for crystal from around the world, and the hands-on **LEGO Imagination Center.** The adjacent Downtown Disney West Side has a three-story **Virgin Megastore** (with more than 300 listening stations) and a half-dozen boutiques like **Hoypoloi Gallery** for art, **Fuego by Sosa Cigars** for hand-rolled cigars and **Magic Masters,** a re-creation of Harry Houdini's private library. At Disney's BoardWalk, a highlight is **Wyland Galleries'** original ocean art, with other shops carrying limited groceries and basic Disney souvenirs. Downtown Disney stores are open until 11 PM daily.

SKIP THE SCHLEP: If you're staying at one of the WDW hotels, you can request free delivery of theme park purchases to your hotel room. Purchases made prior to 7 PM will be delivered by noon the following day; those made after 7 PM will arrive the second day after. And all park guests can request that in-park purchases be delivered to package pickup, located near the front entrance of each theme park, where they can be retrieved upon exiting.

PHONE IT IN: If you want any item from any WDW shopping locale, just call 407-363-6200 and describe what you saw and where you saw it. The Attractions Merchandise Guest Services Department will locate the item, process the purchase and arrange shipping. It's open weekdays except holidays.

Top Quality

MAGIC KINGDOM
24 Ye Olde Christmas | *Liberty Square*
Uptown Jewelers | *Main Street*
Main Street Confectionery | *Main Street*
Emporium | *Main Street*
Pooh's Thotful Shop | *Fantasyland*

EPCOT
26 Art of Disney | *Future World*
25 Glas Und Porzellan | *World Showcase*
Tea Caddy | *World Showcase*
24 Mouse Gear | *Future World*
Fjording | *World Showcase*

DISNEY'S HOLLYWOOD STUDIOS
26 Sweet Spells | *Sunset Boulevard*
25 Animation Gallery | *Animation Courtyard*
24 Mickey's of Hollywood | *Hollywood Boulevard*
23 Keystone Clothiers | *Hollywood Boulevard*
It's a Wonderful Shop | *Streets of America*

DISNEY'S ANIMAL KINGDOM
24 Island Mercantile | *Discovery Island*
23 Disney Outfitters | *Discovery Island*
Caricature Connection | *Discovery Island*
Outpost Shop | *Main Entrance*
22 Mombasa Marketplace | *Africa*

RESORT AREAS
25 Wyland Galleries | *multiple locations*
BouTiki | *Polynesian Resort, Magic Kingdom Area*
Zawadi Marketplace | *Animal Kingdom Lodge, Animal Kingdom Area*
24 Jackson Square Gifts | *Port Orleans-French Q, Downtown Disney Area*
Wilderness Lodge Mercantile | *Wilderness Lodge, Magic Kingdom Area*

DOWNTOWN DISNEY
26 Art of Disney | *Marketplace*
25 Disney's Days of Christmas | *Marketplace*
World of Disney Store | *Marketplace*
Arribas Brothers | *Marketplace*
24 LEGO Imagination | *Marketplace*

Ratings & Symbols

Quality, **Display** and **Service** are rated on the Zagat 0 to 30 scale.

Cost reflects our surveyors' estimate of each store's price range:

| I | Inexpensive | E | Expensive
| M | Moderate | VE | Very Expensive

In the Parks

MAGIC KINGDOM

ADVENTURELAND

Agrabah Bazaar　　　　　　　21 | 23 | 20 | M

"Fitting right into the ambiance" of Adventureland, this "interesting" open-air Middle Eastern souk entices visitors to "get out of the heat and browse" for Aladdin and Jasmine costumes, Lion King goodies, safari clothing, African baskets and carved wooden animals – many of which "you can't find elsewhere in the park"; N.B. it connects to Zanzibar, which sells much of the same inventory.

Pirate's Bazaar　　　　　　　21 | 24 | 20 | M

Booty-seeking buccaneers treasure this open-air street market located at the exit from the Pirates of the Caribbean attraction; the "neat, easy-to-browse" bounty ranges from swashbuckling swords, eye patches and plastic hooks to faux jewels for "damsels", but perplexed parents may bellow "aargh" – "it's hard to get kids out of here!"

FANTASYLAND

Pooh's Thotful Shop　　　　　24 | 23 | 22 | M

A "Pooh-lover's paradise", this whimsical corner of Fantasyland pleases fans with its "adorable" toys, baby clothes and souvenirs – pooh pundits pronounce it "the best place for Eeyore" and "the elusive Heffalumps and Woozles"; but since crowds "get dumped" into the "cramped" spot after exiting the Winnie-the-Pooh ride, it can be "hard to navigate."

Seven Dwarfs' Mine　　　　　20 | 18 | 21 | M

"Hi-ho, hi-ho, it's Seven Dwarfs' stuff to go" sing shoppers who've mined the merchandise at this kiosk next to Snow White's Scary Adventures; however, some Sleepy surveyors yawn that it's just a "typical Disney-character end-of-ride gift shop", while the Grumpy contingent gripes that it's "too small" and doesn't sell "much of anything at all."

Sir Mickey's　　　　　　　　23 | 23 | 23 | M

Though it's "tiny", fans say this Fantasyland shop just outside Cinderella Castle boasts a "well-selected" inventory of "cool" merchandise – it's a "great place to get that 'goofy' (pardon the pun) hat" and also carries other Disney-themed clothes, autograph books, mugs and pens.

	QUALITY	DISPLAY	SERVICE	COST

Tinker Bell's Treasures
23 | 24 | 21 | M

"Just outside the Peter Pan ride" behind the Fantasyland castle, this "heaven" for "wannabe princesses" and "little pixies" carries "cute girlie things" (jewelry, toys, costumes) "in abundance"; in the area that resembles the Darlings' nursery, you can peek into the "dresser drawer" where Tinker Bell sleeps to glimpse the fairy, who occasionally "flies through the shop as a spray of light."

FRONTIERLAND

Briar Patch
22 | 23 | 22 | M

Near the exit from Splash Mountain, this "charming" Frontierland shop carries *Song of the South*–themed wares (e.g. "Brer Rabbit storybooks") along with "items you might want after getting soaked", such as dry clothing and towels; other Magic Kingdom–related goodies include a "wide variety" of Pooh products particularly suited to "Tigger fans."

Frontierland Trading Post
22 | 22 | 22 | M

This "often overlooked" Old West–style storefront in Frontierland wins points as "one of the Magic Kingdom's best trading-pin sources"; though it's "pint-sized", surveyors say it's "rarely crowded" and carries a wide selection of the collectibles.

LIBERTY SQUARE

Heritage House
▽ 25 | 24 | 24 | M

Loyalists laud this "patriotic store" next door to Liberty Square's Hall of Presidents that proudly carries star-spangled souvenirs – from flags and campaign buttons to Statue of Liberty miniatures – as well as reproductions of "great Americana", such as the Declaration of Independence and historic stamps.

Yankee Trader, The
22 | 22 | 22 | M

"Sort of hidden" in Liberty Square along the way to Fantasyland, this "quaint, quiet little shop" puts a Colonial American spin on Disney-themed seasonal merchandise, collectible pins, scrapbooking supplies and a "nice selection of kitchen items."

Ye Olde Christmas Shoppe
24 | 25 | 22 | M

"Feel holly and jolly any time of year" enthuse elves who "forget all about the hot, humid weather" outside when they step into this "winter wonderland", a "quaint" "Victorian"-themed shop in Magic Kingdom's Liberty Square; though "small", it stocks a "beautiful display of ornaments" and other holiday supplies at prices that "aren't too bad", and the "accommodating" staff is "big on heart."

MAIN STREET, U.S.A.

Chapeau, The
22 | 21 | 23 | M

To top your noggin with a "classic souvenir" or simply to "prevent sunburn on that bald spot", head to this "tiny" Main Street, U.S.A. hatter for "the best selection" of "good old-fashioned" Mickey ears, embroidered "immediately" with your name; non-Mouseketeers can choose from "100 or so" other headgear styles, such as visors, baseball caps and straw hats – consequently "lines can be long."

QUALITY | DISPLAY | SERVICE | COST

Disney Clothiers
23 | 23 | 22 | E

Set on Main Street, U.S.A, this expansive outfitter has you covered with "the finest merchandise for your Mouseketeers" ("all the Disney-character T-shirts in one place") plus "more upscale" apparel for adults; since this busy part of the Magic Kingdom can get "crazy", practiced pros suggest shopping here when everyone else is busy watching "parades and shows."

☒ Emporium
24 | 23 | 21 | M

"You can't visit the Magic Kingdom and not go" to this "super-busy" Mickey "megastore" comprising "several smaller shops" that offer "anything and everything Disney"; surveyors laud the "vast assortment" of "souven-ears" at a "range of prices", but warn that the "crush of shoppers" at day's end makes help "hard to find" (tip: "it's a ghost town during the parade").

Engine Co. 71 Firehouse Gift Shop
22 | 22 | 23 | M

This "little" shop in Main Street, U.S.A.'s faux firehouse pays tribute to "all-American heroes" of the hook-and-ladder variety; among the gear are Mickey figurines, clothing and "cute" *101 Dalmatians* items, but perhaps most popular is the display of badges from engine companies around the nation – which sparks some folks' desire for "more fire-fighter-related merchandise" and "fewer pet products."

Main Street Athletic Club
23 | 22 | 21 | M

Join Mickey's team in this "adorably themed" Main Street logo mart selling "great men's clothes", team apparel and "cute activewear" emblazoned with Disney characters playing golf, tennis, basketball or other sports; wannabes can have their photos taken in front of an athletic backdrop and pretend they've been drafted by their favorite club.

Main Street Cinema
20 | 19 | 19 | M

Designed to resemble an old movie palace, this "small" Main Streeter reels in shoppers seeking videos, toys and pins; it also offers "make-your-own music CDs" and online Virtual Magic Kingdom game play (plus info on VMK-related park quests), but some find the "limited" merchandise mix "odd" and "wish they were still showing the old shorts here."

Main Street Confectionery
24 | 24 | 22 | M

Sugar addicts are drawn to Main Street, U.S.A.'s "bright, cheery", "nostalgic" sweetery for "Disney-inspired confections" ("Mickey-shaped Rice Krispie treats") as well as candy classics ("fantastic" peanut brittle, "awesome caramel apples", "fudge to die for"), many prepared in the shop's glass-walled kitchen; given that "the smells alone are divine", it's no surprise you can expect "long lines, especially when the park is closing."

Market House
23 | 23 | 21 | E

The appeal is clear at this "wonderful" Main Street, U.S.A. longtimer (formerly called Crystal Arts) where the glassy-eyed can watch artisans create vitreous valuables "with skill and artistry" and buy custom-etched mugs and keepsakes; given all the "breakable" displays of "expensive" crystal goods, some are "afraid to breathe" and suggest it's "not a good spot for kids" – or klutzes.

	QUALITY	DISPLAY	SERVICE	COST

Town Square Exposition Hall
| 22 | 20 | 22 | M |

A large selection of camera supplies, plus collectible pins and lanyards, can be found in the stalls of this expansive Main Street, U.S.A. hall next to Tony's Restaurant; in the back, there's a "cute" photo op area with "all kinds of classic Disney movie scenes", character cutouts, interactive kiosks and live characters, plus "a little movie theater playing golden oldies."

⚄ Uptown Jewelers
| 24 | 23 | 23 | E |

Aficionados praise the "wonderful collectibles" (e.g. personalized one-of-a-kind watches, silver and gold charms, china figurines and "a great selection of pins") and the customer service at this "busy" Main Streeter; some say that many keepsakes are "surprisingly not that expensive", making it "easy" to "add some WDW to your home."

MICKEY'S TOONTOWN FAIR

County Bounty
| ▽ 24 | 24 | 23 | M |

True to its name, this "terrific" store in Toontown's carnival-style Judge's Tent offers "everything – and I mean everything" – from candy to clothing to "trinkets for younger children"; it's also the place where small fry line up for personal encounters with their favorite characters: princesses, villains or pals of Mickey, played by "cast members who are superb with kids."

Mickey's Toontown Fair Souvenirs
| 24 | 24 | 23 | M |

"Geared to kids" (with displays at "just the right height"), this "huge" county fair in the Magic Kingdom is a "Disneyrific" bonanza, stuffed full of toys, pins, souvenirs, movies, candy and, "of course, the famous personalized Mickey ears"; unsurprisingly, it can be "chaotic" as youngsters grab "all the items they love" and parents try to "put things back without causing a scene."

TOMORROWLAND

Merchant of Venus
| 20 | 19 | 21 | M |

Enthusiastic Earthlings rocket over to this "unique" Tomorrowland shop for Lilo and Stitch trinkets, Buzz Lightyear gear and other "out-of-this-world" sci-fi toys, games and collectible pins; still, not-quite-stellar scores suggest that some feel it's become "just another store."

Mickey's Star Traders
| 22 | 21 | 20 | M |

Tomorrowland Transit Authority's trains "cruise right over" this miniemporium, where "great space-themed souvenirs" (e.g. "freeze-dried" "space food") and "lots of Lilo & Stitch stuff" stand out amid a galaxy of clothing, headgear, toys and other Mouse memorabilia; its futuristic cityscape murals include camouflaged silhouettes of Mickey himself.

EPCOT

FUTURE WORLD

⚄ Art of Disney, The
| 26 | 25 | 23 | VE |

"Perfect for collectors", these Marketplace and Epcot dealers offer "museum-quality" Disney artwork – "rare" and "beautiful cels, photo prints, original sculpture", "high-end" paintings and more – that are "worth every penny" "if your bank account can handle it"; folks "without bottomless wallets" like to just "drool over" the "pure eye candy", noting "knowledgeable" staffers "welcome questions even if it's clear you won't be buying"; N.B. the "almost hidden" Future World branch is "often overlooked."

Camera Center
21 | 19 | 20 | E

For "essential" supplies or solutions to "regular- and video-camera problems", shutterbugs swarm to this "busy" Future World shop, also a "convenient" stop for viewing Disney PhotoPass shots or snaps by the park's pro photogs; employees readily "help in a pinch", so to wallet-watchers who warn you'll "pay through the nose (or should I say ears)" revelers retort "time is money too."

Gateway Gifts
22 | 20 | 22 | M

This oft-"overlooked" nook in the walkway beneath Spaceship Earth has the right stuff for "panic shopping before you leave Epcot"; its galaxy of "last-minute gifts" encompasses "hard-to-find Spaceship Earth items", Epcot apparel, character memorabilia and disposable cameras.

ImageWorks
22 | 20 | 21 | M

The image of Figment, a purple dragon, adorns many "fun and clever" gift items in this petite Imagination! Pavilion place, and your likeness can too; the photo studio proffers "nifty" shots of visitors superimposed against Disney backdrops, "laser pictures etched in crystal" and "cool 3D pictures worth checking out even if you don't know the people" depicted.

Inside Track
20 | 20 | 21 | M

"Car enthusiasts" are revved up about this shop at the exit to Future World's Test Track, where "nifty and unique" "auto-related items" run the gamut from "child-friendly souvenirs" (e.g. $5 photo licenses, antenna toppers) to more "expensive" GM logo gear; the factory-style setting is full of "cute" displays too.

Mission: SPACE Cargo Bay
19 | 19 | 20 | M

"When you have to have astronaut ice cream", take one small step from the Mission: SPACE attraction to this module proffering a galaxy of "neat" NASA-related toys, IMAX DVDs and other "educational Disney paraphernalia"; "friendly" service has some parents over the moon, even as longtimers lament "the merchandise's originality has gotten lost in space."

◪ Mouse Gear
24 | 24 | 22 | M

From character "postcards to clothing to fine watches and home goods", "you name it, they've got it" at this "vast", "comprehensive" faux factory in Future World; a "roomy", "well-organized" setup that makes it "easy to find whatever you want", plus cast members who "always" seem to be "in a good mood" – even if there are "too few" of them – have partisans proclaiming that it "rivals the World of Disney" as their "all-time favorite theme-park shop."

Pin Central
24 | 22 | 22 | M

Collectors who are "hooked on pin trading" "could spend the mortgage" on the "vast selection" of "hard-to-find" pins at this "convenient" shop near the entrance to Epcot; "at least one" of the "friendly" cast members on duty is "an experienced pin trader" who can help you with "all the ins and outs", but even novices can tell "when they're selling a limited edition pin – there's a line around the cash register."

Sea Base Alpha Gift Shop
| 20 | 18 | 21 | M |

It's not too hard finding Nemo – in the form of "cute" character toys, clothing and other "kiddie" faves – within this "small" inlet at the Seas With Nemo & Friends pavilion; fans of the film are hooked, but saltier sorts sigh the marine merchandise "lacks originality" and "variety" while the "afterthought" "hallway" setting "needs easier access."

WORLD SHOWCASE

Artesanias Mexicanas
| 20 | 23 | 20 | M |

Browse "authentic" merchandise like pottery, candles and glassware while you bask in the "lively market atmosphere" at this "huge indoor bazaar" in the Mexico Pavilion of Epcot's World Showcase; resembling a "pueblo town square", it may be "slightly kitschy" ("love the giant sombreros") but amigos assert it's "worth a walk-through", even if critics carp "don't expect south-of-the-border prices."

Club COOL
| 19 | 19 | 18 | I |

"How often do you get to use 'free' and 'Disney' in the same sentence?" posit parched park-goers who stop by this World Showcase spot to try gratis "Coke samples from around the globe"; experiencing "new tastes" is "fun" ("the watermelon is delicious"), and you can buy make-your-own character cups too, though a few chillier critics wish it sold a "greater variety" of colas and contend that it lacks the "cool factor."

Crown and Crest, The
| 23 | 23 | 22 | E |

Anglophiles adore this "bit of Olde England" ensconced in the "quaint" U.K. Pavilion where suits of armor, shields and swords share space with themed chess sets, pub coasters and (natch) a "huge selection" of tea; ok, it's "pricey", but many items are otherwise "unavailable Stateside"; P.S. "genealogy buffs" can "find your family's tartan or crest" here and have it "beautifully framed."

Das Kaufhaus
| 22 | 22 | 20 | E |

In a replica of Freiburg's historic Kaufhaus market plaza, this Germany pavilion shop specializes in eggs, including giant ostrich eggs, painted by an artist who is on hand most days; other highlights are German-made clocks and "beautiful, authentic beer steins and glassware."

Delizie Italiane
| 23 | 21 | 22 | E |

Partisans who prefer this Italy Pavilion courtyard chocolateria say "the Swiss have nothing on these guys" when it comes to bene bonbons; candy cravers "can't stop looking" because they "always find new things to want", enabled by "informative" personnel.

Der TeddyBar
| 24 | 24 | 21 | E |

"Wunderbear" declare devotees of the Germany Pavilion's "truly lovely" old-world toy trove overflowing with "darling", "authentic" Deutschland playthings ("gorgeous" Steiff teddies, "special" custom-made dolls) and entertaining mechanical displays; the goods are "expensive" ("$53 for a small stuffed giraffe!") but those willing to splurge reason "your child will have these keepsakes forever."

Die Weihnachts Ecke   24 | 24 | 20 | E

Surveyors say "if you're looking for a Christmas pickle" or other "authentic" Deutschland treats ("amazing glass ornaments, cool nutcrackers", cookies, candy), polka on over to this elegant Yuletide shop in the Germany Pavilion; Euro-minded folks swear "it's just like shopping in Germany" – but maybe "more expensive."

Fjording, The   24 | 22 | 21 | E

If not exactly af-fjordable, the "high-quality" imports at this gabled Scandinavian store in the Norway Pavilion are certainly "authentic" and "beautiful", ranging from holiday ornaments to Helly Hansen skiing and sailing garb that's hard to find "in the States"; shoppers who don't "catch a sale" console themselves by "putting on a Viking helmet" at a nearby photo-op spot "and having their picture taken with a 10-ft. troll."

Glas Und Porzellan   25 | 23 | 21 | E

"Great for any collector", this Germany Pavilion shop with a giant Hummel figurine in the window sells – surprise – porcelain keepsakes, including signature Disney characters; the pretty showroom holds WDW's "best selection" of the statuettes, but since they come at a price, it's perhaps "not the best" spot "for little ones or the clumsy"; N.B. an artist sometimes paints items on the premises.

Il Bel Cristallo   ▽ 22 | 21 | 19 | E

You'll "leave smelling like a Milan runway" fawn fashionistas who favor this elegant Italy Pavilion boutique that's set in a reproduction of the Venetian Doge's Palace; besides fragrances, the "quality merchandise at quality prices" runs to imported handbags, glassware and porcelain – "if you love Italian leather and couture, you will love it here."

La Bottega Italiana   23 | 23 | 21 | E

La bella vita can be found in this upscale tile-roofed shop at the entrance to Epcot's Italy Pavilion in the form of Murano glassware, chocolates, Venetian masks, a "great selection of perfumes and makeup" and fine wine; just don't bring the little ones, as the store is "almost impossible to navigate with a stroller."

Les Vins de France   23 | 22 | 21 | E

Sample vintages as you scope out the "Gallic-style wining and dining accessories" and *parlez* with "super-friendly" staffers in this corner of the France Pavilion; though perhaps best "for the non-connoisseur", the "decent selection of *vins*" includes "a few interesting bottles", but some oenophiles "choke on the prices"; N.B. there's a nominal fee for tastings.

Mitsukoshi Department Store   23 | 24 | 22 | M

"Prepare to swoon" as you "wander around" this "little piece of real Japan", an "entertaining" World Showcase satellite of the famed Tokyo department store; respondents rhapsodize about "high-quality" merchandise ("unusual" Hello Kitty items, "sake serve ware", "gorgeous kimonos", "amazing" animated clocks, Mikimoto pearls), and report that staffers, who will "write your name in Japanese for free, on anything", "couldn't be more lovely."

	QUALITY	DISPLAY	SERVICE	COST

Souvenirs de France
19 | 19 | 16 | M

After viewing the film in the France Pavilion, Francophiles are funneled into this nondescript store selling "typical souvenirs you'd find" in Paris, from Eiffel Tower miniatures, tote bags and postcards, to French-music CDs; while perhaps it lacks that je ne sais quoi, "the name says it all."

Tea Caddy, The
25 | 24 | 23 | M

"This is my cup of tea" spout sippers who've leafed through the "large selection" of bags and infusions at this "quaint", "veddy, veddy English" World Showcase "treasure" that seemingly offers "every kind of tea under the sun", including some "Twinings not available in stores"; you can also find china pots and cups, biscuits and special imports, all of which makes Anglophiles feel they've "jumped the pond."

Toy Soldier, The
23 | 23 | 22 | M

A habitat of Winnie the Pooh and friends ("check for character meet and greets"), this "unique store" in the U.K. Pavilion doubles as a "Gepetto's playland" of "adorable", "not-run-of-the-mill" wooden toys; "kids will love" it, but you might not if you're "price-sensitive."

Yong Feng Shangdian
▽ 20 | 20 | 21 | M

Just about "anything made in China", from lavish silk rugs and mahogany furniture to "beautiful jade figures" to "inexpensive souvenirs" like chopsticks and bowls, can be found at this Street of Good Fortune emporium that's among the biggest stores in the World Showcase; you can browse for quite "a while" here and odds are you'll turn up "something for everyone."

DISNEY'S HOLLYWOOD STUDIOS

ANIMATION COURTYARD

ⓩ Animation Gallery
25 | 24 | 22 | E

"One-of-a-kind" cels, lithographs, "high-end" figurines and other "Disneyana" "geared toward the collector" predominate at this "museumlike" Animation Courtyard shop, but "inexpensive posters" found here also "look great framed" and will "fit anyone's budget"; "friendly", "attentive" cast members provide "excellent" service to boot; N.B. given all the tempting "breakables", careful customers may want to "hold children's hands."

ⓩ Disney Studio Store
22 | 22 | 21 | M

While this open-air Animation Courtyard shop is "Disney to the core" ("my favorite place to buy Mickey ears"), it also "feels like an expensive boutique", selling clothes "you could wear to work on a casual day" plus scads of film-related souvenirs; a few folks plead for "more Disney Studio logo stuff."

In Character
22 | 22 | 22 | M

"Exceptionally kid-friendly" thanks to its "patient" cast members, this open-air spot in Animation Courtyard lets you "dress up your little princess" as her fave fairy-tale heroine in costumes that fans find "high on quality"; weary wanderers report the location is also "handy" for "killing time while you wait" to get into the nearby Little Mermaid theater.

ECHO LAKE

Indiana Jones Adventure Outpost
| 19 | 21 | 19 | M |

"A must" for "any little boy who idolizes Indiana Jones" and wants a "dead-on" Indy-style fedora of his own, this snug stand at the eponymous attraction carries a "wide range" of the hero's souvenirs – but the high "kitsch" quotient means it's "not exactly the place to dig for treasures"; P.S. some say the fake well is the "real draw."

Sorcerer Hat Shop
| 22 | 21 | 21 | M |

"So many pins, so little time" sigh enthusiasts of this "busy" Hollywood Studios spot "underneath" Sorcerer Mickey's "giant blue hat" that conjures up a "diverse supply" of those special trinkets that "you just have to find"; it's "pretty self-service", but it's "worth the stop" for collectors who can "usually find the ones that they want."

Tatooine Traders
| 21 | 22 | 19 | M |

"*Star Wars* freaks" unleash "their inner nerds" in this emporium of Empire toys, T-shirts, replicas and cels; "serious fans can drop thousands" on "difficult-to-find" collectibles, while kids "spend their allowance" on trinkets or buy photos of themselves in iconic SW scenes; the dark side: Star Tours passengers exit the ride here, generating "awful crowds" that sometimes "overwhelm" the staff.

HOLLYWOOD BOULEVARD

Adrian and Edith's Head to Toe
| ▽ 22 | 23 | 22 | E |

You've joined a cast of thousands, so you may as well dress the part of a Disney tourist with a new outfit from this tiny Hollywood Boulevard clothier; "pick just the right hat", clotheshorses counsel, and you can have it personalized by a staff that is happy to "take time to help you."

Celebrity 5 & 10
| 23 | 23 | 23 | M |

Get your mouse ears personalized at this old-fashioned emporium on Hollywood Boulevard in Hollywood Studios; regulars regard it as a "perfect" stop for Disneyfied utensils, mugs, aprons and other housewares, though wallet-watchers underscore the obvious: "this isn't a true five-and-10 – unless they mean $5 and $10."

Darkroom, The
| 22 | 22 | 22 | E |

"Helpful" cast members focus on your concerns at this deco-design Hollywood Boulevard shop offering "everything you need" in camera equipment and supplies, plus photo finishing; satisfied shutterbugs say it gets "an A+ in my album", though some suggest "in these digital times, they should call it the Card Slot."

Keystone Clothiers
| 23 | 23 | 22 | E |

At this art deco-style Hollywood Boulevard boutique, "adults who don't want a T-shirt" can get decked out in "upscale" Disney duds (collared shirts, jackets, silk Mickey ties), including many "not found anywhere else"; yes, the stuff's "expensive", but clotheshorses contend "excellent quality" makes it "worth the high cost."

Mickey's of Hollywood
| 24 | 24 | 23 | M |

There's no racy lingerie at this spacious Hollywood Boulevard emporium next door to Keystone Clothiers – just lots of that "must-have mouse gear", including character plush toys, Hollywood Studios T-shirts, movie-themed socks, mugs, sunglasses and "anything a wannabe Mouseketeer would ever need"; the real turn-ons here are the "reasonable" prices.

MAIN ENTRANCE

Movieland Memorabilia
22 | 22 | 22 | E

Tinseltown fanatics find "so much to choose from" at this open-air kiosk by the Hollywood Studios entrance; the goods include "pricey" "one-of-a-kind offerings", "cool movie posters" and "signed, framed photos", plus basics like hats, pins, sunglasses and autograph books.

Sid Cahuenga's One of a Kind
22 | 21 | 19 | E

"You never know what you'll find" at this "Hollywood junk shop" housed in a bungalow at Hollywood Studios; Tinseltown devotees deem the store "an attraction in itself" thanks to its "authentic, memorable" merchandise (think autographed film stills, rare movie posters, "cool TV props", costumes), however, longtimers lament it's "lost its quirky appeal over the years", now selling "run-of-the-mill" "celebrity garbage."

PIXAR PLACE

AFI Studio Showcase
22 | 23 | 22 | M

"Movie buffs" coming off the backlot tram tour can scope out this scene featuring "unique" memorabilia from classic films (*The Wizard of Oz, Gone with the Wind*) and TV shows (*I Love Lucy*) plus mementos from some current releases; even those not in the mood to spend say "cool costume exhibits" near the entrance "make this a great walk-through."

STREETS OF AMERICA

It's a Wonderful Shop
23 | 24 | 22 | M

"Every time a bell rings, a Disney dollar gets its wings" at this Disney's Days of Christmas "clone" nestled near the Hollywood Studios New York backlot; service that garners solid scores combined with the shop's sleighful of "super-cute" ornaments, decorations and toys will "put you in the Yuletide spirit even when it's 90 degrees out."

Stage One Company Store
22 | 23 | 22 | M

Even Kermit and Miss Piggy might agree that "for everything Muppet" – from toys to apparel – this Hollywood Studios backlot kiosk "is the place"; *Sesame Street*-savvy shoppers also appreciate the "cute puns and visual jokes in the decor", which nicely "carry over the theme" from the nearby Muppets attraction.

Writer's Stop, The
22 | 23 | 21 | M

It's "more a coffee shop than a bookstore" or stationer, but either way this "cute" Streets of America nook is a welcome stopover "off the beaten track"; bibliophiles feel "free to browse" the books and magazines, then – having "maneuvered through" "unmanageable" queues – "grab a chair" in a "heavenly little corner" and "recoup" over hot chocolate and pastries.

	QUALITY	DISPLAY	SERVICE	COST

Youse Guys Moychindice
22 | 23 | 23 | M

A "straightforward" array of "the usual" Hollywood Studios "goodies" populates this Brooklyn-accented outdoor "corner shop" in Streets of America, but the name "gets your attention" and even wise guys like the "funny presentation" and "appealing" cast members who "ham it up."

SUNSET BOULEVARD

Once Upon A Time
- | - | - | M

Curios including puffy, white-glove oven mitts and a vast selection of Mickey-themed home accessories – from martini shakers and measuring spoons to drawer pulls and drain stoppers – make this marquis-fronted faux theater on Sunset Boulevard a mouse-lover's mecca; the rotunda-shaped foyer holds a huge collection of WDW mugs, as well as an artist who custom-sketches characters while you wait.

Sunset Club Couture
∇ 25 | 25 | 24 | M

This replica of LA's art deco Carthay Circle Theatre on Sunset Boulevard (near the Beauty and the Beast stage) abounds in "jewelry you won't see outside the parks" and "hard-to-find" WDW watches; what's more, cast members "go above and beyond" to please.

☒ Sweet Spells
26 | 26 | 24 | M

At this art deco–style confectioner at the corner of Hollywood Studios' Sunset and Hollywood boulevards "a sweet spell falls over" snackers, cast by "marvelous candy apples", "oatmeal-raisin cookies to die for" and other handmade delights; since it's "hard to pass by" without buying "something delicious", "the lines can get long – but it's worth the wait."

Tower Hotel Gifts
22 | 23 | 21 | M

"Prove you survived the ride" with "offbeat" mementos from The Twilight Zone Tower of Terror shop; its "awesome Hollywood Tower Hotel theming" encompasses "scary gifts" ("everything from robes to service bells" and "T-shirts with great one-liners"), "outstanding atmosphere" and cast members who will "play with you."

Villains in Vogue
23 | 24 | 23 | M

"Admit it, you love Disney villains" like Cruella De Vil and *Sleeping Beauty*'s Maleficent, and at this Sunset Boulevard lair devoted to the classic antagonists, "your evil side" can delight in deliciously demonic costumes and souvenirs (including books that "tell the villain's side of the story"); employees are "always at hand" to help, but with so many "witches and beasts" to "adore", there's "just not enough room."

DISNEY'S ANIMAL KINGDOM

AFRICA

Mombasa Marketplace/Ziwani Traders
22 | 24 | 22 | M

The "native musical instruments", African woodcarvings, hand-painted boxes and many other "beautiful", "affordable" and "exotic" souvenirs "reflect the true nature of Animal Kingdom" agree aficionados who consider these conjoined markets a "must-stop"; also appreciated are "well-done" theme decor and "super-friendly" staffers who "go out of their way to assist"; N.B. pins traded here.

QUALITY DISPLAY SERVICE COST

ASIA

Serka Zong Bazaar
▽ 22 | 22 | 22 | M

After conquering Expedition Everest, remember your peak experience at this souvenir shop in the elaborately designed mythical village of Anadapur; the "massive amount" of "great merchandise" includes "Asian-themed gifts" and the extensive Yeti line of "plush" white abominable snowman hats, backpacks and slippers.

DINOLAND U.S.A.

Chester and Hester's Dinosaur Treasures
20 | 22 | 20 | M

DinoLand's "wacky" "Disney-style" take on a "tacky roadside" shop features an "eclectic" array of souvenirs, trinkets and dinosaur playthings; you might have to "muscle your way past the kids" to take your "stroll down toy-memory lane", and though some snobs snub it as too "corny", kitsch-cravers contend "it's not supposed to be classy" – it's just plain "silly fun."

Dino Institute Shop, The
20 | 20 | 20 | M

Satisfying the "gimmes" induced by a visit to Dinosaur!, this "small" shop at the ride's exit in DinoLand U.S.A. pleases pint-sized paleontologists as well as grown-ups who still have some "childish dino love left in them"; it teems with plushies, shirts, hats and some "unique items", but exasperated excavators grumble "don't expect any assistance while digging."

DISCOVERY ISLAND

Caricature Connection
23 | 22 | 22 | M

"Kids really enjoy having their caricatures drawn" at these half-dozen kiosks around the World, where sketchers who "like what they do" "make it fun for you" too; the resulting cartoon is "not that expensive for Disney" – and a "solid value" since you get a "one-of-a-kind memory to bring home"; tip: watch several artists at work, then "choose one with the style you want."

Disney Outfitters
23 | 24 | 23 | M

Expeditions to this shop near the Tree of Life in "the wilds of Lake Buena Vista" can snare you "cool clothing" along with nature-themed gifts, jewelry and even African art; guided by "helpful Disney folk" you can bag some "decent values" among the "fine selection" ("no bargains or clearance merchandise" report scouts).

⊠ Island Mercantile
24 | 24 | 23 | M

"Let the safari begin" at this gigantic retailer on Discovery Island that many say is "the best, most varied souvenir shop in Animal Kingdom"; you can find anything from stickers to watches plus "a good selection of Disney pins", and cast members "enjoy keeping everyone happy" in this "well-laid-out" space that "never seems overly crowded."

MAIN ENTRANCE

Garden Gate Gifts
▽ 23 | 21 | 21 | M

At the entrance to Disney's Animal Kingdom, this walk-up window stocks "essentials you might have forgotten to pack", such as film and cameras, plus "last-minute souvenirs"; also available are stroller and wheelchair rentals and package pickup.

Outpost Shop, The
23 | **22** | **21** | **M**

An "easy place to stop for gifts after a full morning" in Disney's Animal Kingdom, this outpost just outside the turnstiles tames "last-chance shoppers" with a "large selection" of safari mouse ears, apparel and souvenirs; better still, it's usually "not mobbed" like many of the stores "inside the park."

THE OASIS

Rainforest Cafe Shop
20 | **23** | **18** | **M**

"Even if you're not dining" at the eponymous eateries in Animal Kingdom and Downtown Disney, fans say it's "worth a visit" to these "dark and mysterious" gift shops teeming with animal toys and "environmentally sensitive" souvenirs; "check out the glow-in-the-dark room" too, but note that some dissenters feel soaked by a shop that they claim exists solely "to keep you occupied" while waiting for a table.

At the Resorts

MAGIC KINGDOM AREA

BouTiki
25 | **25** | **23** | **E**

Disney's Polynesian Resort | 1600 Seven Seas Dr.

This "classy-tropical" boutique at the rear of the Polynesian Resort's lobby boasts "terrific tiki theming": colorful carved-wood totems display higher-end island-style clothing ("like Tommy Bahama"), bamboo-and palm-motif accessories and "kitschy" Disney logo wares; though the goods can be "expensive", the decor "makes for great photo ops" at no charge.

Caricature Connection
23 | **22** | **22** | **M**

Disney's Contemporary Resort | 4600 N. World Dr.
Disney's Polynesian Resort | 1600 Seven Seas Dr.
Disney's Wilderness Lodge | 901 Timberline Dr.
See review on page 109.

M. Mouse Mercantile
▽ **24** | **24** | **24** | **M**

Disney's Grand Floridian Resort & Spa | 4401 Floridian Way

The monorail stops right outside the door to this posh, airy second-floor store at Disney's "lovely" Grand Floridian Resort & Spa; its high-end gifts, princess costumes, bath goods and kitchenware appeal to chic souvenir shoppers, some of whom liken it to a "mini-Mouse Gear."

Settlement Trading Post
▽ **23** | **24** | **23** | **M**

Disney's Fort Wilderness Resort & Campground | 4510 N. Ft. Wilderness Trail

A straight-shooting staff "goes out of its way to be helpful" at Fort Wilderness Resort & Campground's rustic general store, a convenient "place to pick up some vittles before taking a bike ride" or to lasso some decent groceries "for cooking at your cabin"; WDW souvenirs and rental movies are also available.

	QUALITY	DISPLAY	SERVICE	COST

Wilderness Lodge Mercantile

24 | 24 | 24 | M

Disney's Wilderness Lodge | 901 Timberline Dr.

An expedition to this big store off the Wilderness Lodge lobby "feels like shopping at Yellowstone" enthuse bargain-hunters who rank it among "the best resort gift shops"; the "always friendly" staff helps you bag "unique offerings not found elsewhere", including Lodge-themed clothing, toys and souvenirs "without Disney-character overkill", but note that "you pay for the convenience" of the in-hotel location.

☑ Wyland Galleries

25 | 25 | 23 | VE

Disney's Polynesian Resort | 1600 Seven Seas Dr.

"Inspiring", "beautifully displayed" dolphin and whale paintings, gi-clée reproductions and sculptures by "famous underwater artist" Wyland (and a dozen or so other artists) are "a feast for the eyes" in these "high-end" galleries, one on the BoardWalk, the other off the lobby of the Polynesian Resort; the staff is "courteous and knowledge-able", but be aware that you'll "need serious money" if you're doing more than just looking.

EPCOT AREA

Beach Club Marketplace

22 | 21 | 21 | M

Disney's Beach Club | 1800 Epcot Resort Blvd.

"Conveniently located on the first floor" of the Beach Club resort, this "relaxed" general store sells a "moderate selection of souvenirs" and hotel logo items plus food packaged "for easy in-room prep"; among the most popular "necessities": refillable "self-service mugs" and "primo gelato."

BoardWalk Character Carnival

23 | 22 | 23 | M

Disney's BoardWalk | 2101 N. Epcot Resort Blvd.

"Every outfit you'd ever want to see" emblazoned with "Mickey, Donald, Minnie or Goofy" (from "kids' clothing to adults' golf" duds) can be had at this BoardWalk shop that strikes boosters as a "carnival of fun"; yet a small faction of bored walkers yawns over "standard" inventory that can be found elsewhere in WDW.

Calypso Trading Post & Straw Market

21 | 21 | 21 | M

Disney's Caribbean Beach Resort | 900 Cayman Way

Offering "cheap beach items and trinkets" (including mail-able coco-nuts), bathing suits and sundries, this spacious shopping area near the food court at Disney's Caribbean Beach Resort strikes some parents as a "good place to set your kids loose with a few dollars"; re-creating the pastel buildings and latticed balconies of a tropical village, its "fun setup" adds to the resort's "island atmosphere."

ESPN Club Store – ESPN The Yard

21 | 20 | 19 | E

Disney's BoardWalk | 2101 N. Epcot Resort Blvd.

"Drop off the guys" at this BoardWalk "sports fans' mecca" that's perfect for groupies looking to "watch a game" while stocking up on "authentic" team gear plus items bearing the eponymous cable network's logo; but still, a few opponents throw a penalty flag at "over-hyped", "overpriced" goods.

Fittings & Fairings Clothes and Notions ▽ 23 | 23 | 21 | E

Disney's Yacht Club Resort | 1700 Epcot Resort Blvd.

Navigators report that this nautically natured shop berthed near the main lobby of the Yacht Club Resort is "the only place to find Yacht Club–branded merchandise", and it also has adult "essentials" such as pint rations of liquor – so comparatively high tariffs don't really take atoll.

Screen Door General Store 23 | 23 | 23 | M

Disney's BoardWalk | 2101 N. Epcot Resort Blvd.

This "handy little store" that "fits well into the mood" of the BoardWalk Resort area carries a "good if limited selection" of "dollhouse-size gro-ceries" and other "home-away-from-home essentials", including ca-sual logo wear that's "more mature and upscale in design" than the norm; "friendly" service is a plus, but some note "you pay a premium for the convenience" of shopping here.

Thimbles & Threads 23 | 22 | 22 | M

Disney's BoardWalk | 2101 N. Epcot Resort Blvd.

With its colorful awning and "nice layout", this BoardWalk clothier beckons bystanders in for "upscale" men's and women's apparel – in-cluding a "decent selection" of Disney Vacation Club merchandise – along with character togs and plush toys for kids; "friendly" cast members call repeat customers "by name" too, so despite wares some term "typical", it sews up most shoppers' affections.

☑ Wyland Galleries 25 | 25 | 23 | VE

Disney's BoardWalk | 2101 N. Epcot Resort Blvd.
See review on page 111.

DISNEY'S ANIMAL KINGDOM AREA

Caricature Connection 23 | 22 | 22 | M

Disney's Animal Kingdom Lodge | 2901 Osceola Pkwy.
See review on page 109.

Everything Pop Shopping & Dining 22 | 22 | 21 | M

Disney's Pop Century Resort | 1050 Century Dr.

Set between the lobby and the food court of Disney's Pop Century Resort, this hopping shop stocks "a little of everything" including pop-culture relics harking back to fads from the '50s to the '90s, Disney-themed souvenirs and sundries; surveyors seeking "last-minute gifts" cop to popping in here.

Maestro Mickey's Merchandise 22 | 21 | 21 | M

Disney's All-Star Music Resort | 1801 W. Buena Vista Dr.

Whether you "forgot it at home" or neglected "to get it in the parks", "they probably have it" at this souvenirs-and-sundries shop next to Intermission Food Court in the lobby of the All-Star Music Resort; you'll find "good variety", consumers contend, but "not at Wal-Mart prices."

Panchito's Gifts & Sundries - | - | - | M

Disney's Coronado Springs Resort | 1000 W. Buena Vista Dr.

Scaled to serve the nearly 2,000 rooms of Disney's Coronado Springs Resort, this large, brightly lit souvenirs and essentials market draws shoppers past the burbling lobby fountain to peruse its offerings: silver jewelry and other Mexican items, logo apparel and watches, games and plush animals, knickknacks, scrapbooking supplies, snacks and sundries.

Zawadi Marketplace

| 25 | 25 | 24 | M |

Disney's Animal Kingdom Lodge | 2901 Osceola Pkwy.

"You feel like you're shopping in Africa, without the inoculations" at this "very thematic" 5,000-sq.-ft. venue at Disney's Animal Kingdom Lodge; its "beautiful" wares include "unique sculptures", instruments, baskets, jewelry and "hand-painted Penzo pottery with Mickeys hidden in the traditional patterns", and prices are "excellent, considering the quality"; add in a "variety" of AK merchandise, a handy mini-mart, pints of popular spirits and "wonderful" staffers, and you get "one of WDW's best hotel stores."

DOWNTOWN DISNEY AREA

Artists Palette, The

| 22 | 21 | 22 | M |

Disney's Saratoga Springs Resort & Spa | 1960 Broadway

"Food and souvenirs in one stop" are a "nice convenience" for Disney Vacation Clubbers and others who appreciate this "small", "friendly" Saratoga Springs Resort shop stocking sundries, groceries and logo merchandise; it's "usually quiet" but during busy times beware "bottlenecks" at the cash register.

Caricature Connection

| 23 | 22 | 22 | M |

Disney's Pop Century Resort | 1050 Century Dr.
See review on page 109.

Conch Flats General Store

| 21 | 19 | 22 | M |

Disney's Old Key West Resort | 1510 N. Cove Rd.

This "one-stop shop" at the Old Key West Resort stocks "typical" souvenirs, Disney Vacation Club merchandise, sundries and groceries; proponents praise "convenience", especially for "last-minute items", but critics complain prices are "no bargain" and carp "good luck getting through the cluttered aisles with your scooter" or stroller – fortunately, "in-park delivery service is excellent."

Fulton's General Store

| 22 | 23 | 23 | M |

Disney's Port Orleans Resort - Riverside | 1252 Riverside Dr.

Surveyors generally appreciate this "large" variety store at the Cajun-inflected, "family-oriented" Port Orleans Riverside Resort because of its "something-for-everyone" inventory: "lots of housewares", clothes, knickknacks, snacks, Mardi Gras items and, of course, "your usual Disney merchandise"; "extremely friendly" employees are a plus.

Jackson Square Gifts and Desires

| 24 | 24 | 22 | M |

Disney's Port Orleans Resort - French Quarter | 2201 Orleans Dr.

This big, easy-to-browse shop off the lobby of Port Orleans French Quarter serves up souvenirs with a "New Orleans flavor" (think Mardi Gras masks and beads), plus a "cross-section of Disney items" as well as a selection of sundries; factor in "friendly" employees, and it's no wonder the good times roll.

QUALITY DISPLAY SERVICE COST

Downtown Disney

MARKETPLACE

Arribas Brothers
`25` `24` `22` `E`

1780 E. Buena Vista Dr.

Clearly "full of treasures and wonders", this "elegant" Marketplace shop "sparkles everywhere" thanks to "highest-quality" lead-crystal showpieces, jewelry at a "range of prices" (including an "extensive" Swarovski selection) and glass keepsakes blown or engraved "before your eyes"; hey guys, it's a "great place to take the wife."

Z Art of Disney, The
`26` `25` `23` `VE`

1780 E. Buena Vista Dr.

See review on page 101.

Basin
`23` `23` `21` `M`

1780 E. Buena Vista Dr.

"Good, clean fun" is in store at this "beautiful" Marketplace venue overflowing with "olfactory delights"; its "delicious-smelling soaps and sea salts", "wonderful bath bombs" and "specialty shampoo bars" will "pamper" you, and may even "get your kid in the tub"; although the merchandise is "not really Disney", many maintain it's a "must-do"; P.S. a few allergy and asthma sufferers say the scents can be "overpowering."

Bibbidi Bobbidi Boutique
`24` `24` `24` `E`

1780 E. Buena Vista Dr.

"Up-and-coming princesses" (ages three and up) who "like to dress up" flock to this Marketplace makeover mecca; sure, the $35 to $175 "royal treatment" – complete with tiara, manicure, "fake hair and makeup" – could drain "a fairy godmother's expense account", but a child's "ear-to-ear grin" when she "realizes she's Cinderella" is "worth every penny"; still, some stern stepmothers scoff at the "assembly-line" aspect, insisting most girls "come out looking the same."

Z Disney's Days of Christmas
`25` `25` `22` `M`

1780 E. Buena Vista Dr.

"You'd need about 68 days of Christmas" to use all the "wonderful" Disney "treasures" – from mouse-ear ornaments to character-print gift wrap to personalized stockings – sold at the Marketplace's "cozy" Noel-themed nook; it "feels like Santa's workshop" year-round, though some carolers comment "Mickey needs more elves" during the holiday season's "hustle and bustle"; P.S. engraving "can take a few days" so "plan accordingly."

Z Disney's Pin Traders
`24` `23` `21` `M`

1780 E. Buena Vista Dr.

Sharp-eyed "fanatics" hooked on the "addictive craze of pin trading" converge on this octagonal, open-air Marketplace kiosk carrying every "character, scene and theme" pin "under the sun" plus a "ridiculous number of accessories"; Disney World's official pin-trading HQ may be a "collector's heaven" but there's "probably more swapping outside than inside", so "bring your game face and your guidebook" and expect to deal with "professionals."

	QUALITY	DISPLAY	SERVICE	COST

Disney's Wonderful World of Memories
23 | **22** | **21** | **M**

1780 E. Buena Vista Dr.

Satisfied scrapbookers salute this small stationer in Downtown Disney Marketplace as a "haven" proffering "special embellishments", albums, picture frames and craft supplies at "prices comparable to those" elsewhere (the "kits are a great deal"); it's also "not as busy as World of Disney", but a few sticklers have memories of a "less-than-stellar selection" ("just overpriced stickers").

Goofy's Candy Shop
23 | **24** | **22** | **M**

1780 E. Buena Vista Dr.

"Sugar shock" may well set in at this Marketplace "dentist's dream" where you can goof around among "tons of handmade goodies" and a "staggering selection" of bulk candy ("every color M&M under the sun") or "create your own concoctions" ("customized caramel apples", slushies in build-your-own Disney character cups); addicts "can't get out of here without spending a bushel", even if some of the stuff "can easily be bought at home."

☑ LEGO Imagination Center
24 | **25** | **20** | **M**

1780 E. Buena Vista Dr.

"Little builders" and other "inventive types" "won't want to leave" this LEGO lodge next door to World of Disney at Downtown Disney Marketplace, where they can "find just the piece or kit they're looking for", "make race cars and test them out" on ramps, or head for the bins on the back wall to "buy in bulk"; also "must-see" are the "amazing" life-size sculptures (the "LEGO T. rex rules!").

Mickey's Mart
22 | **19** | **20** | **M**

1780 E. Buena Vista Dr.

"Don't bother shopping anywhere else" advise budget-minded boosters of this modest Marketplace "hole-in-the-wall" where "everything costs $10 or less", including mystery grab bags; surveyors say some of the plush toys and "stocking-stuffer" mementos are bona fide "bargains", and if others are "not the best quality", hey, "the kids like it."

Mickey's Pantry
23 | **22** | **22** | **M**

1780 E. Buena Vista Dr.

"The best place to Mickey-ize your kitchen", this Downtown Disney destination serves up character-themed tableware and "cooking gadgets" (trivets, pizza cutters, waffle-makers, sink stoppers) that make "fun" "thank-you gifts for whoever's pet-sitting back home"; now that the Pantry has been "downsized", though, some snackers "miss the yummy food it once carried."

☑ Once Upon a Toy
24 | **25** | **23** | **M**

1780 E. Buena Vista Dr.

Adults "relive their childhood" and kids "go wild" in this "huge" Marketplace bazaar that's chock-full of plush animals, board games and other "classic toys with a Disney twist"; it's "kinda pricey", but you "won't find these unusual items anywhere else" and service is "excellent" – you can even "try before buying" in "hands-on play areas" (the popular make-your-own Mr. Potato Head station has an "unsurpassed selection").

	QUALITY	DISPLAY	SERVICE	COST

Pooh Corner
24 | 23 | 22 | M

1780 E. Buena Vista Dr.

Winnie the Pooh, Tigger and the rest of the gang rule at this "adorable" Marketplace shop, which "satisfies" most Milne mavens by supplying character mugs, kids' apparel, plush animals, kitchen items and other bear necessities; however, some grown-ups grouse "bring back the adult line of Pooh clothing and accessories" – "the Hundred-Acre Wood is not just for kids!"

Rainforest Cafe Shop
20 | 23 | 18 | M

1800 E. Buena Vista Dr.

See review on page 110.

Summer Sands
22 | 20 | 19 | E

1780 E. Buena Vista Dr.

"Forgot your board shorts? no problem" – this shore-thing Marketplace source has "top-quality" swimsuits and "trendy" teen fashions by the likes of Roxy and Tommy Bahama; otherwise, some respondents find this place "easy to skip" since there's "no Disney stuff", staffers could be "more helpful" and prices are "a little out of reach."

Team Mickey Athletic Club
23 | 23 | 20 | E

1780 E. Buena Vista Dr.

If dad's the kind of guy who "can never have too many Mickey Mouse hockey jerseys" or "Grumpy golf shirts", squire him over to this "tremendous" Marketplace "fave" that stocks "all the Disney athletic merchandise" for "every major sport" from NASCAR to tennis; finding "great deals" on the clearance rack is easy, but finding a clerk can be "difficult."

☑ World of Disney Store
25 | 24 | 21 | M

1780 E. Buena Vista Dr.

An "attraction in itself", this "mind-boggling" Marketplace behemoth – the Survey's Most Popular store – contains 12 movie-themed sections, all "crammed" with "every type of Disney merchandise you could imagine" "and lots you couldn't", including character memorabilia, clothing, plush toys, housewares and more; when it gets "chaotic" (especially "evenings and weekends"), it can be "hard to find" staffers and "easy to lose your bearings and your little ones", but even so advocates advise "do not leave WDW without stopping here" – just "arrive early" and "pace yourself."

PLEASURE ISLAND

NEW Curl by Sammy Duvall
- | - | - | M

1600 E. Buena Vista Dr.

The surf's always up on Pleasure Island at this cache of coastal cool next to 8 TRAX offering everything from sunglasses and footwear to beach fashions, boogie boards, watches and more; expect established brands like Ray Ban and Maui Jim, as well as über-hip upstarts Electric, Von Zipper and Spy in a minimalist-cool, water-themed space.

Orlando Harley Davidson
21 | 22 | 18 | E

1590 E. Buena Vista Dr.

Motorcycle fans are in Hog heaven at this Pleasure Island purveyor of biker gear (T-shirts, leather jackets, logo merchandise) "sanitized for a family audience"; easy riders can mount a saddle or two and take a gander at custom models, but some opine the selection's "not as wide as at other Harley stores."

WEST SIDE

Cirque du Soleil Boutique

22 | 22 | 19 | E

1478 E. Buena Vista Dr.

Ok, "it's Cirque du Soleil, not Disney", but acrobat aficionados who deem *La Nouba* one of WDW's "best shows" flip over this lobby locale on Downtown Disney's West Side offering soundtracks, costumes and videos; wallet-watchers flip out over "crazy-expensive" prices, but the financially flexible willingly pay to "relive the experience."

DisneyQuest Emporium

18 | 18 | 21 | M

1478 E. Buena Vista Dr.

"The only place" in WDW "to find DisneyQuest pins" is this little shop within the eponymous Downtown Disney West Side attraction, where you can also pick up logo sweatshirts, T-shirts and accessories; N.B. the pins can also be ordered by phone.

Disney's Candy Cauldron

23 | 23 | 21 | M

1478 E. Buena Vista Dr.

Potions as sweet as Snow White herself emerge from this West Side version of the Wicked Queen's dungeon, whose denizens make fudge, candy apples and chocolate-dipped fruit while you watch – "pick up presents" for the folks back home or just "gorge yourself"; the "cramped" shop gets "crowded on summer evenings", but even so its "cute atmosphere is the icing on the mouse ears."

Fuego by Sosa Cigars

21 | 22 | 21 | E

1478 E. Buena Vista Dr.

"Whether you smoke or not", stogie fans urge "stop by to watch cigars being hand-rolled" at this "classic" family-owned tobacconist in a West Side storefront; there's also an "extensive" international selection in the humidor, and "personable" employees will happily help you choose.

House of Blues Company Store

21 | 22 | 19 | M

1478 E. Buena Vista Dr.

At this nook adjoining the House of Blues restaurant on Downtown Disney's West Side, delta devotees "love to browse" the "fun and different" offerings such as original folk art, "funky music", HOB's signature hot sauce and "cool T-shirts"; even folks who consider it an "expensive" "tourist trap" "can't resist" at least a "walk-through."

Hoypoloi Gallery

∇ 24 | 22 | 20 | E

1478 E. Buena Vista Dr.

Ensconced in an arty West Side storefront, what may be WDW's "most interesting shop" displays "first-class", "one-of-a-kind or artist-signed" glass and ceramic *objets*, "funky" sculptures in metal, wood and stone and decorative accessories "you didn't even know you needed"; though no one disputes that the "unique" inventory is "excellent quality", it can also be "pricey" and mouse-maniacs lament that it's "not Disney-themed."

	QUALITY	DISPLAY	SERVICE	COST

Magic Masters

▽ 20 | 25 | 23 | E

1478 E. Buena Vista Dr.

Putting a different spin on the idea of 'Disney magic' this West Side re-creation of Houdini's private library conjures up "tools of the trade" for both "budding" prestidigitators and "serious" sleight-of-handers; "stop by when you see a crowd" gathering for a demo, since the "entertaining" (and "patient") cast members "know what they're talking about" and "will show you any trick", making it "more showplace" than shop.

Magnetron Magnetz

18 | 20 | 18 | I

1478 E. Buena Vista Dr.

"Your refrigerator will never feel naked again" if you succumb to the pull of this West Side trove of more than 20,000 "magnets for every occasion" – from "good, inexpensive souvenirs" to "ultimate" finds for "avid collectors"; with the lights periodically dimming to show off the blinking, glowing, beeping merchandise, few can resist stopping in, so it's "always crowded."

Planet Hollywood on Location

18 | 18 | 17 | M

1478 E. Buena Vista Dr.

Multiplex mavens still "love the atmosphere" of this gift shop in the eponymous West Side restaurant's lobby and consider it a "cool" place to pick up logo merchandise, clothing and other movie-themed souvenirs; but critics find it "nothing really special" and in need of an "update"; N.B. there's a smaller version on Sunset Boulevard at Hollywood Studios.

Starabilias

23 | 22 | 18 | VE

1478 E. Buena Vista Dr.

"You could spend hours" browsing the "rare" and "historic" artifacts at this "must-see" West Side collection that comprises nostalgic pop-culture memorabilia (restored jukeboxes, vintage Coke machines) and "thousands" of objects autographed or once owned by film, TV, music and sports celebs; surveyors say the "crowded" confines abound with "gifts you won't find anyplace else", but "bring your AmEx Black card" if looking to buy.

Virgin Megastore

23 | 21 | 17 | M

1478 E. Buena Vista Dr.

"If you must buy non-Disney music" while at Walt Disney World, surveyors suggest you boogie on over to this "huge" West Side teen "magnet" where live DJs rock out amid a "mind-boggling" inventory of "hard-to-find CD imports", "soundtracks to every movie ever made" and "offbeat DVDs"; the second-floor book section feels "more like a corner store" than a chain, with a "nice" balcony for coffee-drinking and "people-watching."

HOTELS

Hotels

The 22 Disney-owned and -operated resorts offer a wide range of options, from simple, family-friendly "Value" accommodations like **Disney's Pop Century Resort** – where rooms go for as little as $82 per night – to "Deluxe" properties like the **Grand Floridian,** Disney's flagship resort, where a standard room in high season can set you back as much as 10 times that amount (guest room rates vary based on the time of year and the view). All WDW lodgings have shopping and dining on-site, and some boast 24-hour cafes. The higher-end resorts have (or share) spas, and **Disney's Animal Kingdom Lodge** offers an unusual perk: its own savannah with African animals roaming just outside rooms. **Disney Vacation Club,** or DVC, is Disney's version of time-share, with villas in some of the resorts reserved for vacation club members. The resorts are listed by category below, with a synopsis of what to expect at each level:

DELUXE: Disney's Animal Kingdom Lodge, BoardWalk Inn, Contemporary Resort, Grand Floridian Resort & Spa, Polynesian Resort, Wilderness Lodge, Yacht & Beach Club Resorts, Swan and Dolphin.
Amenities: full-service dining, room service, valet parking, bellhop luggage service, spa access, swimming pools, kids' activities, monorail, bus or boat transport to all parks.

HOME AWAY FROM HOME/VACATION CLUB: Disney's Old Key West Resort, Saratoga Springs Resort & Spa, Beach Club Villas, BoardWalk Villas, the Villas at Wilderness Lodge. All are part of Disney Vacation Club, but accommodations are also rented out to non-DVC members as regular hotel rooms.
Amenities: full kitchen in many units, restaurants, swimming pools, on-site recreation, parking at the front door, bus or boat transportation to all parks.

MODERATE: Disney's Caribbean Beach, Coronado Springs, Port Orleans Riverside and French Quarter.
Amenities: restaurants or food courts, limited room service, bellhop luggage service, swimming pools, on-site recreation.

VALUE: Disney's All-Star Movies, All-Star Music, All-Star Sports, Pop Century Resort.
Amenities: food courts, hourly luggage service, swimming pools, bus transportation to all parks.

CAMPGROUND: Disney's Fort Wilderness Resort & Campground. Options include fully furnished cabins (starting at $249 a night) that sleep up to six and fully equipped tent and RV sites (starting at $41 a night).
Amenities: pony rides, hayrides, a petting farm – and the sheer novelty of being able to camp out in the woods just minutes from the Magic Kingdom.

OTHER PERKS: All resort guests can use Disney's complimentary Magical Express service, which allows them to check bags at their hometown airport, bypass baggage claim at Orlando International Airport and board motor coaches to their Disney resort, where bags are delivered to their room upon check-in. This perk, combined with free transportation around WDW (via buses, monorails and water launches) makes a rental car unnecessary for guests who don't plan to leave the resort area. Also, every day one of the four major theme parks offers Extra Magic Hours – they open one hour early or stay open three hours later just for resort guests, providing bonus time to enjoy select attractions and meet Disney characters.

OTHER HOTELS ON DISNEY PROPERTY: There are several non-Disney-owned hotels near Downtown Disney on Hotel Plaza Boulevard: the **Hilton, Hotel Royal Plaza, DoubleTree Guest Suites, Buena Vista Palace, Regal Sun Resort** and **Best Western Lake Buena Vista Resort.** All offer free transportation to the theme parks as well as other perks such as tickets to Disney and non-Disney theme parks and attractions, and reservations for Disney golf courses, dinner shows and theme park restaurants.

RESERVATIONS: For reservations at any WDW hotel, call 407-934-7639 or a travel agent.

Top Rooms

25 Disney's Saratoga Springs Resort & Spa | *Downtown Disney Area*
24 Disney's BoardWalk Inn | *Epcot Area*
Disney's Old Key West Resort | *Downtown Disney Area*
Disney's Yacht Club Resort | *Epcot Area*
Villas at Disney's Wilderness Lodge | *Magic Kingdom Area*

Top Service

25 Disney's Grand Floridian Resort & Spa | *Magic Kingdom Area*
24 Disney's Wilderness Lodge | *Magic Kingdom Area*
Disney's Animal Kingdom Lodge | *Animal Kingdom Area*
Disney's Yacht Club Resort | *Epcot Area*
Disney's Polynesian Resort | *Magic Kingdom Area*

Top Dining

24 Disney's Grand Floridian Resort & Spa | *Magic Kingdom Area*
23 Disney's Animal Kingdom Lodge | *Animal Kingdom Area*
Disney's Contemporary Resort | *Magic Kingdom Area*
22 Disney's Wilderness Lodge | *Magic Kingdom Area*
Villas at Disney's Wilderness Lodge | *Magic Kingdom Area**

Top Facilities

27 Disney's Animal Kingdom Lodge | *Animal Kingdom Area*
26 Disney's Grand Floridian Resort & Spa | *Magic Kingdom Area*
Disney's Yacht Club Resort | *Epcot Area*
Disney's BoardWalk Inn | *Epcot Area*
Disney's Beach Club Resort | *Epcot Area*

ROOMS | SERVICE | DINING | FACIL. | COST

Ratings & Symbols

Rooms, Service, Dining and **Facilities** are rated on the Zagat 0 to 30 scale.

Cost reflects the hotel's high-season rate for a standard double room. It does not reflect seasonal changes.

🏃 children's programs   ⌐ 18-hole golf course
🅑 kitchens   ⓢ notable spa facilities
🅜 views   🔍 tennis

MAGIC KINGDOM AREA

Disney's Contemporary Resort 🅜ⓢ🔍   21 | 22 | 23 | 21 | $339

4600 N. World Dr. | 407-824-1000 | fax 407-824-3539 | 997 rooms, 11 suites
"One stop away from the Magic Kingdom" on the monorail, this Deluxe, *Jetsons*-ish A-frame (with two additional wings) has the "location, location, location" that "makes life so much easier", and after an overhaul not too long ago, the "futuristic" rooms in this "oldie but goodie" are "finally contemporary for this century", sporting "dark woods and steel trim"; since everyone likes to "come for the food", however, getting into Chef Mickey's or the California Grill can be "tricky without a reservation."

Disney's Fort Wilderness   22 | 22 | 20 | 23 | $67
Resort & Campground 🅑🅜🔍

4510 N. Ft. Wilderness Trail | 407-824-2900 | fax 407-824-3508 | 784 campsites, 409 cabins
"Roughing it Disney-style" is easy at this Magic Kingdom–area "camper's paradise" where you can choose from tent, RV campsites or "roomy" cabins (the "best-kept secret" at the parks) that come with a/c, full kitchens and patio decks; surveyors say "there's so much to do", including "canoeing, hiking, horseback riding" and "making s'mores with Chip 'n' Dale" at nightly campfires, that you may not care that it "takes a while to get to the parks."

🅩 Disney's Grand Floridian   24 | 25 | 24 | 26 | $555
Resort & Spa 🏃🅜ⓢ🔍

4401 Floridian Way | 407-824-3000 | fax 407-824-3186 | 837 rooms, 25 suites
Rated the Survey's No. 1 overall hotel, this "stately" Deluxe "grande dame" boasting "magical" "views of Cinderella Castle" and "enormous fresh flower arrangements" is high on "Southern charm"; reviewers "feel like royalty" thanks to "luxurious" pattern-rich rooms, "superior" service, "outstanding" restaurants (most notably Victoria & Albert's) and a "wonderful spa", all "minutes from the Magic Kingdom on the monorail"; of course, the "price reflects the luxury", but this Victorian-style "jewel" is "Disney's flagship for a reason."

Disney's Polynesian Resort 🏃🅜   21 | 24 | 21 | 24 | $499

1600 Seven Seas Dr. | 407-824-2000 | fax 407-824-3174 | 815 rooms, 32 suites
"Friendly" staff members are "quick with an '*aloha*' from the moment you arrive" at this Deluxe "Polynesian getaway" just a "monorail

hop" from the Magic Kingdom; "one of Disney's oldest resorts" and still "a favorite" of many, this "romantic" "tropical escape" enchants with "meticulously maintained" "torch-lit" grounds", an "exceptional" "volcano pool", "large", "beautifully renovated" rooms (some with flat-screen TVs) and a "must-do luau"; the only trouble in paradise? – "premium prices."

Disney's Wilderness Lodge ⚌ 🛁 | 22 | 24 | 22 | 26 | $335 |

901 Timberline Dr. | 407-824-3200 | fax 407-824-3232 | 700 rooms, 27 suites

"The only thing missing are the buffalo roaming" at this "majestic" Deluxe take on the "rustic mountain lodges" of the American West; rooms strike a "nice balance" of "homey" and "classy", and though even supporters say they run "a little small", compensations include a "breathtaking lobby" (especially "during the holidays"), "top-notch" service and the "fabulous" Silver Creek Springs pool area; as for food, you can dine "in luxury" at the Artist Point restaurant or "family-style" at the "entertaining" Whispering Canyon Cafe.

Shades of Green ⚌ 🔍 | - | - | - | - | $80 |

1950 W. Magnolia Palm Dr. | 407-824-3400 | fax 407-824-3665 | 888-593-2242 | 586 rooms, 11 suites

Open to members of the armed forces, their families and others with military connections, this well-priced resort, adjacent to Disney's Magnolia and Palm golf courses, runs a shuttle bus to the parks and is within walking distance of the Polynesian and its monorail; in addition to large rooms, some with their own balcony, amenities include a children's play area, two heated outdoor pools and five restaurants.

Villas at Disney's Wilderness Lodge, The ⚌ 🐾 🛁 | 24 | 22 | 22 | 25 | $570 |

901 Timberline Dr. | 407-824-3200 | fax 407-824-3232 | 116 villas, 65 studios

A "woodsy atmosphere" gives this "family-pleasing" Disney Vacation Club option a real "Pacific Northwest" feel, yet it's just a "short boat ride from the Magic Kingdom"; praise goes to its "fabulous" villas and studios, "excellent" on-site dining and "magnificent" Silver Creek Springs pool, and though some feel its "secluded" location makes it "too detached from the Lodge", partisans consider it "one of WDW's most impressive resorts", "with or without kids" in tow.

EPCOT AREA

Disney's Beach Club Resort ⚌ 🛁 🔍 | 23 | 23 | 20 | 26 | $475 |

1800 Epcot Resort Blvd. | 407-934-8000 | fax 407-934-3850 | 527 rooms, 56 suites

With a "humongous slide, currents and sand-bottomed pools", the "spectacular" three-acre swimming area at this Deluxe New England-themed complex (sibling to the Yacht Club) is "practically a water park"; a "favorite" of many, it boasts "good-size" rooms done in "calm" nautical colors, an "old-fashioned soda fountain" restaurant and a "fantastic" lakeside location that's "extremely convenient" to both Epcot and Hollywood Studios, so satisfied sun-worshipers would "stay here every time – if they could afford to."

Disney's Beach Club Villas ♔⚲♨♨🔍   24   22   20   25 $429

1800 Epcot Resort Blvd. | 407-934-8000 | fax 407-934-3850 |
171 villas, 109 studios

A "first-class home away from home", this Disney Vacation Club resort evokes a "bright and cheerful" Victorian-era beachfront cottage, albeit one with modern amenities, i.e. "comfortable rooms" with full kitchens ("a real plus") as well as a washer and dryer, making them "excellent for a family with young children"; just as important as the "fantastic location" "an easy walk to Epcot" is access to Stormalong Bay, arguably "Disney's best pool" – one that "most kids won't leave voluntarily."

Disney's BoardWalk Inn ♔🔍   24   23   21   26 $475

2101 N. Epcot Resort Blvd. | 407-939-5100 | fax 407-939-5150 |
357 rooms, 14 suites

Recalling an "old-time Atlantic City" resort (there's even a "great waterslide" designed "like an old-fashioned roller coaster"), this Deluxe lakefront "vacation unto itself" is a "short walk" or boat ride from Epcot and Hollywood Studios; rooms are "pretty", and while those with balconies overlooking the BoardWalk's "amazing restaurants, shops and nightclubs" "can be noisy", the garden suites in back are "quiet"; either way, you're "right in the middle of everything."

Disney's BoardWalk Villas ⚲♨♨🔍   24   23   21   24 $560

2101 N. Epcot Resort Blvd. | 407-939-6200 | fax 407-939-5150 |
372 rooms, 533 villas

Satisfied surveyors "could live in" the "spacious", "homey" villas (with their "own kitchen and laundry") at this "beautiful" Disney Vacation Club option that's a "mix of everything a resort should be"; the "convenient" location is "a huge plus" – "there's always something going on down on the BoardWalk", including a "multitude of restaurant options" – and it's a short stroll to Epcot, but "be ready" for a big "walk to your room."

Disney's Caribbean Beach Resort ♨♨   19   19   16   19 $185

900 Cayman Way | 407-934-3400 | fax 407-934-3288 | 2112 rooms

"Colorful" "island flavor" characterizes this sprawling, Moderate Epcot-area resort, set by a lagoon and featuring "beautiful grounds" complete with "peaceful hammocks"; easygoing types say the "large rooms" and "helpful" staff make it fine for a "festive" family holiday, but faultfinders note that it's "a long walk" to the buses and main building and contend that the "adequate" dining options should be "taken up a notch."

☑ Disney's Yacht Club Resort ♔♨♨🔍   24   24   22   26 $415

1700 Epcot Resorts Blvd. | 407-934-7000 | fax 407-934-3450 |
610 rooms, 11 suites

Sharing an "awesome" "mini–water park" (Stormalong Bay) and other facilities with the adjacent Beach Club, this "quieter, more luxurious" Deluxe option resembles a "New England seaside" hotel from yesteryear and offers "easy access" to Epcot and the BoardWalk (a "definite plus"); enthusiasts extol "exceptional service" and "comfy beds", and if a few find "winding around" the "expansive" (and "expensive") resort a "bit of a hike", they can refuel at the on-site Yachtsman restaurant, which serves some of the "best steaks" in WDW.

	ROOMS	SERVICE	DINING	FACIL.	COST

Walt Disney World Dolphin ♥♥ ⑤ ✎ | 19 | 20 | 20 | 22 | $389

1500 Epcot Resort Blvd. | 407-934-4000 | fax 407-934-4099 |
800-227-1500 | 1509 rooms, 129 suites

This Deluxe postmodern Sheraton designed by Michael Graves boasts
a convenient Epcot-area location offering "easy park access", "lots of
amenities", including a Balinese-style Mandara spa, and a range of
dining options, including Todd English's seafooder bluezoo (No. 2 for
Decor among WDW restaurants); admirers also "love those Heavenly
beds" in the "well-maintained" rooms, but some say the "lack of
Disney theming changes the feel of the vacation", especially when this
Swan sibling is "overrun by conventioneers"; N.B. the health club and
parking cost extra.

Walt Disney World Swan ♥♥ ⑤ ✎ | 19 | 20 | 20 | 21 | $349

1200 Epcot Resort Blvd. | 407-934-3000 | fax 407-934-4499 |
800-227-1500 | 756 rooms, 55 suites

The "Heavenly beds" are as "tempting as the parks" insist admirers
who "unwind" at this Deluxe Westin that some call the "Dolphin's little brother" since it shares many facilities, including an expansive,
grottolike pool; it's within "walking distance of Epcot" and has "good
service" "without the high prices" of resorts on WDW property, but
"hidden fees" – including charges for parking and the health club – ruf-
fle the feathers of critics, and some contend that its "corporate" feel
"lacks that magical quality" found at Disney-themed hotels; N.B. the
above ratings may not reflect a post-Survey lobby redo.

DISNEY'S ANIMAL KINGDOM AREA

Disney's All-Star Movies Resort | 15 | 17 | 15 | 17 | $119

1991 W. Buena Vista Dr. | 407-939-7000 | fax 407-939-7111 | 1920 rooms

"Delight the children" with a stay at this "cute" Value motel in the
Animal Kingdom area that's "geared for young families" "on a limited
budget"; admirers applaud its two "themed pools" and the food
court's "wide variety of choices", and advise "don't forget your camera" "if you're a fan of 101 Dalmatians", Toy Story and other Disney
flicks, since they figure into the decor; still critics give just "one star"
to "nothing fancy" rooms that are "beginning to show wear" and perennial "long lines at check-in."

Disney's All-Star Music Resort | 15 | 17 | 14 | 17 | $119

1801 W. Buena Vista Dr. | 407-939-6000 | fax 407-939-7222 | 1920 rooms

"Kids love all the bright colors" and the "cool" guitar- and piano-
shaped pools at this "wonderfully affordable" Value option in the
Animal Kingdom area, where a "friendly" staff orchestrates your welcome; critics cite off-notes such as "unreasonably long" check-in
lines, "rooms that aren't real roomy" and "noisy" public spaces, but
fans say it can't "be beat for staying on-property" at a low price.

Disney's All-Star Sports Resort | 14 | 16 | 14 | 16 | $119

1701 W. Buena Vista Dr. | 407-939-5000 | fax 407-939-7333 |
1920 rooms

Geared for families with "a sports-loving little one", this "motellike"
Value resort in the Animal Kingdom area scores points with its "amazing" theming (e.g. giant helmets) and "great pools"; fans favor the

food court's "wide variety" as well, but the "small" "no-frills" rooms may not be comfortable for your team, and opponents complain "you get what you pay for", including "loud" "kids of all ages" "running around throwing footballs."

☒ Disney's Animal Kingdom Lodge ⚭ ♨Ⓢ

23	24	23	27	$335

2901 Osceola Pkwy. | 407-938-3000 | fax 407-938-4799 | 1274 rooms, 19 suites

"Wake up to wildebeests outside the window" at this Deluxe "adventure in itself" where every day "feels like a safari"; fans judge it "top-drawer" all around, from the "luxuriously tribal" rooms overlooking the game reserve to the "jaw-dropping" art-filled lobby, not to mention the "exotic" restaurants and "hospitable" staff; though a few find the accommodations "on the small side" "considering the price" and note it's "far from everything else", more agree this "extra-magical experience" is "not to be missed."

Disney's Coronado Springs Resort ♨Ⓢ

20	20	17	21	$185

1000 W. Buena Vista Dr. | 407-939-1000 | fax 407-939-1001 | 1875 rooms, 46 suites

The "Southwestern atmosphere" is "cheery and welcoming" at this Moderate resort in the Animal Kingdom area with "well-maintained" grounds" and a central lake; though it's "very spread out", all that space allows for four pools (including an "unbelievable" one designed like a Mayan temple), a spa and an "extensive gym"; because lots of conventioneers hang their hats in the "nice-size rooms", however, it can be "hectic and loud", and some say the suits "take away from the family feeling."

Disney's Pop Century Resort

18	19	16	19	$119

1050 Century Dr. | 407-938-4000 | fax 407-938-4040 | 2880 rooms

Pop-culture vultures sashay "down memory lane" at this "eye-catching" Animal Kingdom–area Value resort that's packed with "whimsical" "memorabilia" from the past 50 years; most find it "spunky", "economical" and "fun", with three "huge" "kid-friendly" pools, "comfortable" if "utilitarian" rooms and an "adequate food court", but a few curmudgeons complain that this "Disneyfied Motel 6" is "too loud and crowded", at least "if you don't have children."

DOWNTOWN DISNEY AREA

Best Western Lake Buena Vista Resort, Walt Disney World Resort ♨

∇ 15	15	12	13	$239

2000 Hotel Plaza Blvd. | 407-828-2424 | fax 407-828-8933 | 800-348-3765 | 321 rooms, 4 atrium suites

Choose a high-floor room "facing the Magic Kingdom", and you'll be rewarded with "incredible" views of the fireworks; otherwise, while the cost-conscious consider this 18-story Downtown Disney tower "alright for the money", with "adequate dining" choices and complimentary transport to the parks, fussier folk frown on "run-of-the-mill" quarters with "1980s-style tropical" furnishings in "aquas, peaches and pinks"; N.B. a partial renovation post-Survey may outdate the above Facilities rating.

	ROOMS	SERVICE	DINING	FACIL.	COST

Buena Vista Palace, Walt Disney World Resort ♨⑤✎

▽ 19 | 17 | 16 | 21 | $159

1900 N. Buena Vista Dr. | 407-827-2727 | fax 407-827-6034 | 866-397-6516 | 888 rooms, 124 suites

With a 10,000-sq.-ft. spa, a 24/7 fitness center, three "good pools" and six restaurants, there's plenty to do at this sprawling, plant-filled complex in a "convenient" Downtown Disney location across from Pleasure Island; adherents also appreciate the "nice-size guestrooms" and "helpful staff"; N.B. the Rooms score may not reflect a post-Survey redo that incorporated spruced-up, minimalist furnishings, pillow-top beds and flat-panel TVs.

Disney's Old Key West Resort ✎♨⑤✎

24 | 22 | 17 | 23 | $485

1510 N. Cove Rd. | 407-827-7700 | fax 407-827-7710 | 761 villas

The first Vacation Club resort, this "laid-back", pastel-hued, Downtown Disney–area option earns praise as a "true home away from home" with "well-laid-out" rooms that are among "the biggest for the money" in WDW; "set amid the Lake Buena Vista golf course", far "from the hustle and bustle of the parks", it has "lush, green landscaping" that makes it feel "more like an upscale condo community than a hotel" and is staffed by a "courteous" crew, but a few gourmets gripe that "dining choices are limited."

Disney's Port Orleans Resort - French Quarter ♨

21 | 21 | 16 | 21 | $185

2201 Orleans Dr. | 407-934-5000 | fax 407-934-5353 | 1008 rooms

Tricked up with "Mardi Gras jesters" and occasional "jazz and blues" performances, this Moderate resort "really gives you the feeling" you're in the Crescent City ("without the drunken revelers outside your room"); reachable from Downtown Disney via water shuttle, it's a "nice compromise between price and quality", with an "intimate" feel, "lovely" landscaping and "wonderfully decorated" quarters; just don't expect to feast like a Cajun: there's "only a small food court", albeit one with "yummy beignets."

Disney's Port Orleans Resort - Riverside ♨

21 | 21 | 19 | 22 | $185

1251 Riverside Dr. | 407-934-6000 | fax 407-934-5777 | 2048 rooms

Citing such down-home amenities as a "fantastic fishin' hole" and "amazing pools" that "10 outta 10 kids love", river rats rave about the "combo of activity and serenity" at the French Quarter's larger next-door neighbor, which shares its Moderate pricing and its "direct access to Downtown Disney by boat"; the "nice-size" rooms in a "picturesque" setting earn kudos, as does the staff that "transports you back to the olden days on the Mississippi" with its "genuine Southern hospitality."

☑ Disney's Saratoga Springs Resort & Spa ♨⑤✎

25 | 22 | 16 | 23 | $485

1960 Broadway | 407-827-1100 | fax 407-827-4444 | 552 villas, 288 studios

"Saddle up to stay" at the "newest" Disney Vacation Club property, a "sprawling" complex modeled after upstate New York's horse-y resort; the "elegantly decorated" rooms (ranked No. 1 in the WDW Survey) have "plenty of space for the whole family", and other assets include a "cordial" staff, "fantastic" pool and "excellent" spa; the one hitch may be the "limited selection" at the Artist's Palette restaurant, but it's an "easy" trot to Downtown Disney's many eateries.

DoubleTree Guest Suites, Walt Disney World Resort ♨️🐾

▽ 22	21	13	19	$309

2305 Hotel Plaza Blvd. | 407-934-1000 | fax 407-934-1015 | 229 suites

"Having an extra room" "works well" for families say those who appreciate this "brightly decorated" all-suites chain hotel in the Downtown Disney area; there's transportation to the parks throughout the day (and to Pleasure Island in the evenings), and kids can also amuse themselves on-site in the game room, playground or pool; despite nothing-special food choices, it's considered a "good alternative to staying" with the Mouse.

Hilton Walt Disney World ♨️🍴Ⓢ

20	20	17	21	$209

1751 Hotel Plaza Blvd. | 407-827-4000 | fax 407-827-3890 | 800-782-4414 | 708 rooms, 106 suites

This "reasonably priced" "alternative to a Disney hotel" has comfortable rooms and is just a "short walk to Downtown Disney" (buses make periodic runs to the parks as well); while the dining options may not be gourmet, its seven restaurants include an Italian, a Japanese steakhouse and a sports bar, plus there's a weekly character breakfast; other assets include two pools and a "polite staff."

Hotel Royal Plaza, Walt Disney World Resort 🍴✎

▽ 23	21	16	19	$279

1905 Hotel Plaza Blvd. | 407-828-2828 | fax 407-827-3977 | 371 rooms, 23 suites

Habitués hail this "lovely" 17-story tan-and-pink tower as a "best-kept secret", particularly after renovations not long ago enhanced the already "large rooms" with "super-comfy" pillow-top beds and "huge bathrooms" stocked with Bath & Body Works toiletries; family-friendly features include free transportation to the parks, a heated outdoor pool and complimentary breakfast for kids under 10, plus Downtown Disney's restaurants and nightlife are just a short walk away.

🆕 Regal Sun Resort ♨️🍴✎

-	-	-	-	$119

1850 Hotel Plaza Blvd. | 407-828-4444 | fax 407-828-8192 | 800-624-4109 | 619 rooms, 7 suites

A 2007 makeover revitalized this 19-story Hotel Plaza Boulevard stalwart (formerly the Grosvenor) with a modern-tropical motif: bright-red bedspreads and light walls spruce up the guestrooms, while the lobby's bamboo flooring and Caribbean-green ceilings create a breezy welcome; though the structure's unfortunate bones remain – narrow hallways, no balconies – an expanded pool-playground area, tower-room views of nightly fireworks and thrice-weekly character breakfasts at the on-site LakeView Restaurant are pluses.

GOLF

Golf

THE COURSES: The granddaddies of golf at WDW are the **Magnolia** and **Palm** courses, located on the northern side of the resort near Magic Kingdom; they were designed by Joe Lee and opened along with the resort in 1971. The following year, Lee added the **Lake Buena Vista** course, next to what is now Downtown Disney. WDW's newest course is **Osprey Ridge,** introduced in 1992 and designed by renowned golf course architect Tom Fazio. Rounding out Disney's golf offerings is **Oak Trail,** a family-play nine-hole walking course. The **Celebration Golf Club** is the centerpiece of an upscale gated community developed by Disney in the 1990s – it's a 15-minute drive from the WDW resort area, but it's open to the public too.

HOSTS AND STEWARDS: Disney has hosted the PGA TOUR for a fall Classic annually since 1971. Currently, the event, called the Disney Classic at Walt Disney World Resort, is played on the Magnolia and Palm courses. All five on-site courses have earned the "Certified Audubon Cooperative Sanctuary" designation, meaning they meet Audubon International's criteria as "stewards of the environment."

GREENS FEES: A round of golf can cost as much as $169 at WDW's premier courses, but reduced rates are offered in summer, when late afternoon/early evening rounds can be played for as little as $38. During certain times of the year, discounts are also available for morning rounds beginning after 10 AM. Transportation to all courses is complimentary for WDW resort guests, as is club storage and transfer. Rental clubs and shoes are also available.

FLASH SOME GREEN: Sometimes, to be treated like a king you need to show the money. Golf isn't a high-paying industry unless your name is Tiger or Jack, so a few bucks' tip can often make a difference in how you're treated (TIP means To Improve Performance).

RESERVING AND LEARNING: For tee times, call 407-939-4653. Guests with a resort confirmation number can reserve tee times up to 90 days ahead; day visitors can book up to 30 days ahead. Private or group golf instruction from PGA Professionals is available, as well as one-on-one Video Computer Swing Analysis.

TAP-INS – A FEW FINAL THOUGHTS: Getting stuck on the back nine during a downpour without a jacket can ruin any round, so don't forget the rain gear and pack an extra pair of golf shoes if you're playing more than three rounds. A good travel planner can also make your life easier, as will calling the course a few days in advance to double-check your tee time, make sure the greens aren't being aerated that day and so on. Lastly, and we can't stress this enough – enjoy yourself no matter how you play. After all, it sure beats working!

P.S.: All WDW courses have on-site restaurants that will allow you to replace the calories that you burn off following your ball.

COURSE FACIL. SERVICE VALUE COST

Ratings & Symbols

Course, Facilities, Service and **Value** are rated on the Zagat 0 to 30 scale.

Cost reflects the price per non-member or non-guest to play 18 holes on a weekend in high season, i.e. the highest price of play. Yardage, USGA Rating and Slope are listed after each address.

🏌 caddies/forecaddies   ⚬⟋ guests only
🛒 carts only

Celebration Golf Club
| 23 | 22 | 23 | 21 | $145 |

701 Golfpark Dr. | 407-566-4653 | www.celebrationgolf.com | 6772/4949; 73/68.5; 135/121

A "picturesque" layout "designed by the Jones boys" (Robert Trent Jones Sr. and Jr.), this "perfectly manicured course" plays through "beautiful homes" "in the center of 'Pleasantville'" – aka the "planned community" of Celebration southwest of Orlando; while a few "expected more" from what they call a "not overly challenging" experience, most find it "a fair test" featuring "huge, sloped greens" and "fairways lined with ball-eating grass"; even better, it has "an exceptionally nice staff" providing "typical Disney service."

Walt Disney World, Lake Buena Vista 🛒
| 22 | 24 | 25 | 20 | $149 |

2200 Club Lake Dr. | 407-939-4653 | www.disneyworldgolf.com | 6749/5194; 73/69.9; 133/122

"Probably the easiest" of the Disney courses is this "pleasant surprise" "designed for all skill levels" where you "tee off next to boats and canals" and "wind through Old Key West and Saratoga Springs" resorts; though nitpickers note "it's a little hard to get to" and is "getting closed in by time-share development", loyalists laud the "laid-back atmosphere" and say it's a "nice variation" from "other WDW courses."

Walt Disney World, Magnolia 🛒
| 23 | 23 | 23 | 19 | $169 |

1950 Magnolia Palm Dr. | 407-939-4653 | www.disneyworldgolf.com | 7516/5232; 76.4/70.5; 140/123

With holes that "require high shots over bunker-fronted greens", "the mighty Mag will test your skills" say swingers satisfied by this "beautiful, relaxing" links, home to both the final rounds of the PGA Tour's FUNAI Classic and the "famed Mickey Mouse sand trap" at the par-3 sixth; while wallet-watchers insist it's "awfully pricey", you get "great facilities" and "world-class" service as part of the deal.

Walt Disney World, Oak Trail
| ▽ 21 | 22 | 22 | 23 | $38 |

1950 W. Magnolia-Palm Dr. | 407-939-4653 | www.disneyworldgolf.com | 2913/2532

"It's more than a golf course – it's like an outdoor reserve" gush nature-lovers of this "well-laid-out" links with what some call "the most interesting greens at WDW"; it's "great to take the kids" "for a quick nine holes", and while most praise the "top-notch facilities" and "wonderful Disney service", some caution "once you leave the clubhouse, there's no cart service", so stock up on beverages before you set out.

	COURSE	FACIL.	SERVICE	VALUE	COST

Walt Disney World, Osprey Ridge 🏌

| 26 | 24 | 24 | 20 | $169 |

3451 Golf View Dr. | 407-939-4653 | www.disneyworldgolf.com |
7101/5402; 74.4/71.3; 131/127

"Hills, slopes, elevated tees – this is Florida?" ask swingers enamored with this "excellent", "serene" Tom Fazio–designed links featuring "lots of water" and "large sand wastelands lining the lush fairways"; add "first-class service" and many call it "Disney's best course", so even though a few find it "overpriced" and warn of "rookies with rental equipment" ("be prepared for a five-hour round"), that doesn't daunt devotees who say "if you can play only one course here, make it this one."

Walt Disney World, Palm 🏌

| 22 | 24 | 24 | 19 | $149 |

1950 Magnolia Palm Dr. | 407-939-4653 | www.disneyworldgolf.com |
6957/5311; 73.9/70.4; 138/124

This "beautiful", "well-groomed" track (which, along with Magnolia, hosts the PGA Tour's FUNAI Classic) is "fun" as well as "challenging", boasting a 36-year-old Joe Lee design "cut through trees and lakes" with a watery par-4 sixth hole that may be the "hardest at WDW"; though it's a "good experience overall" complete with "friendly" service, some say "world-class prices" mean it's "not much of a value" and herpetologically minded hackers advise "watch out for gators."

DISNEY
CRUISE LINE

Disney Cruise Line

THE SHIPS: Disney Cruise Line has two almost-identical ships, the **Disney Magic,** launched in July 1998, and the **Disney Wonder,** launched in July 1999. Both generally sail from Port Canaveral, Florida, to the Caribbean (Magic) and the Bahamas (Wonder) except when temporarily "repositioned" to another port. Italian-designed, the ships have similar interiors, restaurants and entertainment venues, and feature Mickey Mouse's famed silhouette on their red stacks. Both have 877 staterooms, from Standard to Deluxe, that are about 25% larger than on most cruise ships. Almost three-quarters are outside rooms and all are no smoking.

ACTIVITIES: Kids get royal treatment, with (collectively) nearly an entire deck's worth of space dedicated to youth activities. Disney characters are a big part of the action, appearing in Broadway-style shows and at themed deck parties like Pirates In the Caribbean. Parents can escape the kids at adult-only areas including a spa (make reservations on boarding day, as slots go quickly), swimming pool, nightclubs and Castaway Cay beach (see below). Also, there's an experienced staff to care for infants and toddlers when mom and dad want a romantic dinner alone.

DINING: Meals are served in three themed restaurants, and DCL's "rotation" dining means your waiters move with you from one venue to the next. The adults-only restaurant, **Palo** (on both ships), requires a jacket for men; make reservations as soon as you board, as seats go quickly. There are buffets for breakfast, lunch, snacks and kids' dinners. With the exception of a $10 surcharge at Palo, all onboard food and snacks are included in the cruise cost, as is 24-hour room service, but name-brand snacks and canned/bottled beverages are extra.

CASTAWAY CAY: This 1,000-acre, private Bahamian island with powdery white sand beaches is a favorite stop, with a family beach plus a secluded stretch of sand for guests 18 and older with massage cabanas, a lunch buffet and a bar. Activities include parasailing, snorkeling, kayaking, swimming with stingrays, sailing and bicycling, with supervised activities for kids three–17.

THE TERMINAL: Disney has its own cruise terminal at Port Canaveral, about an hour's drive from Orlando. Shuttle transportation from Orlando International Airport to the port is provided, and many visitors combine a cruise with a Disney World vacation – made easy with just one check-in (your key even works in both places). If you're planning a cruise-and-land stay, consider cruising last if you want a more restful end to your vacation.

RESERVATIONS: A three-day cruise for a family of four aboard Disney Cruise Line can start at $1,416, excluding taxes and miscellaneous fees. The fare includes accommodations, onboard entertainment, meals, snacks and most nonalcoholic drinks. Shore excursions, spa treatments, and specialty and alcoholic drinks cost extra. For best prices, book a year in advance. Fall offers the best value, but also the risk of hurricanes.

ROOMS SERVICE DINING FACIL.

Ships

Disney Magic

| 25 | 26 | 25 | 26 |

Length: 964 ft. | 877 staterooms

An "aura of class" prevails on Disney Cruise Line's flagship – the first of its minnie-fleet of two – where "top-notch" dining, "spacious" art deco–style cabins and "out-of-this-world" service add up to a "magical adventure"; "plenty" of "secret" "adults-only" hideouts and a smartly designed "family setup" mean "well-occupied" kids are "rarely seen or heard", creating a "memorable" (even "romantic") experience that "thrills all ages" – so even though it's far from cheap, converts fall under its spell "time and time again."

Disney Wonder

| 26 | 25 | 24 | 26 |

Length: 964 ft. | 877 staterooms

"Kick back" and be "pampered" aboard this "*Wonder*-ful", "almost identical" twin of the *Disney Magic* that "takes you back to the heyday of cruising"; "gorgeous" art nouveau touches throughout and "majestic", "well-thought-out" staterooms "as big as a Manhattan studio apartment" please cruisers, as does "read-your-mind" service, "outstanding" dining and "amazing" shows and excursions; "phenomenal children's programs", a toddlers' pool that DCL's other ship lacks and "secret" parents-only "getaways" are more reasons why it's "fun for the whole family, together or apart."

Activities & Entertainment

Ratings: Child Appeal, Adult Appeal, Thrill

Castaway Cay:
Castaway Ray's Stingray Adventure

▽ | 29 | 26 | 22 |

Disney Magic, Disney Wonder | Interactive Attraction | Duration: 60 min

Cruisers seeking a unique, "safe" "encounter with sea life" will "love" this interactive experience; after an educational briefing, participants don snorkel gear and dive into the lagoon where they "feed and swim with stingrays", making for an "amazing" underwater adventure that's memorable for "adults and kids" (who "still talk about it six months later"); N.B. $29 for ages five–nine, $35 ages 10 and up; children under 16 must be accompanied by an adult.

Castaway Cay: Serenity Bay

| - | 28 | 12 |

Disney Magic, Disney Wonder | Beach

On the opposite end of Castaway Cay from Family Beach sits this "romantic", "peaceful" "adults-only" "paradise" where DCL guests 18 and older can "recharge" "away from the noise of the kids"; visitors can enjoy grown-up perks like "open-air massages" and "cocktails in the sun" or just be "lulled to sleep by soft breezes and lapping water"; some say "it's one of the best ideas Disney ever had" (though "more hammocks for the older set" "would be nice").

Castaway Family Beach

| 28 | 27 | 19 |

Disney Magic, Disney Wonder | Beach

Castaways contend there's "something to do for everyone" on DCL's "postcard-perfect" 1,000-acre "private" "paradise", from "enjoying the sun" on a "pristine" "white-sand beach lined with palm trees" to snorkeling "Disney-style" in "a crystal clear lagoon" with "old 20,000 Leagues Under the Sea submarines"; there's also biking, hiking and personal watercraft rentals available on this stop in "Shangri-la" that many call "the best day" of their cruise – now if only one could spend "a week."

Disney Dreams   28 | 26 | 20
Disney Magic, Disney Wonder | Live Show | Duration: 50 min
"Quite possibly the best Disney show on land or water", this "first-rate" "Broadway-style" production staged in Walt Disney Theatre explores the "magical" "power of dreams" through music; audiences encounter "many well-known characters" (like Aladdin, Ariel, Cinderella, Peter Pan and Simba) who bring beloved songs to life in "awesome" fashion, leading fans to call it a "highlight of the cruise" – just "bring a tissue", since it can "transform even the most jaded adults into starry-eyed kids."

Do Si Do with Snow White   ∇ 26 | 13 | 15
Disney Magic, Disney Wonder | Interactive Attraction | Duration: 60 min
"Little princesses" will love participating in "special activities" like learning the "Dance of the Seven Dwarfs" and experiencing the "thrill" of meeting one of Disney's most beloved characters at Oceaneer Club; parents say the experience is "perfect magic" for kids ages three to four and "exactly why you want to go on a DCL cruise" – but "sign up well in advance" to avoid having Snow White fans melt into tears.

Flubber   ∇ 27 | 15 | 22
Disney Magic, Disney Wonder | Interactive Attraction | Duration: 60 min
Junior scientists don "cool lab coats" and perform "amazing" "experiments" with solid liquids in this Oceaneer Lab activity designed for ages eight to 12; led by the "very funny" Professor Goo, kids make their own Flubber, which they "get to take home" ("my daughter kept hers in the fridge for months!") and learn something in the process.

Golden Mickeys, The   27 | 26 | 18
Disney Magic, Disney Wonder | Live Show | Duration: 50 min
From the "red carpet walk" to "guest interviews" "on the big screen", this "original", "fun-tastic" "twist on the Oscars" has attendees "feeling like celebrities"; the "spectacular" "multimedia and stage show" "brings together scenes" and music from 75 years of "classic" Disney films and features appearances by "favorite" characters, "including the villains" ("Ursula's dramatic appearance alone is worth showing up for"); "big kids" may be "bored" but adults can expect "a lump in the throat."

Hercules - A Muse-ical Comedy   25 | 24 | 17
Disney Wonder | Live Show | Duration: 50 min
The son of Zeus "steals the show" in this "hysterically funny" vaudeville-esque interpretation of the "obscure cartoon"; a "far cry above standard cruise ship" shows (indeed, fans say it "could rank alongside *The Lion King* and *Beauty and the Beast*"), it features "upbeat" music, "magnificent" costumes and lots of "general silliness" – though "most of the jokes will go over kids' heads", adults will be "laughing for the rest of the trip."

Magical Farewell

▽ 28 | 27 | 22

Disney Magic | Live Show | Duration: 50 min

Disney Magic passengers can relive the ship's "outstanding" stage shows in this "superb" musical revue featuring excerpts from *Disney Dreams*, *The Golden Mickeys* and *Hercules – A Muse-ical Comedy*; surveyors say it's "great to see all the characters one last time" to "get pics and autographs", ensuring a "wonderful" end to the voyage.

Twice Charmed - An Original Twist on the Cinderella Story

▽ 27 | 26 | 18

Disney Magic | Live Show | Duration: 50 min

Considered a highlight of the *Magic*'s shipboard entertainment, this "first-rate" musical puts a "wonderful twist" on the classic story; smitten spectators say new songs and surprising plot developments (such as the existence of a Fairy God*father*) along with "amazing" "theatrical" details ("wonderful use of scrims") make the show "entertaining" and "even a little edgy" – "at least by Disney standards."

Welcome Aboard! Variety Show

▽ 23 | 24 | 16

Disney Magic | Live Show | Duration: 50 min

Passengers get the cruise off to a "good start" while getting a "taste of what's to come" via this "excellent" variety show on the *Disney Magic*; the "memorable" revue features singing and dancing cast members, familiar characters and a preview of the comedy acts in the ship's clubs, which leaves some "laughing" all the way out to sea.

Dining

Ratings: Food, Decor, Service

Animator's Palate   *Californian*

22 | 26 | 26

Disney Magic, Disney Wonder | Table service | Serves alcohol | B, D

A "feast for the palate" as well as the palette, this "magical" show-restaurant's "animated decor" actually "comes alive": as dinner progresses, "the music builds" and the "black-and-white" space "gradually changes color" ("waiters' costumes as well"), making for "spectacular" visuals; the Californian fare is deemed "excellent" by many, and even the less impressed agree "it's all about the show", anyway; P.S. this "masterpiece" only runs "on the first dining rotation", so "don't skip it."

Beach Blanket Buffet   *Eclectic*

19 | 17 | 20

Disney Wonder | Counter service | Serves alcohol | B, L, D

Presenting "a different theme each day" in "laid-back surroundings" that include outside tables with "views of the ocean and ports of call", this "huge" Eclectic buffet spread on Deck 9 of the *Wonder* "has enough variety" so that "everyone can find something they'll enjoy"; surveyors laud "efficient service" and say it's especially good for breakfast thanks to "made-to-order omelets" and "fresh" fruits; P.S. kids have a separate line at dinner.

Cove Cafe   *Bakery/Coffeehouse*

▽ 21 | 21 | 23

Disney Magic, Disney Wonder | Counter service | Serves alcohol | S

Java junkies jeer "Starbucks could learn a thing or two" from this "inviting" cafe/bar/bakery in the "adults-only section" on the DCL ships where parents escape for "excellent" coffees, cocoas and specialty alcoholic drinks bound to put a "wobble in your legs"; it's a "comfortable" spot to "go online", watch TV or "wind down" "away from the family" when "all that blue sky and blue water get to be too much."

Goofy's Galley *Sandwiches* ▽ 19 | 16 | 21

Disney Magic, Disney Wonder | Counter service | Serves alcohol | B, L, D, S
Salads, "fresh" fruit and "delish" wraps make this "convenient", "no-frills" snack and sandwich bar near the Goofy pool fine for "a quick bite" and a "healthy" "alternative" to "heavier items" from counter-service places; soft-serve ice cream, panini and chicken nuggets please seafarers in more indulgent moods.

Lumiere's *Continental* 23 | 24 | 25

Disney Magic | Table service | Serves alcohol | B, L, D
A "distinctive" "escape from the madding crowd" on Deck 3 of the *Magic,* this "sister of [the *Wonder*'s] Triton's" is "first class all the way", with "excellent" "upscale" Continental dishes and "elegant, fairy-tale" art deco decor "inspired by *Beauty and the Beast*" that makes diners feel like Belle of the ball – an impression reinforced by the "extremely attentive" service.

Palo *Italian* 26 | 25 | 26

Disney Magic, Disney Wonder | Table service | Reservations: Required | Serves alcohol | D
"Something special on a cruise full of special", this "phenomenal" Northern Italian on Deck 10 of the *Magic* and the *Wonder* – voted No. 1 for Food and Service on DCL – "rivals top restaurants" on land or sea; "hide out from the kids for a night" in the "elegant", "relaxing" dining room with the "best view of the ocean on the ship" and let the "cream of the crop" staff "make you feel like the only ones" onboard; all in all, it's well "worth the extra $10 charge"; P.S. "make reservations as soon as you board."

Parrot Cay *Caribbean* 21 | 22 | 25

Disney Magic, Disney Wonder | Table service | Serves alcohol | B, L, D
Cruisers crow "you can almost feel the island breezes" at this "cheerfully decorated" "Bahamian-themed" spot where cast members "dance around and entertain" to "calypso rhythms"; the "islandy" Caribbean menu is "nothing too over the top" but mostly "done well", and it's especially appealing at breakfast, "when most of the young ones are at the Beach Blanket Buffet."

Pinocchio's Pizzeria *Pizza* ▽ 16 | 15 | 18

Disney Magic, Disney Wonder | Counter service | Serves alcohol | L, D
This counter near the Goofy pool slings "all-you-want" "Pizza Hut"-like slices (pepperoni, cheese and a daily special) while providing "much-needed relief from the heat"; though "pie snobs" complain of "doughy", "mediocre" fare, it's "good for the kids" and service is generally "very fast."

Room Service *Eclectic* 19 | 15 | 21

Disney Magic, Disney Wonder | Serves alcohol | B, L, D
While the ships' room service menu has a "limited selection" of Eclectic fare, concierge-level cruisers can "order anything from any of

the restaurants" onboard, "a secret" that lets them avoid "noisy dining rooms" or sate "3 AM cravings"; either way, "nothing compares" to dining "on your private veranda", especially when everything but the tip is part of the cruise package.

Topsider Buffet *Eclectic*   18 | 16 | 20

Disney Magic | Counter service | Serves alcohol | B, L, D

Cruisers "love the view" and "eating outside" at this "standard cruise buffet" in a "convenient location" on Deck 9 of the *Magic*; maybe the Eclectic fare's "nothing stellar", but there are "lots of choices" and it's a handy "alternative to the dining rooms" "when you don't want to get dressed up" – "just beware of being trampled on your way past the giant shrimp."

Triton's *Seafood*   24 | 24 | 26

Disney Wonder | Table service | Serves alcohol | B, L, D

You "feel like you're dining under the sea" seated below the "beautiful" "mosaic of Ariel and her friends" in this *Little Mermaid*–themed sea-fooder on Deck 3, where *Wonder* voyagers enjoy an experience "fit for a king" of the deep; with "excellent" food and "outstanding" service, it offers a "degree of elegance in a whirlwind of kids" – "show up in jeans and you'll feel underdressed."

Nightlife & Deck Parties

Ratings: Appeal, Decor, Service

Cadillac Lounge   23 | 23 | 23

Disney Wonder

Like "sitting in the coolest car you'll ever own", this "relaxing" lounge in the *Disney Wonder*'s Route 66 entertainment district is loaded with touches like chrome, Caddy fins and two-tone bucket seats lining the bar; "one of the very few quiet spots on the ship", it's "geared for adults" with "high-end liquors", champagne by the glass and caviar, and come evening it shifts into "piano bar" gear as a keyboardist revs up the "standards."

Diversions   22 | 22 | 22

Disney Magic, Disney Wonder

"Die-hard sports fans" can "relax" and never miss a play thanks to these laid-back bars in the fore of both DCL ships, where the big-screen plasma TVs show ESPN and team memorabilia decks the walls; even if the "game of your choice" isn't on, special tables for playing backgammon, checkers and chess provide substitute diversion.

Pirates In the Caribbean Deck Party   25 | 24 | 23

Disney Magic, Disney Wonder

A "high-seas" "highlight" "for all ages", this deckfest on the two Disney liners provides a "rollicking good time" "in the pirate spirit" with "loads of food", "dancing" and "character visits" featuring ship-mates from Captain Hook to "the main mouse himself" (who "flies be-tween the smokestacks"); to seal its appeal as "the best night" spent aboard, it's "topped off" by a "fireworks display off the bow" that's so "spectacular" "you'll be saying 'argggh' for days."

Rockin' Bar D

Disney Magic

▽ 21 | 19 | 22

Concert posters, LP covers and colored lights lend a roadhouse feel to this dance club/cabaret on the *Disney Magic*'s Beat Street, a D-tour for "adult entertainment" in the form of DJs, live pop bands and "themed" events like the '80s Time Warp or '70s Disco Party – i.e. all the makings for a "rockin'" night.

Sail Away Celebration

Disney Magic, Disney Wonder

26 | 24 | 23

The DCL ships "go all out" with this topside "bon voyage party", which "sets the tone" for an "energizing" adventure with "reasonably priced" "sail-away drinks", appearances by "Mickey and pals" and "dancing and music" for "adults and kids" alike; "the crew really gets things going" "on that Disney note": when they play "'When You Wish Upon a Star' from the ship's horns", "how can you not get excited?"

Sessions

Disney Magic

▽ 19 | 19 | 23

When it's time for "adults to hang out", this deco lounge on the *Magic*'s Beat Street provides "outstanding service" and "relaxing" vibes (think low lights, comfy seating and ocean-view portholes); personal listening stations by day and a jazzy evening pianist enhance the laid-back groove, and if action-seekers find it "the sleepiest" of spots, it's fine for a "chill-out" session after you "put the kids to bed."

WaveBands

Disney Wonder

22 | 20 | 21

Tune into some "entertainment for grown-ups" at this club in the Route 66 section of the *Disney Wonder,* where decor featuring vintage radios sets the stage for a "variety" of "themed" events like "karaoke", "'70s and '80s nights" and Top 40 DJs and live music; in the later hours it's "no kids allowed", so both cruisers and "crew members" can "party every night like it's 1999."

INDEXES

Park abbreviations run as follows: DAK=Disney's Animal Kingdom;
DD=Downtown Disney; DHS=Disney's Hollywood Studios;
MK= Magic Kingdom.

disneyworld.com | 407-824-4321   141

Attractions Types

Includes attraction names and locations. ⛤ indicates places with the highest ratings, popularity and importance.

ANIMATRONIC SHOW

Carousel of Progress | **MK, Tomorrowland**

Country Bear Jamboree | **MK, Frontierland**

Enchanted Tiki Room | **MK, Adventureland**

Hall of Presidents | **MK, Liberty Sq**

BOAT RIDE

NEW Gran Fiesta Tour | **Epcot, World Showcase**

it's a small world | **MK, Fantasyland**

Jungle Cruise | **MK, Adventureland**

Liberty Sq. Riverboat | **MK, Liberty Sq**

Living with the Land | **Epcot, Future World**

Maelstrom | **Epcot, World Showcase**

⛤ Pirates/Caribbean | **MK, Adventureland**

Sea Raycer Boats | **MK Area**

CAR/TRAM RIDE

⛤ Buzz Lightyear's Spin | **MK, Tomorrowland**

Great Movie Ride | **DHS, Hollywood Blvd**

⛤ Haunted Mansion | **MK, Liberty Sq**

Journey/Imagination | **Epcot, Future World**

⛤ Kilimanjaro Safaris | **DAK, Africa**

Many Adventures of Pooh | **MK, Fantasyland**

Peter Pan's Flight | **MK, Fantasyland**

⛤ Seas with Nemo | **Epcot, Future World**

Snow White/Adventures | **MK, Fantasyland**

Spaceship Earth | **Epcot, Future World**

Studio Backlot Tour | **DHS, Pixar Pl**

Tomorrowland Indy Spdwy. | **MK, Tomorrowland**

Tomorrowland Transit | **MK, Tomorrowland**

NEW Toy Story Mania! | **DHS, Pixar Pl**

Universe of Energy | **Epcot, Future World**

EXHIBIT

American Adventure | **Epcot, World Showcase**

Canada Pavilion | **Epcot, World Showcase**

China Pavilion | **Epcot, World Showcase**

Dino-Sue | **DAK, DinoLand**

France Pavilion | **Epcot, World Showcase**

Germany Pavilion | **Epcot, World Showcase**

Italy Pavilion | **Epcot, World Showcase**

Japan Pavilion | **Epcot, World Showcase**

Leave a Legacy | **Epcot, Future World**

Mexico Pavilion | **Epcot, World Showcase**

Morocco Pavilion | **Epcot, World Showcase**

Norway Pavilion | **Epcot, World Showcase**

United Kingdom Pavilion | **Epcot, World Showcase**

FIREWORKS

IllumiNations | **Epcot, World Showcase**

⛤ Wishes Spectacular | **MK Park**

FLUME/WHITEWATER

Kali River Rapids | **DAK, Asia**

⛤ Splash Mountain | **MK, Frontierland**

INTERACTIVE ATTRACTION

Affection Section | **DAK, Africa**

Ariel's Grotto | **MK, Fantasyland**

Boneyard | **DAK, DinoLand**

Camp Minnie-Mickey Trails | **DAK, Minnie-Mickey**

Conservation Station | **DAK, Africa**

Discovery Is. Trails | **DAK, Discovery Is**

Donald's Boat | **MK, Toontown**

Fairytale Garden | **MK, Fantasyland**

Habitat Habit! | **DAK, Africa**

Honey, I Shrunk/Kids | **DHS,
Sts of America**
ImageWorks | **Epcot, Future World**
Innoventions | **Epcot, Future World**
NEW Journey/Narnia | **DHS,
Pixar Pl**
Judge's Tent | **MK, Toontown**
Kidcot Fun Stops | **Epcot,
World Showcase**
Maharajah Jungle Trek | **DAK, Asia**
Mickey's Country Hse. | **MK,
Toontown**
Minnie's Country Hse. | **MK,
Toontown**
Monsters, Inc. | **MK, Tomorrowland**
Oasis Exhibits | **DAK, Oasis**
Pangani Forest | **DAK, Africa**
Pooh's Playful Spot | **MK,
Fantasyland**
Swiss Family Treehse. | **MK,
Adventureland**
Tom Sawyer Is. | **MK, Frontierland**
Toontown Hall/Fame | **MK,
Toontown**
Z Turtle Talk | **Epcot, Future World**
Walt Disney: One Man's Dream |
DHS, Pixar Pl

LIVE SHOW

Beauty/Beast | **DHS, Sunset Blvd**
NEW Block Party Bash | **DHS Park**
British Invasion | **Epcot,
World Showcase**
Cirque du Soleil | **DD, W Side**
Disney Dreams | **MK Park**
Dragon Legend Acrobats | **Epcot,
World Showcase**
Dream with Mickey | **MK,
Fantasyland**
Z Fantasmic! | **DHS, Sunset Blvd**
Z Festival of the Lion King | **DAK,
Minnie-Mickey**
Finding Nemo: The Musical | **DAK,
DinoLand**
Indiana Jones | **DHS, Echo Lake**
JAMMitors | **Epcot, Future World**
Lights, Motors, Action! | **DHS,
Sts of America**
Magic/Disney Animation | **DHS,
Animation Courtyard**
Mariachi Cobre | **Epcot,
World Showcase**
Matsuriza | **Epcot, World Showcase**
Mickey's Jammin' Parade | **DAK,
Africa**
Miyuki | **Epcot, World Showcase**

MO'ROCKIN | **Epcot, World Showcase**
Off Kilter | **Epcot, World Showcase**
Oktoberfest Musik | **Epcot,
World Showcase**
Pam Brody | **Epcot,
World Showcase**
Z Playhouse Disney | **DHS,
Animation Courtyard**
Pocahontas/Friends | **DAK,
Minnie-Mickey**
SpectroMagic Parade | **MK Park**
Spirit of America Fife | **Epcot,
World Showcase**
Voices of Liberty | **Epcot,
World Showcase**
Voyage/Little Mermaid | **DHS,
Animation Courtyard**
World Showcase Players | **Epcot,
World Showcase**

MINI-GOLF

Disney's Winter Summerland |
Blizzard Bch
Fantasia Gardens | **Epcot Area**

MOVIE/MULTIMEDIA

Circle of Life | **Epcot, Future World**
Honey I Shrunk/Audience | **Epcot,
Future World**
Impressions de France | **Epcot,
World Showcase**
It's Tough/Bug | **DAK, Discovery Is**
Z Mickey's PhilharMagic | **MK,
Fantasyland**
Muppet Vision 3-D | **DHS,
Sts of America**
O Canada! | **Epcot,
World Showcase**
Reflections of China | **Epcot,
World Showcase**
Sounds Dangerous | **DHS,
Echo Lake**
Stitch's Great Escape! | **MK,
Tomorrowland**

POOL

Castaway Creek | **Typhoon Lagoon**
Cross Country Creek | **Blizzard Bch**
Ketchakiddee Creek |
Typhoon Lagoon
Melt-Away Bay | **Blizzard Bch**
Shark Reef | **Typhoon Lagoon**
Ski Patrol Training | **Blizzard Bch**
Tike's Peak | **Blizzard Bch**
Z Typhoon Lagoon Pool |
Typhoon Lagoon

ROLLER COASTER/ THRILL RIDE

Barnstormer Goofy's | **MK, Toontown**

Ⓩ Big Thunder Mtn. | **MK, Frontierland**

Ⓩ DINOSAUR | **DAK, DinoLand**

Ⓩ Expedition Everest | **DAK, Asia**

Ⓩ Mission: SPACE | **Epcot, Future World**

Primeval Whirl | **DAK, DinoLand**

Ⓩ Rock 'n' Roller Coaster | **DHS, Sunset Blvd**

Ⓩ Space Mountain | **MK, Tomorrowland**

Star Tours | **DHS, Echo Lake**

Ⓩ Test Track | **Epcot, Future World**

Ⓩ Twilight Zone Tower | **DHS, Sunset Blvd**

SIMULATOR

Ⓩ Soarin' | **Epcot, Future World**

SPINNING/ ORBITING RIDE

Astro Orbiter | **MK, Tomorrowland**

Cinderella's Carrousel | **MK, Fantasyland**

Dumbo | **MK, Fantasyland**

Mad Tea Party | **MK, Fantasyland**

Magic Carpets/Aladdin | **MK, Adventureland**

TriceraTop Spin | **DAK, DinoLand**

TOUR

Around the World Segway | **Epcot, World Showcase**

Backstage Magic | **multi.**

Backstage Safari | **DAK Park**

Behind the Seeds | **Epcot, Future World**

Disney's Family Magic | **MK Park**

Disney's Keys/Kingdom | **MK Park**

Disney's Magic/Trains | **MK Park**

Dolphins in Depth | **Epcot, Future World**

Epcot DiveQuest | **Epcot, Future World**

Epcot Seas Aqua | **Epcot, Future World**

UnDISCOVERed Future | **Epcot, Future World**

VIP Tour | **multi.**

Yuletide Fantasy | **Epcot, Future World**

TRAIN

Walt Disney Railroad | **MK, Main St**

WATERSLIDE

Bay Slides | **Typhoon Lagoon**

Ⓩ Crush 'n' Gusher | **Typhoon Lagoon**

Downhill Double Dipper | **Blizzard Bch**

Gangplank Falls | **Typhoon Lagoon**

Ⓩ Humunga Kowabunga | **Typhoon Lagoon**

Keelhaul Falls | **Typhoon Lagoon**

Mayday Falls | **Typhoon Lagoon**

Runoff Rapids | **Blizzard Bch**

Slush Gusher | **Blizzard Bch**

Snow Stormers | **Blizzard Bch**

Storm Slides | **Typhoon Lagoon**

Ⓩ Summit Plummet | **Blizzard Bch**

Ⓩ Teamboat Springs | **Blizzard Bch**

Toboggan Racers | **Blizzard Bch**

OTHER TYPES OF ATTRACTIONS

Chairlift | Chair Lift | **Blizzard Bch**

DisneyQuest | Arcade | **DD, W Side**

Parasailing | Parasailing | **MK Area**

Ⓩ Richard Petty Driving | NASCAR Racing | **MK Area**

Sandy White Beach | Beach | **Typhoon Lagoon**

Wide World/Sports | Sports Venue | **MK Area**

Attractions Special Features

Includes attraction names and locations. ☑ indicates places with the highest ratings, popularity and importance.

ADDITIONS

(Properties added since the last edition of the book)

Block Party Bash | **DHS Park**

Gran Fiesta Tour | **Epcot, World Showcase**

Journey/Narnia | **DHS, Pixar Pl**

Toy Story Mania! | **DHS, Pixar Pl**

EDUCATIONAL

Carousel of Progress | **MK, Tomorrowland**

Circle of Life | **Epcot, Future World**

Conservation Station | **DAK, Africa**

☑ DINOSAUR | **DAK, DinoLand**

Dolphins in Depth | **Epcot, Future World**

Epcot DiveQuest | **Epcot, Future World**

Epcot Seas Aqua | **Epcot, Future World**

Habitat Habit! | **DAK, Africa**

Hall of Presidents | **MK, Liberty Sq**

Innoventions | **Epcot, Future World**

Kidcot Fun Stops | **Epcot, World Showcase**

☑ Kilimanjaro Safaris | **DAK, Africa**

Living with the Land | **Epcot, Future World**

Magic/Disney Animation | **DHS, Animation Courtyard**

Maharajah Jungle Trek | **DAK, Asia**

Pangani Forest | **DAK, Africa**

Shark Reef | **Typhoon Lagoon**

Spaceship Earth | **Epcot, Future World**

Universe of Energy | **Epcot, Future World**

Walt Disney: One Man's Dream | **DHS, Pixar Pl**

GUIDED TOURS

Around the World Segway | **Epcot, World Showcase**

Backstage Magic | **multi.**

Backstage Safari | **DAK Park**

Behind the Seeds | **Epcot, Future World**

Disney's Family Magic | **MK Park**

Disney's Keys/Kingdom | **MK Park**

Epcot Seas Aqua | **Epcot, Future World**

VIP Tour | **multi.**

MUST-SEES

☑ Big Thunder Mtn. | **MK, Frontierland**

☑ Buzz Lightyear's Spin | **MK, Tomorrowland**

Cirque du Soleil | **DD, W Side**

☑ Crush 'n' Gusher | **Typhoon Lagoon**

☑ DINOSAUR | **DAK, DinoLand**

☑ Expedition Everest | **DAK, Asia**

☑ Fantasmic! | **DHS, Sunset Blvd**

☑ Festival of the Lion King | **DAK, Minnie-Mickey**

☑ Haunted Mansion | **MK, Liberty Sq**

☑ Humunga Kowabunga | **Typhoon Lagoon**

IllumiNations | **Epcot, World Showcase**

☑ Kilimanjaro Safaris | **DAK, Africa**

☑ Mickey's PhilharMagic | **MK, Fantasyland**

☑ Mission: SPACE | **Epcot, Future World**

☑ Pirates/Caribbean | **MK, Adventureland**

☑ Rock 'n' Roller Coaster | **DHS, Sunset Blvd**

☑ Soarin' | **Epcot, Future World**

☑ Space Mountain | **MK, Tomorrowland**

☑ Splash Mountain | **MK, Frontierland**

☑ Summit Plummet | **Blizzard Bch**

☑ Test Track | **Epcot, Future World**

☑ Twilight Zone Tower | **DHS, Sunset Blvd**

RAINY DAY APPROPRIATE

Carousel of Progress | **MK, Tomorrowland**

Country Bear Jamboree | **MK, Frontierland**

DisneyQuest | **DD, W Side**

NEW Gran Fiesta Tour | **Epcot, World Showcase**

Great Movie Ride | **DHS,
Hollywood Blvd**

Hall of Presidents | **MK, Liberty Sq**

Honey I Shrunk/Audience | **Epcot,
Future World**

ImageWorks | **Epcot, Future World**

Innoventions | **Epcot, Future World**

Living with the Land | **Epcot,
Future World**

Magic/Disney Animation | **DHS,
Animation Courtyard**

Ⓩ Mickey's PhilharMagic | **MK,
Fantasyland**

Ⓩ Mission: SPACE | **Epcot,
Future World**

Muppet Vision 3-D | **DHS,
Sts of America**

Ⓩ Pirates/Caribbean | **MK,
Adventureland**

Ⓩ Playhouse Disney | **DHS,
Animation Courtyard**

Spaceship Earth | **Epcot,
Future World**

🆕 Toy Story Mania! | **DHS,
Pixar Pl**

Ⓩ Turtle Talk | **Epcot, Future World**

Universe of Energy | **Epcot,
Future World**

Voyage/Little Mermaid | **DHS,
Animation Courtyard**

Walt Disney: One Man's Dream |
DHS, Pixar Pl

TEENS TOO
(13 & Above)

Ⓩ DINOSAUR | **DAK, DinoLand**

DisneyQuest | **DD, W Side**

Dolphins in Depth | **Epcot,
Future World**

Ⓩ Expedition Everest | **DAK, Asia**

Ⓩ Humunga Kowabunga |
Typhoon Lagoon

Kali River Rapids | **DAK, Asia**

Ⓩ Kilimanjaro Safaris | **DAK, Africa**

Lights, Motors, Action! | **DHS,
Sts of America**

Ⓩ Mission: SPACE | **Epcot,
Future World**

Parasailing | **MK Area**

Ⓩ Rock 'n' Roller Coaster | **DHS,
Sunset Blvd**

Ⓩ Space Mountain | **MK,
Tomorrowland**

Ⓩ Splash Mountain | **MK,
Frontierland**

Star Tours | **DHS, Echo Lake**

Ⓩ Summit Plummet | **Blizzard Bch**

Ⓩ Test Track | **Epcot, Future World**

Ⓩ Twilight Zone Tower | **DHS,
Sunset Blvd**

TODDLERS
(3 & Under)

Affection Section | **DAK, Africa**

Ariel's Grotto | **MK, Fantasyland**

Astro Orbiter | **MK, Tomorrowland**

🆕 Block Party Bash | **DHS Park**

Boneyard | **DAK, DinoLand**

Ⓩ Buzz Lightyear's Spin | **MK,
Tomorrowland**

Camp Minnie-Mickey Trails | **DAK,
Minnie-Mickey**

Cinderella's Carrousel | **MK,
Fantasyland**

Disney Dreams | **MK Park**

Dumbo | **MK, Fantasyland**

Fairytale Garden | **MK, Fantasyland**

Ⓩ Festival of the Lion King | **DAK,
Minnie-Mickey**

🆕 Gran Fiesta Tour | **Epcot,
World Showcase**

it's a small world | **MK, Fantasyland**

Judge's Tent | **MK, Toontown**

Ketchakiddee Creek |
Typhoon Lagoon

Magic Carpets/Aladdin | **MK,
Adventureland**

Many Adventures of Pooh | **MK,
Fantasyland**

Ⓩ Playhouse Disney | **DHS,
Animation Courtyard**

Pooh's Playful Spot | **MK,
Fantasyland**

Ⓩ Seas with Nemo | **Epcot,
Future World**

SpectroMagic Parade | **MK Park**

Tike's Peak | **Blizzard Bch**

Toontown Hall/Fame | **MK,
Toontown**

Ⓩ Turtle Talk | **Epcot, Future World**

Voyage/Little Mermaid | **DHS,
Animation Courtyard**

Ⓩ Wishes Spectacular | **MK Park**

YOUNG CHILDREN
(Ages 4–7)

Barnstormer Goofy's | **MK,
Toontown**

🆕 Block Party Bash | **DHS Park**

Ⓩ Buzz Lightyear's Spin | **MK,
Tomorrowland**

Camp Minnie-Mickey Trails | **DAK, Minnie-Mickey**

Cinderella's Carrousel | **MK, Fantasyland**

Disney's Family Magic | **MK Park**

Disney's Winter Summerland | **Blizzard Bch**

Dumbo | **MK, Fantasyland**

Ⓩ Festival of the Lion King | **DAK, Minnie-Mickey**

NEW Gran Fiesta Tour | **Epcot, World Showcase**

Ketchakiddee Creek | **Typhoon Lagoon**

Kidcot Fun Stops | **Epcot, World Showcase**

Ⓩ Kilimanjaro Safaris | **DAK, Africa**

Many Adventures of Pooh | **MK, Fantasyland**

Ⓩ Playhouse Disney | **DHS, Animation Courtyard**

Pooh's Playful Spot | **MK, Fantasyland**

Primeval Whirl | **DAK, DinoLand**

SpectroMagic Parade | **MK Park**

Ⓩ Teamboat Springs | **Blizzard Bch**

Tike's Peak | **Blizzard Bch**

Tomorrowland Indy Spdwy. | **MK, Tomorrowland**

Ⓩ Turtle Talk | **Epcot, Future World**

Ⓩ Wishes Spectacular | **MK Park**

Dining Cuisines

Includes restaurant names and locations. ☑ indicates places with the highest ratings, popularity and importance.

AFRICAN

☑ Boma | **DAK Area**
☑ Jiko/Cooking Place | **DAK Area**
Tusker House | **DAK, Africa**

AMERICAN (NEW)

☑ Flying Fish Cafe | **Epcot Area**
☑ Victoria & Albert's | **MK Area**

AMERICAN (TRADITIONAL)

Artist's Palette | **DD Area**
Backlot Express | **DHS, Sts of America**
Beach Club Mktpl. | **Epcot Area**
Beaches & Cream | **Epcot Area**
Big River Grille | **Epcot Area**
Cape May Cafe | **Epcot Area**
Captain's Grille | **Epcot Area**
Capt. Cook's | **MK Area**
Columbia Harbour Hse. | **MK, Liberty Sq**
Cosmic Ray's Starlight Cafe | **MK, Tomorrowland**
Earl of Sandwich | **DD, Mktpl**
Electric Umbrella | **Epcot, Future World**
End Zone Food Ct. | **DAK Area**
ESPN Club | **Epcot Area**
Everything Pop | **DAK Area**
☑ 50's Prime Time | **DHS, Echo Lake**
FoodQuest | **DD, W Side**
Garden Grove Cafe | **Epcot Area**
Gasparilla Grill | **MK Area**
Ghirardelli | **DD, Mktpl**
Grand Floridian | **MK Area**
Harambe Fruit Mkt. | **DAK, Africa**
Hollywood & Vine | **DHS, Hollywood Blvd**
☑ Hollywood Brown Derby | **DHS, Hollywood Blvd**
Intermission Food Ct. | **DAK Area**
Liberty Tree | **MK, Liberty Sq**
Lunching Pad | **MK, Tomorrowland**
Mara, The | **DAK Area**
Old Port Royale | **Epcot Area**
Olivia's Cafe | **DD Area**
Pecos Bill Café | **MK, Frontierland**
Pinocchio Vill. | **MK, Fantasyland**
Pizzafari | **DAK, Discovery Is**

Planet Hollywood | **DD, W Side**
Plaza Rest. | **MK, Main St**
Rainforest Cafe | **multi.**
NEW Riverside Mill Food Ct. | **DD Area**
Roaring Fork | **MK Area**
Rosie's All-American | **DHS, Sunset Blvd**
Sandtrap B&G | **MK Area**
Sassagoula Floatworks | **DD Area**
Sci-Fi Dine-In Theater | **DHS, Echo Lake**
Shutter's/Port Royale | **Epcot Area**
Starring Rolls | **DHS, Sunset Blvd**
Toluca Turkey | **DHS, Sunset Blvd**
Tomorrowland Terr. Noodle | **MK, Tomorrowland**
Trail's End | **MK Area**
NEW Turf Club Bar & Grill | **DD Area**
Tusker House | **DAK, Africa**
Whispering Canyon | **MK Area**
World Premiere Food Ct. | **DAK Area**

ASIAN

Tomorrowland Terr. Noodle | **MK, Tomorrowland**
NEW Yak & Yeti | **DAK, Asia**

BAKERIES

Boulangerie Pâtisserie | **Epcot, World Showcase**
Kringla Bakeri Og | **Epcot, World Showcase**
Main St. Bakery | **MK, Main St**
Wetzel's Pretzels | **DD, W Side**

BARBECUE

Flame Tree BBQ | **DAK, Discovery Is**
Whispering Canyon | **MK Area**

BRITISH

Garden View Lounge | **MK Area**
Rose & Crown | **Epcot, World Showcase**
Yorkshire County Fish | **Epcot, World Showcase**

CAJUN

House of Blues | **DD, W Side**
NEW Riverside Mill Food Ct. | **DD Area**

CALIFORNIAN

☑ California Grill | **MK Area**
☑ Hollywood Brown Derby | **DHS, Hollywood Blvd**
Wolfgang Puck Café | **DD, W Side**
Wolfgang Puck Express | **DD, Mktpl**

CANADIAN

☑ Le Cellier Steak | **Epcot, World Showcase**

CHINESE

Lotus Blossom | **Epcot, World Showcase**
Nine Dragons | **Epcot, World Showcase**

CUBAN

Bongos Cuban Cafe | **DD, W Side**

ECLECTIC

ABC Commissary | **DHS, Hollywood Blvd**
Mara, The | **DAK Area**
Pepper Mkt. | **DD Area**
Sunshine Season | **Epcot, World Showcase**

FRENCH

Bistro de Paris | **Epcot, World Showcase**
Boulangerie Pâtisserie | **Epcot, World Showcase**
Chefs de France | **Epcot, World Showcase**

GERMAN

Biergarten/Sommerfest | **Epcot, World Showcase**

HAWAIIAN

Kona Cafe | **MK Area**
'Ohana | **MK Area**

HEALTH FOOD

Harambe Fruit Mkt. | **DAK, Africa**

HOT DOGS

Casey's Corner | **MK, Main St**

ICE CREAM/DESSERT

Auntie Gravity's | **MK, Tomorrowland**
Enchanted Grove | **MK, Fantasyland**
Ghirardelli | **DD, Mktpl**
Plaza Ice Cream | **MK, Main St**

IRISH

Raglan Road | **DD, Pleasure Is**

ITALIAN

Il Mulino New York | **Epcot Area**
Mama Melrose's | **DHS, Sts of America**
Pizzafari | **DAK, Discovery Is**
Portobello Yacht Club | **DD, Pleasure Is**
Tony's Town Sq. | **MK, Main St**
NEW Tutto Italia | **Epcot, World Showcase**

JAPANESE

(* sushi specialist)
Kimonos* | **Epcot Area**
Teppan Edo | **Epcot, World Showcase**
Tokyo Dining* | **Epcot, World Showcase**
Yakitori Hse. | **Epcot, World Showcase**

MEDITERRANEAN

Cítricos | **MK Area**
Fresh Med. Mkt. | **Epcot Area**
Spoodles | **Epcot Area**
Studio Catering | **DHS, Echo Lake**

MEXICAN

El Pirata/El Perico | **MK, Adventureland**
San Angel Inn | **Epcot, World Showcase**

MOROCCAN

Rest. Marrakesh | **Epcot, World Showcase**
Tangierine | **Epcot, World Showcase**

NORWEGIAN

Kringla Bakeri Og | **Epcot, World Showcase**

NUEVO LATINO

Maya Grill | **DD Area**

PACIFIC NORTHWEST

☑ Artist Point | **MK Area**

PIZZA

Pizzafari | **DAK, Discovery Is**
Toy Story Pizza | **DHS, Sts of America**

SANDWICHES

Artist's Palette | **DD Area**
Earl of Sandwich | **DD, Mktpl**
Starring Rolls | **DHS, Sunset Blvd**

SEAFOOD

Cape May Cafe | **Epcot Area**
Cap'n Jack's | **DD, Mktpl**
Columbia Harbour Hse. | **MK,
    Liberty Sq**
Coral Reef | **Epcot, Future World**
🆉 Flying Fish Cafe | **Epcot Area**
Fulton's Crab Hse. | **DD, Pleasure Is**
Narcoossee's | **MK Area**
🆉 Todd English's bluezoo |
    Epcot Area
🆉 Yachtsman Steak | **Epcot Area**

SOUTHERN

Boatwright's | **DD Area**
House of Blues | **DD, W Side**

STEAKHOUSES

Captain's Grille | **Epcot Area**
🆉 Le Cellier Steak | **Epcot,
    World Showcase**
Shula's Steak | **Epcot Area**
🆉 Yachtsman Steak | **Epcot Area**

TEAROOMS

Garden View Lounge | **MK Area**

Dining Special Features

Listings cover the best in each category and include restaurant names and locations. Multi-location restaurants' features may vary by branch.
☑ indicates places with the highest ratings, popularity and importance.

ADDITIONS

(Properties added since the last edition of the book)
Riverside Mill Food Ct. | **DD Area**
Turf Club Bar & Grill | **DD Area**
Tutto Italia | **Epcot, World Showcase**
Yak & Yeti | **DAK, Asia**

ADULT APPEAL

☑ Artist Point | **MK Area**
Big River Grille | **Epcot Area**
☑ California Grill | **MK Area**
Chefs de France | **Epcot,
World Showcase**
Cítricos | **MK Area**
Coral Reef | **Epcot, Future World**
ESPN Club | **Epcot Area**
☑ Flying Fish Cafe | **Epcot Area**
Fresh Med. Mkt. | **Epcot Area**
☑ Hollywood Brown Derby | **DHS,
Hollywood Blvd**
House of Blues | **DD, W Side**
☑ Jiko/Cooking Place | **DAK Area**
Kimonos | **Epcot Area**
Narcoossee's | **MK Area**
Raglan Road | **DD, Pleasure Is**
Shula's Steak | **Epcot Area**
Tangierine | **Epcot,
World Showcase**
Teppan Edo | **Epcot,
World Showcase**
Tokyo Dining | **Epcot,
World Showcase**

BREAKFAST

(Other than hotels)
Pizzafari | **DAK, Discovery Is**
Spoodles | **Epcot Area**
Starring Rolls | **DHS, Sunset Blvd**
Sunshine Season | **Epcot,
World Showcase**

BRUNCH

☑ Boma | **DAK Area**
House of Blues | **DD, W Side**

BUFFET SERVED

(Check availability)
Biergarten/Sommerfest | **Epcot,
World Showcase**
☑ Boma | **DAK Area**

Cape May Cafe | **Epcot Area**
Fresh Med. Mkt. | **Epcot Area**
Garden Grove Cafe | **Epcot Area**
Hollywood & Vine | **DHS,
Hollywood Blvd**
House of Blues | **DD, W Side**

DESSERT

☑ Artist Point | **MK Area**
Beaches & Cream | **Epcot Area**
Bistro de Paris | **Epcot,
World Showcase**
Boulangerie Pâtisserie | **Epcot,
World Showcase**
☑ California Grill | **MK Area**
Cítricos | **MK Area**
FoodQuest | **DD, W Side**
Ghirardelli | **DD, Mktpl**
Kringla Bakeri Og | **Epcot,
World Showcase**
Main St. Bakery | **MK, Main St**
Plaza Ice Cream | **MK, Main St**
Starring Rolls | **DHS, Sunset Blvd**
☑ Victoria & Albert's | **MK Area**

DINING ALONE

(Other than hotels and places with counter service)
☑ Flying Fish Cafe | **Epcot Area**
Wolfgang Puck Café | **DD, W Side**

ENTERTAINMENT

(Call for days and times of performances)
Biergarten/Sommerfest | **Bavarian
music | Epcot, World Showcase**
Garden View Lounge | piano |
MK Area
House of Blues | bands | **DD, W Side**
Kimonos | karaoke | **Epcot Area**
Planet Hollywood | DJ | **DD, W Side**
Raglan Road | Irish bands | **DD,
Pleasure Is**
☑ Victoria & Albert's | harpist |
MK Area

FAMILY-STYLE

Biergarten/Sommerfest | **Epcot,
World Showcase**
☑ Boma | **DAK Area**
Cape May Cafe | **Epcot Area**

Hollywood & Vine | **DHS, Hollywood Blvd**
Liberty Tree | **MK, Liberty Sq**
Mama Melrose's | **DHS, Sts of America**
Nine Dragons | **Epcot, World Showcase**
'Ohana | **MK Area**
Teppan Edo | **Epcot, World Showcase**
Whispering Canyon | **MK Area**

LATE DINING

(Weekday closing hour)
Big River Grille | 12:30 AM | **Epcot Area**
Bongos Cuban Cafe | 11:30 PM | **DD, W Side**
Capt. Cook's | 24 hrs. | **MK Area**
End Zone Food Ct. | 12 AM | **DAK Area**
ESPN Club | 1 AM | **Epcot Area**
Everything Pop | 12 AM | **DAK Area**
Gasparilla Grill | 24 hrs. | **MK Area**
House of Blues | 2 AM | **DD, W Side**
Intermission Food Ct. | 12 AM | **DAK Area**
Kimonos | 12 AM | **Epcot Area**
Planet Hollywood | 2 AM | **DD, W Side**
Raglan Road | 1:30 AM | **DD, Pleasure Is**
NEW Riverside Mill Food Ct. | 12 AM | **DD Area**
Roaring Fork | 12 AM | **MK Area**
Sassagoula Floatworks | 12 AM | **DD Area**
Spoodles | 12 AM | **Epcot Area**
World Premiere Food Ct. | 11:30 PM | **DAK Area**

LOCAL FAVORITES

Z Artist Point | **MK Area**
Big River Grille | **Epcot Area**
Z Boma | **DAK Area**
Bongos Cuban Cafe | **DD, W Side**
Cap'n Jack's | **DD, Mktpl**
Z Flying Fish Cafe | **Epcot Area**
Fulton's Crab Hse. | **DD, Pleasure Is**
Z Hollywood Brown Derby | **DHS, Hollywood Blvd**
House of Blues | **DD, W Side**
Z Jiko/Cooking Place | **DAK Area**
Planet Hollywood | **DD, W Side**
Portobello Yacht Club | **DD, Pleasure Is**

Shula's Steak | **Epcot Area**
Z Todd English's bluezoo | **Epcot Area**
Z Victoria & Albert's | **MK Area**
Wolfgang Puck Café | **DD, W Side**
Z Yachtsman Steak | **Epcot Area**

MEET FOR A DRINK

Big River Grille | **Epcot Area**
Bongos Cuban Cafe | **DD, W Side**
Z California Grill | **MK Area**
Cítricos | **MK Area**
Z Flying Fish Cafe | **Epcot Area**
Fulton's Crab Hse. | **DD, Pleasure Is**
Kimonos | **Epcot Area**
Narcoossee's | **MK Area**
Portobello Yacht Club | **DD, Pleasure Is**
Rose & Crown | **Epcot, World Showcase**
Z Todd English's bluezoo | **Epcot Area**
NEW Turf Club Bar & Grill | **DD Area**
NEW Yak & Yeti | **DAK, Asia**

NOTABLE CHEFS

Z Todd English's bluezoo | *Todd English* | **Epcot Area**
Z Victoria & Albert's | *Scott Hunnel* | **MK Area**
Wolfgang Puck Café | *Wolfgang Puck* | **DD, W Side**

OUTDOOR DINING

(G=garden; P=patio; S=sidewalk; T=terrace)
Bongos Cuban Cafe | T | **DD, W Side**
Boulangerie Pâtisserie | S | **Epcot, World Showcase**
Flame Tree BBQ | P | **DAK, Discovery Is**
Z Hollywood Brown Derby | P | **DHS, Hollywood Blvd**
Kringla Bakeri Og | P | **Epcot, World Showcase**
Lotus Blossom | P | **Epcot, World Showcase**
Portobello Yacht Club | P | **DD, Pleasure Is**
NEW Riverside Mill Food Ct. | S | **DD Area**
Rose & Crown | P | **Epcot, World Showcase**
NEW Turf Club Bar & Grill | P | **DD Area**

NEW Tutto Italia | P | **Epcot, World Showcase**
Wolfgang Puck Café | P | **DD, W Side**
NEW Yak & Yeti | G | **DAK, Asia**

PRIX FIXE MENUS

(Call for prices and times)
Chefs de France | **Epcot, World Showcase**
☑ Victoria & Albert's | **MK Area**

QUICK BITES

ABC Commissary | **DHS, Hollywood Blvd**
Artist's Palette | **DD Area**
Auntie Gravity's | **MK, Tomorrowland**
Backlot Express | **DHS, Sts of America**
Beach Club Mktpl. | **Epcot Area**
Beaches & Cream | **Epcot Area**
Big River Grille | **Epcot Area**
Boulangerie Pâtisserie | **Epcot, World Showcase**
Cap'n Jack's | **DD, Mktpl**
Captain's Grille | **Epcot Area**
Capt. Cook's | **MK Area**
Casey's Corner | **MK, Main St**
Cosmic Ray's Starlight Cafe | **MK, Tomorrowland**
Earl of Sandwich | **DD, Mktpl**
Electric Umbrella | **Epcot, Future World**
El Pirata/El Perico | **MK, Adventureland**
Enchanted Grove | **MK, Fantasyland**
ESPN Club | **Epcot Area**
Flame Tree BBQ | **DAK, Discovery Is**
FoodQuest | **DD, W Side**
Gasparilla Grill | **MK Area**
Ghirardelli | **DD, Mktpl**
Harambe Fruit Mkt. | **DAK, Africa**
Kringla Bakeri Og | **Epcot, World Showcase**
Lotus Blossom | **Epcot, World Showcase**
Lunching Pad | **MK, Tomorrowland**
Main St. Bakery | **MK, Main St**
Mara, The | **DAK Area**
Old Port Royale | **Epcot Area**
Pecos Bill Café | **MK, Frontierland**
Pepper Mkt. | **DD Area**
Pinocchio Vill. | **MK, Fantasyland**
Pizzafari | **DAK, Discovery Is**

Plaza Ice Cream | **MK, Main St**
NEW Riverside Mill Food Ct. | **DD Area**
Roaring Fork | **MK Area**
Rosie's All-American | **DHS, Sunset Blvd**
Sassagoula Floatworks | **DD Area**
Starring Rolls | **DHS, Sunset Blvd**
Studio Catering | **DHS, Echo Lake**
Sunshine Season | **Epcot, World Showcase**
Tangierine | **Epcot, World Showcase**
Teppan Edo | **Epcot, World Showcase**
Toluca Turkey | **DHS, Sunset Blvd**
Tomorrowland Terr. Noodle | **MK, Tomorrowland**
Toy Story Pizza | **DHS, Sts of America**
Trail's End | **MK Area**
Wetzel's Pretzels | **DD, W Side**
Wolfgang Puck Express | **DD, Mktpl**
NEW Yak & Yeti | **DAK, Asia**
Yakitori Hse. | **Epcot, World Showcase**
Yorkshire County Fish | **Epcot, World Showcase**

QUIET CONVERSATION

☑ Artist Point | **MK Area**
Bistro de Paris | **Epcot, World Showcase**
Cap'n Jack's | **DD, Mktpl**
Cítricos | **MK Area**
Fresh Med. Mkt. | **Epcot Area**
☑ Jiko/Cooking Place | **DAK Area**
Kimonos | **Epcot Area**
Olivia's Cafe | **DD Area**
Sandtrap B&G | **MK Area**
☑ Victoria & Albert's | **MK Area**

ROMANTIC PLACES

Bistro de Paris | **Epcot, World Showcase**
☑ California Grill | **MK Area**
Cítricos | **MK Area**
Coral Reef | **Epcot, Future World**
☑ Flying Fish Cafe | **Epcot Area**
Kimonos | **Epcot Area**
☑ Todd English's bluezoo | **Epcot Area**
Tokyo Dining | **Epcot, World Showcase**
☑ Victoria & Albert's | **MK Area**

SPECIAL OCCASIONS

Bistro de Paris | **Epcot, World Showcase**
Bongos Cuban Cafe | **DD, W Side**
🔁 California Grill | **MK Area**
Cítricos | **MK Area**
Garden View Lounge | **MK Area**
🔁 Hollywood Brown Derby | **DHS, Hollywood Blvd**
🔁 Jiko/Cooking Place | **DAK Area**
🔁 Todd English's bluezoo | **Epcot Area**
🔁 Victoria & Albert's | **MK Area**
🔁 Yachtsman Steak | **Epcot Area**

TEEN APPEAL

Auntie Gravity's | **MK, Tomorrowland**
Backlot Express | **DHS, Sts of America**
Beaches & Cream | **Epcot Area**
Capt. Cook's | **MK Area**
Casey's Corner | **MK, Main St**
Cosmic Ray's Starlight Cafe | **MK, Tomorrowland**
Electric Umbrella | **Epcot, Future World**
El Pirata/El Perico | **MK, Adventureland**
ESPN Club | **Epcot Area**
🔁 50's Prime Time | **DHS, Echo Lake**
Gasparilla Grill | **MK Area**
Ghirardelli | **DD, Mktpl**
Mama Melrose's | **DHS, Sts of America**
Mara, The | **DAK Area**
Old Port Royale | **Epcot Area**
Pecos Bill Café | **MK, Frontierland**
Planet Hollywood | **DD, W Side**
Rainforest Cafe | **multi.**
Sci-Fi Dine-In Theater | **DHS, Echo Lake**
Sunshine Season | **Epcot, World Showcase**
Teppan Edo | **Epcot, World Showcase**

THEME RESTAURANTS

🔁 Artist Point | **MK Area**
Beaches & Cream | **Epcot Area**
Biergarten/Sommerfest | **Epcot, World Showcase**
Boatwright's | **DD Area**
🔁 Boma | **DAK Area**
Cape May Cafe | **Epcot Area**

Coral Reef | **Epcot, Future World**
ESPN Club | **Epcot Area**
🔁 50's Prime Time | **DHS, Echo Lake**
Fulton's Crab Hse. | **DD, Pleasure Is**
🔁 Hollywood Brown Derby | **DHS, Hollywood Blvd**
🔁 Le Cellier Steak | **Epcot, World Showcase**
Liberty Tree | **MK, Liberty Sq**
Mama Melrose's | **DHS, Sts of America**
Nine Dragons | **Epcot, World Showcase**
'Ohana | **MK Area**
Planet Hollywood | **DD, W Side**
Raglan Road | **DD, Pleasure Is**
Rainforest Cafe | **multi.**
Rest. Marrakesh | **Epcot, World Showcase**
Rose & Crown | **Epcot, World Showcase**
San Angel Inn | **Epcot, World Showcase**
Sci-Fi Dine-In Theater | **DHS, Echo Lake**
Teppan Edo | **Epcot, World Showcase**
Tony's Town Sq. | **MK, Main St**
Whispering Canyon | **MK Area**

VIEWS

Bistro de Paris | **Epcot, World Showcase**
🔁 California Grill | **MK Area**
Cap'n Jack's | **DD, Mktpl**
Cítricos | **MK Area**
Coral Reef | **Epcot, Future World**
Fulton's Crab Hse. | **DD, Pleasure Is**
Narcoossee's | **MK Area**
Portobello Yacht Club | **DD, Pleasure Is**
NEW Riverside Mill Food Ct. | **DD Area**
Rose & Crown | **Epcot, World Showcase**
NEW Turf Club Bar & Grill | **DD Area**
Wolfgang Puck Café | **DD, W Side**
NEW Yak & Yeti | **DAK, Asia**

WATERSIDE

Big River Grille | **Epcot Area**
Cap'n Jack's | **DD, Mktpl**
Fulton's Crab Hse. | **DD, Pleasure Is**
Ghirardelli | **DD, Mktpl**

Portobello Yacht Club | **DD,**
Pleasure Is
NEW Riverside Mill Food Ct. |
DD Area
Rose & Crown | **Epcot,**
World Showcase
NEW Turf Club Bar & Grill |
DD Area
Wolfgang Puck Café | **DD, W Side**

WINNING WINE LISTS

Z Artist Point | **MK Area**
Bistro de Paris | **Epcot,**
World Showcase
Z Boma | **DAK Area**
Z California Grill | **MK Area**

Cítricos | **MK Area**
Z Flying Fish Cafe | **Epcot Area**
Z Hollywood Brown Derby | **DHS,**
Hollywood Blvd
Il Mulino New York | **Epcot Area**
Z Jiko/Cooking Place | **DAK Area**
Z Le Cellier Steak | **Epcot,**
World Showcase
Shula's Steak | **Epcot Area**
Z Todd English's bluezoo |
Epcot Area
NEW Tutto Italia | **Epcot,**
World Showcase
Z Victoria & Albert's | **MK Area**
Z Yachtsman Steak | **Epcot Area**

DINING

SPECIAL FEATURES

Nightlife Special Features

Listings cover the best in each category and include names and locations.
Z indicates places with the highest ratings, popularity and importance.

ADDITIONS

(Properties added since the last
edition of the book)

Fuego/Sosa Cigars | **DD,
   Pleasure Is**

Rix Lounge | **DAK Area**

DANCING

Atlantic Dance Hall | **Epcot Area**
BET SoundStage | **DD, Pleasure Is**
Z 8 TRAX | **DD, Pleasure Is**
Jellyrolls | **Epcot Area**
Mannequins | **DD, Pleasure Is**
Motion | **DD, Pleasure Is**
NEW Rix Lounge | **DAK Area**

DJs

Atlantic Dance Hall | **Epcot Area**
BET SoundStage | **DD, Pleasure Is**
Z 8 TRAX | **DD, Pleasure Is**
House of Blues | **DD, W Side**
Mannequins | **DD, Pleasure Is**
Motion | **DD, Pleasure Is**
NEW Rix Lounge | **DAK Area**

DRINK SPECIALISTS

Belle Vue Room | Cocktails |
   Epcot Area
Bongos Cuban Cafe | Rum | **DD,
   W Side**
California Grill | Wine by the Glass |
   MK Area
Cape Town Lounge | Wine by the
   Glass | **DAK Area**
Crew's Cup | Beer | **Epcot Area**
Dawa Bar | Beer | **DAK, Africa**
NEW Fuego/Sosa Cigars | Wine by
   the Glass | **DD, Pleasure Is**
Martha's Vineyard | Wine by the
   Glass | **Epcot Area**
Mizner's | Cocktails | **MK Area**
Outer Rim Lounge | Cocktails |
   MK Area
Z Raglan Road | Beer | **DD,
   Pleasure Is**
NEW Rix Lounge | Cocktails |
   DAK Area
Rose & Crown | Beer | **Epcot,
   World Showcase**
Shula's Steak | Wine by the Glass |
   Epcot Area

Tune-In Lounge | Cocktails | **DHS,
   Echo Lake**
Victoria Falls | Wine by the Glass |
   DAK Area

FINE FOOD TOO

California Grill | **MK Area**
Magic Mushroom Bar | **DD, Mktpl**
Z Raglan Road | **DD, Pleasure Is**
Rose & Crown | **Epcot,
   World Showcase**
Shula's Steak | **Epcot Area**

OUTDOOR SPACES

Dawa Bar | **DAK, Africa**
NEW Fuego/Sosa Cigars | **DD,
   Pleasure Is**
Z Raglan Road | **DD, Pleasure Is**

QUIET CONVERSATION

Ale & Compass | **Epcot Area**
Belle Vue Room | **Epcot Area**
Cape Town Lounge | **DAK Area**
Crew's Cup | **Epcot Area**
Garden View Lounge | **MK Area**
Kimonos | **Epcot Area**
Martha's Vineyard | **Epcot Area**
Mizner's | **MK Area**
Outer Rim Lounge | **MK Area**
Territory | **MK Area**
Turf Club | **DD Area**

ROMANTIC

Atlantic Dance Hall | **Epcot Area**
Bongos Cuban Cafe | **DD, W Side**
Garden View Lounge | **MK Area**
House of Blues | **DD, W Side**
Kimonos | **Epcot Area**
Martha's Vineyard | **Epcot Area**
Mizner's | **MK Area**

VIEWS

Belle Vue Room | **Epcot Area**
Bongos Cuban Cafe | **DD, W Side**
California Grill | **MK Area**
Cap'n Jack's | **DD, Mktpl**
Garden View Lounge | **MK Area**
Mizner's | **MK Area**
Narcoossee's | **MK Area**
Portobello Yacht Club | **DD,
   Pleasure Is**
Stone Crab | **DD, Pleasure Is**

Shopping Merchandise

Includes store names and locations. ☑ indicates places with the highest ratings, popularity and importance.

ACCESSORIES

Adrian & Edith's | **DHS, Hollywood Blvd**
Agrabah Bazaar | **MK, Adventureland**
Calypso Trading | **Epcot Area**
Celebrity 5 & 10 | **DHS, Hollywood Blvd**
Chapeau | **MK, Main St**
☑ Emporium | **MK, Main St**
Everything Pop | **DAK Area**
Main St. Athletic Club | **MK, Main St**
Merchant of Venus | **MK, Tomorrowland**
Mickey's Star Traders | **MK, Tomorrowland**
☑ Mouse Gear | **Epcot, Future World**
Sorcerer Hat Shop | **DHS, Echo Lake**
Sunset Club Couture | **DHS, Sunset Blvd**
Team Mickey Athletic | **DD, Mktpl**

ANTIQUES

Der TeddyBar | **Epcot, World Showcase**
☑ Once Upon a Toy | **DD, Mktpl**

ART

☑ Animation Gallery | **DHS, Animation Courtyard**
☑ Art of Disney | **multi.**
Caricature Connection | **multi.**
Disney's Wonder/Memories | **DD, Mktpl**
Fjording | **Epcot, World Showcase**
House of Blues | **DD, W Side**
Hoypoloi Gallery | **DD, W Side**
Mombasa Mktpl. | **DAK, Africa**
Movieland Memorabilia | **DHS, Entrance**
☑ Wyland Galleries | **multi.**
Zawadi Mktpl. | **DAK Area**

BED/BATH

Basin | **DD, Mktpl**

BOOKS

Main St. Cinema | **MK, Main St**
Virgin Megastore | **DD, W Side**
Writer's Stop | **DHS, Sts of America**

CAMERAS/VIDEO

Camera Center | **Epcot, Future World**
Darkroom | **DHS, Hollywood Blvd**
Main St. Cinema | **MK, Main St**

CHILDRENSWEAR

Bibbidi Bobbidi | **DD, Mktpl**
BoardWalk Carnival | **Epcot Area**
BouTiki | **MK Area**
Conch Flats | **DD Area**
Disney Clothiers | **MK, Main St**
Disney Outfitters | **DAK, Discovery Is**
Keystone Clothiers | **DHS, Hollywood Blvd**
La Bottega Italiana | **Epcot, World Showcase**
Pooh Corner | **DD, Mktpl**
Pooh's Thotful Shop | **MK, Fantasyland**
Seven Dwarfs' Mine | **MK, Fantasyland**
Sir Mickey's | **MK, Fantasyland**
Stage One | **DHS, Sts of America**
Tinker Bell's Treasures | **MK, Fantasyland**
☑ Uptown Jewelers | **MK, Main St**

CHINA/CRYSTAL

Arribas Brothers | **DD, Mktpl**
Market House | **MK, Main St**

CIGARS

Fuego/Sosa Cigars | **DD, W Side**

COLLECTIBLES/ SOUVENIRS

AFI Studio | **DHS, Pixar Pl**
☑ Animation Gallery | **DHS, Animation Courtyard**
Artesanias Mex. | **Epcot, World Showcase**
☑ Art of Disney | **multi.**
Briar Patch | **MK, Frontierland**
Caricature Connection | **multi.**
Chapeau | **MK, Main St**
Cirque du Soleil Boutique | **DD, W Side**
Club COOL | **Epcot, World Showcase**
County Bounty | **MK, Toontown**

Crown & Crest | **Epcot,**
World Showcase

Das Kaufhaus | **Epcot,**
World Showcase

Der TeddyBar | **Epcot,**
World Showcase

Die Weihnachts Ecke | **Epcot,**
World Showcase

Dino Institute Shop | **DAK, DinoLand**

☑ Disney's Days/Christmas | **DD,**
Mktpl

☑ Disney's Pin Traders | **DD, Mktpl**

☑ Disney Studio Store | **DHS,**
Animation Courtyard

Engine Co. 71 | **MK, Main St**

ESPN Club Store | **Epcot Area**

Frontierland Trading | **MK,**
Frontierland

Heritage House | **MK, Liberty Sq**

House of Blues | **DD, W Side**

ImageWorks | **Epcot, Future World**

In Character | **DHS,**
Animation Courtyard

Indiana Jones Outpost | **DHS,**
Echo Lake

Inside Track | **Epcot, Future World**

☑ Island Mercantile | **DAK,**
Discovery Is

Jackson Sq. Gifts | **DD Area**

Maestro Mickey's Merc. |
DAK Area

Merchant of Venus | **MK,**
Tomorrowland

Mickey's Mart | **DD, Mktpl**

Mickey's Star Traders | **MK,**
Tomorrowland

Mickey's Toontown | **MK, Toontown**

M. Mouse Merc. | **MK Area**

☑ Mouse Gear | **Epcot,**
Future World

Movieland Memorabilia | **DHS,**
Entrance

Once Upon A Time | **DHS,**
Sunset Blvd

Orlando Harley Davidson | **DD,**
Pleasure Is

Outpost Shop | **DAK, Entrance**

Panchito's Gifts | **DAK Area**

Pin Central | **Epcot, Future World**

Planet Hollywood/Location | **DD,**
W Side

Screen Door General | **Epcot Area**

Sea Base Alpha | **Epcot,**
Future World

Serka Zong Bazaar | **DAK, Asia**

Settlement Trading | **MK Area**

Seven Dwarfs' Mine | **MK,**
Fantasyland

Sid Cahuenga's | **DHS, Entrance**

Sir Mickey's | **MK, Fantasyland**

Sorcerer Hat Shop | **DHS, Echo Lake**

Souvenirs de France | **Epcot,**
World Showcase

Stage One | **DHS, Sts of America**

Starabilias | **DD, W Side**

Tatooine Traders | **DHS, Echo Lake**

Tower Hotel Gifts | **DHS,**
Sunset Blvd

Town Square | **MK, Main St**

Villains in Vogue | **DHS,**
Sunset Blvd

Wilderness Lodge Merc. | **MK Area**

☑ World of Disney Store | **DD,**
Mktpl

Yankee Trader | **MK, Liberty Sq**

Ye Olde Christmas | **MK, Liberty Sq**

Youse Guys | **DHS, Sts of America**

Zawadi Mktpl. | **DAK Area**

GADGETS AND GIZMOS

Camera Center | **Epcot,**
Future World

Chester/Hester's Dinos. | **DAK,**
DinoLand

Magic Masters | **DD, W Side**

Magnetron Magnetz | **DD, W Side**

Mission: SPACE | **Epcot,**
Future World

☑ Once Upon a Toy | **DD, Mktpl**

HOBBY SHOPS

Magic Masters | **DD, W Side**

HOME FURNISHINGS

Artesanias Mex. | **Epcot,**
World Showcase

Die Weihnachts Ecke | **Epcot,**
World Showcase

Fjording | **Epcot, World Showcase**

Glas Und Porzellan | **Epcot,**
World Showcase

Hoypoloi Gallery | **DD, W Side**

Il Bel Cristallo | **Epcot,**
World Showcase

It's a Wonderful Shop | **DHS,**
Sts of America

Mickey's Pantry | **DD, Mktpl**

Mitsukoshi Dept. Store | **Epcot,**
World Showcase

Once Upon A Time | **DHS,**
Sunset Blvd

Tea Caddy | **Epcot,**
World Showcase

Ye Olde Christmas | **MK, Liberty Sq**

Yong Feng | **Epcot, World Showcase**

JEWELRY

Keystone Clothiers | **DHS,**
Hollywood Blvd

Mitsukoshi Dept. Store | **Epcot,**
World Showcase

Z Uptown Jewelers | **MK, Main St**

MENS/WOMENSWEAR

(Stores carrying both)

Agrabah Bazaar | **MK,**
Adventureland

BoardWalk Carnival | **Epcot Area**

BouTiki | **MK Area**

Conch Flats | **DD Area**

Disney Clothiers | **MK, Main St**

Disney Outfitters | **DAK,**
Discovery Is

Fittings & Fairings | **Epcot Area**

Fulton's General | **DD Area**

Gateway Gifts | **Epcot,**
Future World

In Character | **DHS,**
Animation Courtyard

Indiana Jones Outpost | **DHS,**
Echo Lake

Z Island Mercantile | **DAK,**
Discovery Is

La Bottega Italiana | **Epcot,**
World Showcase

Main St. Athletic Club | **MK,**
Main St

Mickey's of Hollywood | **DHS,**
Hollywood Blvd

Mitsukoshi Dept. Store | **Epcot,**
World Showcase

M. Mouse Merc. | **MK Area**

Mombasa Mktpl. | **DAK, Africa**

Orlando Harley Davidson | **DD,**
Pleasure Is

Planet Hollywood/Location | **DD,**
W Side

Team Mickey Athletic | **DD, Mktpl**

Thimbles & Threads | **Epcot Area**

Yong Feng | **Epcot, World Showcase**

MUSIC/DVDS

Main St. Cinema | **MK, Main St**

Virgin Megastore | **DD, W Side**

POSTERS/PRINTS

AFI Studio | **DHS, Pixar Pl**

SPECIALTY FOODS

Beach Club Mktpl. | **Epcot Area**

Delizie Italiane | **Epcot,**
World Showcase

Disney's Candy Cauldron | **DD,**
W Side

Z Disney's Days/Christmas | **DD,**
Mktpl

Goofy's Candy | **DD, Mktpl**

Les Vins de France | **Epcot,**
World Showcase

Main St. Confection | **MK, Main St**

Mickey's Pantry | **DD, Mktpl**

Z Sweet Spells | **DHS, Sunset Blvd**

Tea Caddy | **Epcot,**
World Showcase

SWIMWEAR

Beach Club Mktpl. | **Epcot Area**

Calypso Trading | **Epcot Area**

NEW Curl by Sammy Duvall | **DD,**
Pleasure Is

Summer Sands | **DD, Mktpl**

Thimbles & Threads | **Epcot Area**

TOYS

Chester/Hester's Dinos. | **DAK,**
DinoLand

Z Emporium | **MK, Main St**

Z LEGO Imagination | **DD, Mktpl**

Merchant of Venus | **MK,**
Tomorrowland

Mickey's Mart | **DD, Mktpl**

Mickey's of Hollywood | **DHS,**
Hollywood Blvd

M. Mouse Merc. | **MK Area**

Pirate's Bazaar | **MK,**
Adventureland

Pooh Corner | **DD, Mktpl**

Pooh's Thotful Shop | **MK,**
Fantasyland

Rainforest Cafe Shop | **multi.**

Sea Base Alpha | **Epcot,**
Future World

Serka Zong Bazaar | **DAK, Asia**

Tatooine Traders | **DHS, Echo Lake**

Tinker Bell's Treasures | **MK,**
Fantasyland

Toy Soldier | **Epcot,**
World Showcase

Hotel Special Features

Indexes list the best in each category and include Hotel names and locations.
Ƶ indicates places with the highest ratings, popularity and importance.

ADDITIONS

(Properties added since the last edition of the book)

Regal Sun Resort | **DD Area**

BEAUTIFUL GROUNDS

Ƶ Disney's Animal King. Lodge | **DAK Area**

Disney's Bch. Club | **Epcot Area**

Disney's Bch. Club Villas | **Epcot Area**

Ƶ Disney's Grand Floridian | **MK Area**

Disney's Old Key West | **DD Area**

Disney's Polynesian | **MK Area**

Disney's Wilderness | **MK Area**

Ƶ Disney's Yacht Club | **Epcot Area**

Villas/Disney's Wilderness | **MK Area**

DESTINATION SPA

Buena Vista Palace | **DD Area**

FISHING

Disney's Bch. Club Villas | **Epcot Area**

Disney's BoardWalk Villas | **Epcot Area**

Disney's Caribbean Bch. | **Epcot Area**

Disney's Contemporary | **MK Area**

Disney's Coronado Spgs. | **DAK Area**

Disney's Fort Wilderness | **MK Area**

Ƶ Disney's Grand Floridian | **MK Area**

Disney's Old Key West | **DD Area**

Disney's Port Orleans/French Q. | **DD Area**

Disney's Port Orleans/Riverside | **DD Area**

Ƶ Disney's Yacht Club | **Epcot Area**

Villas/Disney's Wilderness | **MK Area**

JACUZZIS

(In-room)

Ƶ Disney's Animal King. Lodge | **DAK Area**

Disney's BoardWalk Inn | **Epcot Area**

Ƶ Disney's Grand Floridian | **MK Area**

Hotel Royal Plaza | **DD Area**

SAILING

Disney's Bch. Club Villas | **Epcot Area**

Disney's Caribbean Bch. | **Epcot Area**

Disney's Contemporary | **MK Area**

Ƶ Disney's Grand Floridian | **MK Area**

Disney's Old Key West | **DD Area**

Disney's Polynesian | **MK Area**

Disney's Port Orleans/French Q. | **DD Area**

Disney's Port Orleans/Riverside | **DD Area**

Walt Disney Swan | **Epcot Area**

SPA FACILITIES

Buena Vista Palace | **DD Area**

Ƶ Disney's Animal King. Lodge | **DAK Area**

Disney's Contemporary | **MK Area**

Disney's Coronado Spgs. | **DAK Area**

Ƶ Disney's Grand Floridian | **MK Area**

Disney's Old Key West | **DD Area**

Ƶ Disney's Saratoga | **DD Area**

Hilton Walt Disney | **DD Area**

Walt Disney Dolphin | **Epcot Area**

Walt Disney Swan | **Epcot Area**

VILLAS

Disney's Bch. Club Villas | **Epcot Area**

Disney's BoardWalk Villas | **Epcot Area**

Disney's Old Key West | **DD Area**

Ƶ Disney's Saratoga | **DD Area**

Villas/Disney's Wilderness | **MK Area**

ALPHABETICAL
PAGE INDEX

Attractions

Dining

Character Dining & Dinner Shows

Nightlife

Shopping

Hotels

Golf

Disney Cruise Line

See reviews beginning on page 135

subscribe to ZAGAT.com

WDW MAPS & PHOTOS

MAGIC KINGDOM
Date opened: **1971**
Size: **107 acres**
Architectural icon: **Cinderella Castle**

The "heart and soul of Disney World", this "granddaddy" of Orlando theme parks strikes fans as an "enchanting" "escape from reality" where "fairy tales, Wild West adventures and jungle expeditions meet visions of the future"; the "storybook" atmosphere and "classic" "cartoon-based rides" make it "best for young children", but the "mountain tripleheader" (Space, Splash and Thunder) and "retro" attractions like The Haunted Mansion appeal to all ages, as do the "breathtaking" Wishes fireworks; "immaculate" grounds, "amazing attention to detail" (especially in Cinderella Castle) and "knowledgeable" cast members are pluses, and though mouse-bashers grouse it's "perpetually" crowded, "too tame" for "thrill-seekers" and "shows signs of aging", its "old-fashioned charm" works magic for most.

EPCOT

Date opened: **1982**
Size: **300+ acres**
Architectural icon: **Spaceship Earth** *(aka: "the giant golfball")*

Though not the utopian 'Experimental Prototype Community of Tomorrow' Walt envisioned, this "educational playground" offers an "unusual" "mix of culture, science" and thrills; World Showcase features 11 "mini-countries" replicating the "sights, sounds and smells" of each via "authentic" architecture, entertainment and native cuisine "from sushi to schnitzel", while Future World "wows" with innovative "high-intensity" rides like Mission: SPACE, Test Track and the Survey's Most Popular attraction, Soarin', plus hands-on exhibits exploring man's relation to nature; it's very "spread out" ("bring hiking boots") and some find it "not Disney enough", but defenders point to "recent additions" (e.g. Turtle Talk with Crush, The Seas with Nemo & Friends) that have upped its kid appeal and "improved" what they call "Orlando's most unique theme park."

DISNEY'S HOLLYWOOD STUDIOS

Date opened: **1989**
Size: **135 acres**
Architectural icon: **12-story Sorcerer's Hat**

Old-school "Hollywood" meets modern-day "movie magic" in this "imaginative" Tinseltown tribute (fka Disney-MGM Studios) where the starry-eyed can "pretend to be anyone" "from Ariel to a Wookie" and learn "behind-the-scenes secrets" on "backstage" visits; other draws include "gravity-defying" rides (Tower of Terror, Rock 'n' Roller Coaster), live-action shows (Fantasmic!, Playhouse Disney – Live on Stage!), as well as a new interactive street spectacular, Block Party Bash; a few critics contend that the park lacks "age cross-over appeal" (especially since the "working studio aspect of the original concept" is gone) and note that onetime "showstoppers" (Star Tours, the Indiana Jones Stunt Spectacular) can seem "dated", but newcomers like Toy Story Mania! may pique their interest – and all appreciate exploring "without the huge crowds" found elsewhere in WDW.

THE PARKS

DISNEY'S ANIMAL KINGDOM
Date opened: **1998**
Size: **500 acres**
Architectural icon: **Tree of Life**

Though "everyone thinks 'zoo'", Disney's newest and "most ambitious" theme park is an "ingenious" mix of "animals and ambiance" that allows visitors to "hang out with tigers, see Broadway-caliber shows" and "climb Mount Everest" all on the same day; "lush", "sprawling" grounds encompass six "lands", each with "breathtaking landscaping" and attractions such as the "imagination-defying" Expedition Everest roller coaster (the Survey's top-rated attraction for Adult Appeal) and Kilimanjaro Safaris, a Serengeti jeep-trek offering "up-close" wildlife "encounters"; though potshots are taken at its dearth of activities "for young children", lack of "real" restaurants, "narrow pathways" and "super-early" closing time, the many admirers of this "half-day" park and its 1,700 creatures consider it a "roaring success."

TYPHOON LAGOON/BLIZZARD BEACH
Date opened: **1989/1995**
Size: **56 acres/66 acres**
Architectural icon: **Mount Mayday/Mount Gushmore**

Sure, some view these water parks as little more than "breaks" from the big guys, but their "unique" "slip 'n' slide" rides leave many fearing they "may not make it back" to dry land; themed around a "freak Florida snowstorm", Blizzard Beach boasts the likes of Summit Plummet – the Survey's No. 1 Thrill – which sends "macho men" and others on a "scary" high-speed "plunge", while the "tropical"-motif Typhoon Lagoon, though more "relaxing" and "quiet", also features "powerful" attractions like "roller-coaster waterslides" and the "infamous" Surf Pool with "scream"-inducing six-ft. waves; wet blankets bemoan "long lines", "mile-high climbs", "hot concrete" and a lack of shade and lounge chairs (especially at Blizzard Beach), but overall they're a "refreshing" change of pace.

❶ SUMMIT PLUMMET *Disney's Blizzard Beach*

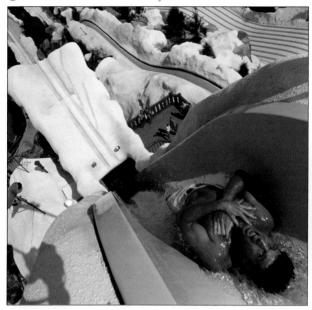

PROS: "the bomb" ... "absolute bestest!"
CONS: "the wedgiemaker" ... "not for the faint of heart"

❷ TWILIGHT ZONE TOWER OF TERROR *Hollywood Studios*

PROS: "terrifically terrifying" "heart-in-your-throat" "free-fall"
CONS: "my son was so scared he bit me"

❸ ROCK 'N' ROLLER COASTER *Hollywood Studios*

PROS: "bone-jarring" "blastoff" ... "Space Mountain on 'roids"
CONS: "long wait, short ride"

❹ EXPEDITION EVEREST *Disney's Animal Kingdom*

PROS: "unpredictable" "Matterhorn of the new millennium"
CONS: "you must enjoy going backwards"

❺ MISSION: SPACE *Epcot*

PROS: "if you can handle it, there's nothing else like it"
CONS: "barf bags are there for a reason"

❻ SPACE MOUNTAIN* *Magic Kingdom*

PROS: a "classic" ... "gets the blood flowing"
CONS: "a little jerky"   *Closing in early 2009 for refurbishment.*

❼ HUMUNGA KOWABUNGA *Typhoon Lagoon*

PROS: "scarier for adults than kids" ... "bragging rights"
CONS: "painful landing"

❽ SPLASH MOUNTAIN *Magic Kingdom*

PROS: "adorable animatronics" ... "heckuva plunge" ... "a scream"
CONS: "gratuitously soaked"

❾ CRUSH 'N' GUSHER *Typhoon Lagoon*

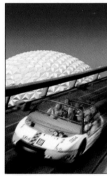 

PROS: "thrilling", "inventive" "water-coaster"
CONS: "tough on the behind"

❿ TEST TRACK *Epcot*

PROS: "exhilarating" ... "blasting" "through a wall"
CONS: "fun...when it's working"

⓫ DINOSAUR *Disney's Animal Kingdom*

PROS: "realistic" ... "you'll swear" they could "gobble you up"
CONS: "I've seen *adults* cry"

⑫ SOARIN' *Epcot*

PROS: "breathtakingly beautiful" ... "appeals to young and old"
CONS: "get your Fastpass early or you won't be riding"

⑬ BIG THUNDER MOUNTAIN RAILROAD *Magic Kingdom*

PROS: "adrenaline rushes"..."first-rate theming"..."family favorite"
CONS: "beginners' coaster" ... "no loops or big-ride thrills"

⑭ SLUSH GUSHER *Blizzard Beach*

PROS: "cool family ride" ... "Summit Plummet's little brother"
CONS: "may be too fast for little ones"

TOP 20 THRILLS

⑮ RICHARD PETTY DRIVING EXPERIENCE
WDW Speedway, Magic Kingdom Area

PROS: "speed-tacular" ... "ultimate thrill"
CONS: "way over my budget"

⑯ TYPHOON LAGOON SURF POOL *Typhoon Lagoon*

PROS: "unbelievable" waves "without the salt and sand"
CONS: "you better hold on" to the "little ones"

⑰ DOWNHILL DOUBLE DIPPER *Blizzard Beach*

PROS: "adults and kids alike" "love it – repeatedly"
CONS: "short"

18 KALI RIVER RAPIDS *Disney's Animal Kingdom*

PROS: "refreshing" ... "worth the wet"
CONS: "even your sneakers" will "get thoroughly soaked"

19 LIGHTS, MOTORS, ACTION! EXTREME STUNT SHOW
Hollywood Studios

PROS: "action-packed" ... "jaw-dropping" stunts
CONS: "can be hot" "in the bleachers"

20 CIRQUE DU SOLEIL LA NOUBA *Downtown Disney West Side*

PROS: "spectacular" ("how do people do that with their bodies?")
CONS: "very expensive"

❶ DISNEY'S GRAND FLORIDIAN RESORT & SPA
Also: No. 1 Service, No. 1 Dining

PROS: "Grande dame" ... "magical" "views of Cinderella Castle" ... "WDW's flagship for a reason"
CONS: "the price reflects the luxury"

❷ DISNEY'S ANIMAL KINGDOM LODGE
Also: No. 1 Public Facilities

PROS: "adventure in itself" ... "wake up to wildebeests outside the window" ... "like you're on safari"
CONS: "far from everything else"

❸ DISNEY'S YACHT CLUB RESORT

PROS: "easy access" to Epcot ... "awesome" "mini-water park"
CONS: "a bit of a hike" to your room

❹ DISNEY'S BOARDWALK INN

PROS: "right in the middle of everything"
CONS: "can be noisy"

❺ DISNEY'S WILDERNESS LODGE

PROS: "breathtaking lobby" ... "nice balance" of "homey" and "classy"
CONS: rooms "a little small"

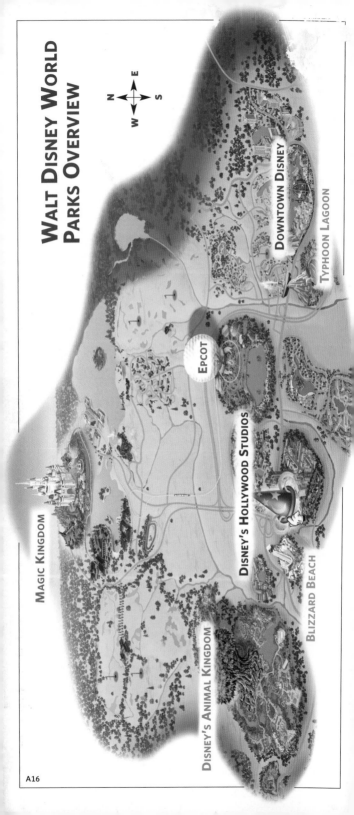

WALT DISNEY WORLD PARKS OVERVIEW

N
W — E
S

MAGIC KINGDOM

DISNEY'S ANIMAL KINGDOM

EPCOT

DISNEY'S HOLLYWOOD STUDIOS

BLIZZARD BEACH

DOWNTOWN DISNEY

TYPHOON LAGOON